FOUL!

THE SECRET WORLD OF FIFA: BRIBES, VOTE RIGGING AND TICKET SCANDALS

ANDREW JENNINGS

HarperSport

An Imprint of HarperCollinsPublishers

First published in hardback in 2006 by
HarperSport
an imprint of HarperCollins
London

First published in paperback in 2007

1

A CIP catalogue record for this book is
available from the British Library

ISBN-13 978-0-00-720869-2
ISBN-10 0-00-720869-3

Set in Linotype Sabon by
Rowland Phototypesetting Ltd, Bury St Edmunds, Suffolk
Printed and bound in Great Britain by
Clays Ltd, St Ives plc

The HarperCollins website address is
www.harpercollins.co.uk

For more on FIFA, see the author's website at
www.transparencyinsport.org

This book is proudly printed on paper which contains wood
from well-managed forests, certified in accordance with
the rules of the Forest Stewardship Council.
For more information about FSC,
please visit www.fsc.org

Mixed Sources
Product group from well-managed
forests and other controlled sources
www.fsc.org Cert no. SW-COC-1806
© 1996 Forest Stewardship Council
FSC

For the bears and for the fans

ANDREW JENNINGS is an internationally acclaimed investigative journalist and film-maker. His exposé of sleaze at the International Olympic Committee, *The Lords of the Rings*, is ranked among *Sports Illustrated's* Top 100 Sports Books of All Time. It was translated into 13 languages and earned him a five-day jail sentence from a judge in the IOC's home town of Lausanne.

Foul! has so far been translated into 12 languages and Jennings' BBC *Panorama* documentary *The Beautiful Bung*, based on the book, has been screened worldwide. See more at www.transparencyinsport.org.

CONTENTS

CONTENTS

ABOUT THE AUTHOR

When children ask me what it is I do exactly, I tell them I've made a life and a living out of chasing bad men.

I've investigated corrupt police-officers, corrupt governments and professional criminals, I've won awards for my work on secret British involvement in the Iran/Contra scandal and crooked cops. And when I turned forty I started looking into sport.

Sport? Some of my comrades in investigative journalism asked me, had I gone soft?

Not a bit of it. Sport belongs to the people. It's part of our culture, the social cement that holds us together.

And just as corruption in government and among police officers causes public concern, so, too, it matters when bad men take control of the people's sport and use it for their own personal ends.

So I trawled the waters of sport politics and came up with one gigantic fish, rotting, as fish tend to, from the head. It was, of all things, the Olympics.

I revealed that Juan Antonio Samaranch, leader of the Olympics, had been a career fascist, a minister in the government of the murderous Spanish dictator Franco. And I discovered that among the men who stood behind him in his International Olympic Committee were some who should have been behind bars (and have since spent time there) and many for whom Olympic politics was not a way to serve the people, but self-service, big time – and supersize that.

Investigative reporters don't always live to see bad men get their comeuppance, but the whole world saw Olympic corruption blow up back in 1998 and when the US Senate investigated the scandal they invited me to testify in Washington.

I might have left it there. But then I got a call from Colin Gibson, sports editor of the *Daily Mail*, asking would I take a look at the people running international football. 'Ah, come off it, Colin,' I said. 'Football is *big*. It would take years to find out what's going on inside FIFA.'

It's taken years. The things I've discovered have shocked even me. Some bad guys have been in there taking what they can. It's still the beautiful game, of course. They can't take that away from us. But, as you'll read here, there's been some ugly business going on. I'd like to see the beautiful game get the leadership it deserves. In that spirit I dedicate this book to the fans.

PREFACE

Click, click, click
Candid snapshots from inside world football's fortress
But stop
That's not allowed in the villa up on Sunny Hill

They say it's the people's game
Don't ask, how much the boss pays himself
Or who got the kickback, who got the contract
Don't ask, who got all those World Cup tickets

They're based in Switzerland
Where whistle-blowing is a crime
Their documents are forever hidden
Nobody ever gets the evidence

This isn't a history of FIFA
Just a taste of the truth
Here are snapshots of how it really is
How it's been for the last quarter century
For the good of the game.

Andrew Jennings
February 2006

BLATTER'S TICKING TIME-BOMB

A kickback lands on Sepp's desk

FIFA Headquarters, Zurich, winter 1998. It's just turned seven o'clock in the morning at Sunny Hill, the white-walled, red-tiled mansion perched on a hillside high above the city at Sonnenberg. Down in the warm basement mailroom, secretaries gather to collect the post and telexes and overnight faxes. News of football results, player transfers, tournaments, travel schedules, pleas for subsidies from national associations, appointments with heads of state – just an ordinary day's business at the world's largest sports organisation.

Heads of department pop in, eager to pick up some tit-bit of news they can take upstairs and present, personally, to the boss, in exchange for some small favourable comment, or just a nod of approval. Here comes Erwin Schmid, FIFA's Director of Finance, a broad-shouldered bear of a man, who gets more dishevelled as the day goes on, his shirt-tail escaping from his trousers. Here comes Erwin, with the usual happy greetings.

He picks up an envelope. It's from the head office of FIFA's bankers, the Union Bank of Switzerland. Erwin tears it open and looks at the enclosed document, a notification of a payment. His plump face pales. He reads it again. Something is not right. Something is most irregular. Erwin leaves the mailroom and heads for the elevator, gripping the document in one tight, nervous hand.

Two floors up, FIFA General Secretary Joseph S Blatter, known universally as 'Sepp', reclines behind his leather-topped desk, in a high-backed black leather chair, performing his morning ritual of reading the *Neue Zurcher Zeitung*. The big JVC television is silent, too early for the tennis he loves to watch.

At 61 years of age Blatter has the air of a man who's in charge. He's a round man, round face, round body, a little on the short side, going bald. But his well-cut suit, his two-tone shirt, his solid gold cufflinks, his heavy, premium wristwatch, his don't-waste-my-time stare, all say: *I've been the boss for 17 years. Now, what can you do for me?* President Joao Havelange has an office just above but today he's an ocean away, at home in Brazil. Sepp is in charge.

Blatter enjoys the villa's finest views. A gigantic picture window frames the distant Alps, the wooded ridge and, far below, the lake and the old city, its church steeples squeezed between the valley shoulders. He might stroll across to the side window and gaze down on a steep vineyard and secluded villas whose high gates open now and then as a trickle of dark Mercedes saloons carry their owners to the city.

But this is no day to enjoy the view. His finance director has bad news for the boss who is also his good friend, indeed, his best friend. Erwin Schmid tells colleagues, 'I have only one friend in my life and that is JSB.' And now Erwin has the kind of news that can tear friendships apart. As the elevator rises, Erwin's spirits sink.

For the past three years Blatter himself has overseen the sale of rights for the World Cups of 2002 and 2006: the rights to show the games on television in every country in the world, the rights to put FIFA's badge and the magic words 'World Cup' on soft drinks, beer, burgers, razors and trainers. They're all in FIFA's gift. And senior people within FIFA have overseen a whopping US$2.3 billion worth of business to old friends in a secretive company a few Alpine ranges to the south.

Sitting at No 10 Marktstrasse in the little tax-haven city of Sarnen, this company goes by the name of International Sport and Leisure, or ISL.

Erwin steps out of the lift. The document in his hand threatens to blow FIFA apart. Over the years there's been unkind talk of the relationship between FIFA and ISL, rumours of kickbacks and bribes. Loyal fellows like Erwin have dismissed that talk. Special relationships always attract gossip, don't they? Bad losers often complain. And there's been no evidence of wrongdoing. But now, there's this piece of paper. A payment has landed some-where it shouldn't.

Erwin pads along the carpeted corridor. He reaches Blatter's door, knocks and waits for the call. In he goes. Erwin wastes no time. He hands the document to Blatter. It is a standard USB form, stating that ISL has transferred one million Swiss francs (some £400,000) into FIFA's account. It's the payee's name that makes acid churn in the belly. He's a senior official in football. It's a very fat 'thank you'. This is most improper (but not illegal in Switzerland, as long as it is declared to the taxman).

'My God,' Blatter groans. He stands up. 'This is a problem . . .'

'*It does not belong to us.*'

Erwin knows that. But what will Blatter do? Call in the police? Report it to FIFA's Executive Committee, to the Finance Committee? That is the least that should be done.

Instead, the money is moved out of FIFA's account to the man named on the payment order. And the record of the transaction sits there. The law says this record must be kept until the winter of 2008. So there it is, a ticking timebomb, waiting to go off.

Tick. Tick. Tick.

Tunis, Abou Nawas Hotel, 23 January 2004. The reporters have come from Cairo and Cape Town, Yaounde and Nairobi, some wearing city suits, some in white desert jalabiyyas, others in colourful West African agbadas, all sitting in rows, notebooks at the ready, waiting for the words of the most powerful man in world football.

High above the podium in the brightly lit function room is the portrait that dominates public buildings, restaurants and shops in this country. President Zine El Abidine Ben Ali stands erect and unsmiling, sports a helmet of implausibly jet-black hair and wears a long dress-coat, studded with medals. In the Tunisia he has led since 1987 no serious political opposition is permitted, no critical opinion tolerated, and hundreds of people rot in jail after unfair trials. There are elections here: Ben Ali wins them every time, claiming 99 per cent of the vote.

But his country always shows a happy face to tourists and, this week, to thousands of fans from Rwanda and Benin, Mali, Zimbabwe and a dozen other countries who've flocked to the stadiums on the Mediterranean coast for non-stop, stadium-shaking drumming, cheering and jeering at the finals of the 2004 African Nations Cup.

Here comes Sepp Blatter, taking his seat at the centre of the podium beneath Ben Ali's portrait. He was general secretary, now he's FIFA president with six years under his belt. Blatter admires

Ben Ali as someone who has earned 'a lot of respect' and praises Tunisia as 'an absolutely open country'.

To Blatter's right sits our host, Issa Hayatou from Cameroon, president of African football for the past sixteen years. A big, broad-chested man, once a champion 800-metre runner, Hayatou looks tired but has a nod here and a smile there for men he's laughed and duelled with. Eighteen months ago he challenged Blatter for the FIFA presidency. He promised to 'restore integrity and accountability' to the organisation. Along with others, he wrote to Zurich's public prosecutor accusing Blatter of corruption and demanding an investigation. Hayatou's integrity campaign couldn't beat Sepp's charisma and Blatter won a second term as president. The prosecutor decided not to take Blatter to court, on the basis that there was insufficient evidence for a prosecution to proceed. No charges were brought.

Everyone knew Blatter would strike back. It's his way: *stand in my path and it will cost you*. Yesterday, Hayatou stood for re-election as president of the African confederation. Blatter and his Zurich bag-carriers strongly backed the challenger, Botswana's Ismail Bhamjee. But Hayatou is no pushover. He'd secured his base in the French-speaking countries from Morocco down through West Africa to the Congo, and Bhamjee, who never got any momentum, lost, 46 votes to 6. Still, Blatter's a pro. There's no trace of bitterness in his face. He touches Hayatou's arm and the gesture says, *We're all friends again*. The subtext: *I'll get you next time*.

To Blatter's left sits FIFA General Secretary Urs Linsi who, like his president, sports a diagonally striped tie, blue shirt and dark suit. Like Blatter, from the German-speaking part of Switzerland. Like Blatter, he's balding; one rogue tuft of hair sticks up above his forehead.

Ever since arriving at FIFA, Linsi has been a Blatter-man.

Blatter recruited him as finance director from Credit Suisse years ago in 1999. When then-General Secretary Michel Zen-Ruffinen backed Hayatou for the presidency, Linsi stayed loyal. After the votes were counted in Seoul in May 2002, Blatter growled to a Swiss reporter, 'Tomorrow, we take care of Mr Clean.' Mr Clean, Zen-Ruffinen, was out. Linsi was on his way up. So now, aged 54, Linsi's got two jobs, finance director and general secretary. He's a very powerful man.

At the Abou Nawas Hotel, a question from the floor. What does the president think of African football? Blatter smiles. He says with conviction, 'Africa is the future of football.' (It's a formula that works for him. About the women's game? That firm voice: 'The future of football.' About Asia? 'The future of football.') Blatter's on good form, flashing his warmest charismatic smile. It's a beautiful day.

But there's a party pooper. Me. I've got hold of the roaming microphone. 'A question to President Blatter.' His smile fades, he draws up a fist to support his chin. I'm not his favourite reporter. I know about the ticking time-bomb. And here I go: 'After the last marketing and TV contract was signed with ISL for 2002 and 2006, a secret payment of one million Swiss francs from ISL arrived by accident in FIFA's bank account.'

I draw breath. Sepp's eyes tighten a little. I'm off again. 'It is alleged that you, as general secretary at the time, instructed it was to be moved immediately to a private account of a FIFA official.' Then I ask him who it went to.

Blatter tenses up, gazes down at the table before him and mutters something about the ISL company, now in the hands of a liquidator. Then, he says, frostily, 'I will not enter into discussion here in this press conference and I think also it is totally out of the matter we like to discuss today in Africa together with the African journalists for the development of football in this continent. I'm sorry, please accept this situation as it is and I am sure your colleagues from the African and international press here will agree with me.'

Outside, in an atrium dotted with tall potted palms, I sink into a soft leather settee, sip strong sweet coffee and chat with old acquaintances from the press-room at the previous World Cup. A tall white reporter from South Africa, hurrying to an interview, pauses, waves and calls cheerily, 'I always like to see some theatre!' A lean magazine editor from the Gulf, casual in open-neck shirt and unbuttoned sports coat marvels, 'Blatter's face went green!'

'No,' says a friend from the Kenyan *Daily Nation*, 'He turned yellow.'

Tick. Tick. Tick.

2

GOODBYE SIR STAN

Hello to a New World of Sport

Frankfurt, 10 June 1974. Voters descending through the clouds could see the River Main snaking under bridges and around the toy-town skyscrapers in the distant city. The modest glass tower of their hotel poked up from the pine forest close to the airport. There in his suite their president, Sir Stanley Rous, watched the planes coming in, from other European cities or faraway continents, heard the squealing rubber and bumps of their touch-downs.

Rous was a tall, upright schoolmasterly man with an authoritative grey moustache, a man pushing eighty, reserved as only an Englishman of his generation could be. Would this plane carry men steadfast in their loyalty? Or waverers? Or men open to inducements? Or enemies who wanted him to take his pension and go? Wanted to sweep him away, change everything and bring in a new and totally different way of life?

Sir Stanley leaves the window and returns to the round wooden table that dominates his sitting room. Not long now. Tonight: a big party thrown by the playboy Gunter Sachs, he'd been married to Brigitte Bardot. Tomorrow: the congress and the election, the threat from the Brazilian Joao Havelange ('Jow' he calls himself). Surely Sir Stanley's steady hand, cautiously reforming the laws of the precious game and his determination to protect it from the spivs who wanted their logos plastered everywhere, would prevail against the challenger?

Football was in good heart, Sir Stanley believed. Since becoming FIFA president thirteen years ago in 1961, he'd steered the sporting ship well clear of murky political waters. There was no need to rush to recognise Communist China and he'd been absolutely correct to ban Arsenal from going to play there. He wasn't going to banish Taiwan. And if the natives in places like Sharpeville mobbed the police, tragedies were bound to occur. He'd done his reading and he knew that fellow Mandela was a Red and football would take no benefit from siding with convicts. His mission, as he saw it, was to bring people together, not exclude old friends from the game. And the law was the law. If the elected South African government passed laws saying that blacks and whites shouldn't live together, FIFA had no right to interfere. It was dismaying that here in Frankfurt this week were so many people who couldn't understand that his sensible point of view was in the best interests of the game.

His men at the English FA had distributed his election programme, there really wasn't much more to do. The World Cup was starting in a few days and keeping his eye on that ball was an obligation he wouldn't shirk. Meticulous organisation was essential. That's why he'd received a knighthood, for putting together the joyous Olympic Games in London back in 1948. The Queen had even made him a Commander of the British Empire.

All this fuss about elections and for what? FIFA hadn't needed one before. Rous had taken over from Arthur Drewry, which made for 18 years of English rule at FIFA, a marvellous stretch. Why change things now? But some of the London newspaper reporters had reservations. Was that disloyalty? They were calling him bluff, outspoken, immovable – although that last point wasn't fair, he'd listen to anyone. They harped on about his age but 79 was a good age, he'd got at least four more years in him. He was football's ambassador to the world. There would be more than 120 men from football associations here in Frankfurt for the election and surely enough of them would not be troubled – or even aware – that his campaign was being described in London as 'ponderously inept'. Those chaps had done well to raise the money for their fares. And what was this colossal piece of cheek? Joao Havelange, the challenger, offering him a generous pension!

There's a knock at the door. 'Mr Myers from the United Press International to see you, Sir,' and in bustles Morley Myers, polite, on the short side, in his dark striped suit, crinkly hair and glasses, always scurrying to file another dispatch. Morley comes bearing news Sir Stanley doesn't want to hear, news that no-one else dares tell him.

'Your rival is running very strongly, he's everywhere, there doesn't seem to be much aggression or lobbying on your side.' Morley wants Rous's response: 'How do you feel about this? What's your political platform?'

'I let my record speak for itself,' Rous replies.

JOAO HAVELANGE never missed a chance to speak for himself. For four years he'd tugged sleeves, made his promises, struck his deals. With voting just hours away he couldn't afford to waste time in his suite. Every hour planes landed bearing voters

– new ears to whisper into. The Airport Steigenberger was a modern airy building but pressman Myers, talking to me thirty years on, recalls, 'There were lots of hidey holes and they were all meeting surreptitiously, little plots going on all over the place, and you didn't know who was who. That's where the real election was taking place. You have this antennae and somehow you could sense that FIFA was about to experience this seismic change, an end of a way of life. There was a buzz, you could feel it.'

Sir Stanley's rival was a knight as well, but even more so; three different governments had bestowed the honour on him. He was a Portuguese Knight of Sport, a Knight of the Infant Enrique, and a Swedish Knight of Vasa and, although this wasn't written down anywhere, a darling of the generals who then governed his homeland, Brazil. Havelange was promising to bring some diversion, some prestige to their discredited regime and the generals would help him in any way they could.

Havelange looked presidential, the aristocratic nose a domineering prow cleaving his way through wavelets of lesser beings, the hooded dark eyes penetrating to the depths of their wallets. The tall athletic physique, the gleaming brow, the swept back hair, the rakish curls, the finely-cut clothes, all made for an imposing impression. He looked hungry, a predator with curling lips that hinted at sexual power.

Rous was a great referee, he could run all day and was a man you'd trust with your watch and keys, but he wasn't a work of art. Screaming girl fans didn't lie in wait to tear souvenir strips from his black tunic and shorts. Havelange had swum in the 1936 Olympics and was back again playing water polo in 1952 in Helsinki. He had poise. He had grace and ambition beyond medals. When he climbed the ladder out of the pool for the last time he kept going upwards. Four years later in Melbourne he was Brazil's Chef de Mission, two years on and he'd taken control of the Brazilian Sports Confederation – including football – and in 1963 he joined the select ranks of the International Olympic Committee (IOC). There he learned to network on a global scale and so impressed his colleagues that half a lifetime later, in 1999, the IOC appointed him to their anti-corruption commission.

Havelange at 59 was two decades younger than Sir Stanley, and vibrating with energy and ideas. Unlike the ageing president who only spoke English, Havelange could tell you fluently in any one of four languages how much better off you'd be if you voted for him. He talked of his successful business career. He ran Brazil's biggest bus company, had interests in chemicals and insurance. He promised that with his entrepreneurial dynamism there'd be money galore to create wonderful new competitions and training courses.

Many of the officials flying in to stay at the Steigenberger had met Havelange and liked him. He'd brought Brazil's World Cup winning team to play in a country near them, thoughtfully leaving the gate-money behind with his grateful hosts.

He'd listened to their troubles. Across Africa people were angry that it was so hard to qualify for the World Cup. There were 16 slots for finalists and nine were reserved for Europe. South America had bagged four and that left only three for the rest of the world.

Havelange would set that right. Within eight years, he pledged, there'd be 24 finalists and he dropped strong hints that the extra eight places would go to teams from the developing world. Rous's FIFA, dominated by Europeans for all its 70 years, wouldn't listen to Africa. It was if they couldn't hear non-European voices. At their UEFA congress in Edinburgh earlier in the year they'd made a threat: *increase the number of finalists and Europe withdraws. We'll take our ball away and run a European World Cup*

12

and invite a 'few South Americans'. Sir Stanley, deaf to the sound of voters running towards Havelange, couldn't see a problem with a European World Cup.

Havelange told the press that he'd win, said he had more than 70 votes pledged. 'It won't be on the first ballot,' he said. 'Besides, there are always surprises in elections and, like everyone else, I have to wait.'

THE MAN both Havelange and Rous were waiting for, hoping he would win the election for them, had driven from his offices two hours away in France, checked in to the airport hotel, changed into a plum-coloured suit and mingled with the voters. What neither of the contenders then knew was that both had called for help from this shy but determined man who, backed by his team of fixers, was becoming the most powerful figure in world sport. Morley Myers recalls, 'Horst Dassler was the invisible man, blending into the background, very wealthy but not ostentatious and it was a case of seeing the guy but not knowing what he was doing. We didn't realise then how involved he was.'

Dassler's day job was running his family's Adidas sportswear company. He wanted sports federations to sign contracts that committed their teams to wear Adidas kit. He wanted individual stars to wear the three stripes. And he wanted the world to watch on television and follow their example. To get the contracts, he had to have the sports leaders in debt to him. What better way than to put them in power?

He surveyed the likely candidates, did his private deals, and helped them to victory with Adidas money. He made them presidents and let them remember – charmingly of course – that he could keep them in power, or push them out. All they had to do was play the game, which meant looking out for Adidas. And now power at FIFA was up for grabs. It was a sport shockingly under-sold to the public and Dassler had plans to address that. But first, the elections.

When it came to Rous versus Havelange, Dassler's strategy was to back both horses, at least at first. 'I had to be as close as possible to Havelange,' says Christian Jannette, a small, dark, intense linguist, then a member of Dassler's discreet Adidas international relations team. Jannette had joined Dassler after working for the French team at the Munich Olympics two years before. 'I knew Havelange from my relationships with the IOC,' he said.

Sir Stanley was looked after by the third member of Dassler's platoon at the Steigenberger, John Boulter, the British former 800-metre runner. Boulter, a tall, lean, languages teacher with floppy blonde hair tumbling over his beaky nose, seemed taken aback at being asked what he actually did in the great FIFA war of succession. 'I can't remember a lot from 30 years ago,' he told me. 'I was just nice to Rous. One just helps and is friendly, and why should one not be? Whatever Christian Jannette says, I don't have any specific recollection of being nice to Sir Stanley. I certainly wouldn't be nasty to him. It's a long time ago.'

Jannette's memory is sharper. 'Boulter had to be as close as possible to Stanley Rous – Dassler did not take any risks! Dassler at 38 was very sporty and fit and every morning he jogged with Boulter. This was something new for me. I was always very far behind!' A woman sports official told me once that the first time she met Dassler she was more than impressed, she was mesmerised. It wasn't that he was tall and very well built, it certainly wasn't the sizeable nose. 'It was the eyes,' she said, 'They held you suspended in the air.' Dassler could inspire great devotion and Boulter, a hard veteran of 30 years of sports politics, elections and kit contracts, told me that he wasn't up to writing a biography of Dassler 'because it would be a hagiography'.

Jannette, the unwilling jogger, fondly recalls a charismatic and complex character. 'Power and business were important to Horst. I don't think money was important. He could have had a Rolls-Royce with a driver, but he had none of that. Once we were invited to a big party in Germany and he had no evening dress – he had to rent one. He did not have a lot of taste, nor care about these things. Power in the world of sport meant he could have his people anywhere.' Was he a nice man? 'Not always. He could be very, very charming but he could be very, very bad. Terrible.'

A fourth member of Dassler's team checked in, again with a specific mission. Colonel Hassine Hamouda, a Tunisian athlete who had competed for France in Berlin in 1936 when Havelange swam for Brazil, published a sports magazine for the Francophone countries. It was called *Champion D'Afrique* and it was funded by Dassler. Adidas would never sell a lot of kit in Africa but Dassler gave it away to win the support of officials whose votes could be decisive in elections. Hamouda helped focus attention on his generous boss and his wishes. Morley Myers explains how it worked. 'Rous was unhappy about commercialising the game, that wasn't his world, and he didn't realise the influence of Horst Dassler and Havelange. Horst at the time had good contacts in Africa. He gave away a lot of equipment so that was support the African countries couldn't do without. It seemed pretty obvious that if Havelange didn't get in, you wouldn't be getting any more gear.'

Sir Stanley couldn't speak directly to the voters from the Francophone countries but Havelange could. French was his first language, the one he spoke at home with his parents who had arrived in Brazil as immigrants from Belgium. Not only did Havelange speak their language, he understood French anxieties. France had hosted the founding of FIFA in Paris in 1904, Frenchman Jules Rimet had got his name on the World Cup, but power was slipping away. 'It was clear that France was not supporting Rous. Havelange was their candidate,' says Jannette. 'In that time France was losing power. At the IOC Lord Killanin had defeated Count Jean de Beaumont to be president. There was a big fight between the French and English speakers. French had been the first language at the IOC and English second. Now it was reversed.'

American journalist and fluent French-speaker Keith Botsford, who was in Frankfurt for the London *Sunday Times*, says it wasn't just the French football association backing Havelange. French diplomats had put in a word for Joao in the old French empire. 'I saw a lot of African diplomats in Frankfurt, some of them the cream of the French education system. Some were absolutely not of football, not necessarily voting but influencing their delegations,' said Botsford.

Dassler kept a cautious foot in both camps until the fifth member of his election team turned up and took him to the bar. 'Rous isn't going to win, he's lost a lot of Africa,' he said. He knew because he'd been at the African confederation congress and Havelange had his people there. 'He [Havelange] is catching up fast and I think he may win. You have to talk to him now.'

Dassler then simply distributed a wad of cash among the officials who were holding out or who could bring in other votes to encourage them to back Havelange. There is no evidence that Havelange knew what Dassler was up to. Each was given a few thousand dollars and those who were not in their rooms found an envelope when they got back.

So Dassler was now backing one horse and it was Havelange. Jannette turned up the charm. 'I was there to be as friendly as possible with Havelange and to go to the official reception. I didn't even go to the Congress.' He laughed. 'And I nearly missed the World Cup Final. That day in Munich I had a very nice lunch with Monique Berlioux, Director of the IOC, and Leni Riefenstahl, and we spoke and we spoke and suddenly I noticed I had to be in the stadium and I arrived at the beginning of the second half. Adidas had good seats in the VIP stand and Dassler was not pleased with me.'

AFTER AN EARLY breakfast on the morning of Tuesday 11 June 1974, the voters from 122 national football associations, their hangers-on, the fixers and reporters queued for coaches that took them the 10 km into the city and off-loaded them outside Frankfurt's Kongresshalle, grand in the old style, on the banks of the broad grey Main. They filled only the front few rows of the auditorium.

In their hands they had Havelange's eight-point election programme. Damn the Europeans, the size of the World Cup would be expanded and he would introduce a Junior World Championship. He would go out and find sponsors and with their money he would give cash aid to national associations, courses run by visiting coaches, doctors and referees, new stadiums and more competitions in the developing world for developing clubs. The headquarters in Zurich would be expanded.

If Rous had opened FIFA's door to China that morning he might have split Africa and carried with him the powerful Secretary-General of the Supreme Council for Sport in Africa, Jean-Claude Ganga from the Congo. That might have been enough to secure four more years in power. Instead the usually avuncular Ganga was provoked into striding the gangways of the auditorium haranguing delegates as they came forward to cast their votes. Havelange predicted correctly. It did go to a second ballot. He needed 79 votes for a clear victory on the first round but got only 62 to Sir Stanley's 56. The second round gave

Havelange world football, 68–52, before it was time for lunch.

A few days later Keith Botsford told *Sunday Times* readers what had happened in the Steigenberger and the Kongresshalle. He reported, 'a pungent odour of money and the too-familiar strains of *Rule Britannia* once again sinking beneath the waves'. And he wrote of 'little brown envelopes being passed around with such fraternal sentiments as "if that's not enough, please tell me"'. Things could only get worse, he feared. 'Sir Stanley was a bulwark protecting football against the twin evils of Too Much Money and Too Much Politics. Havelange is a creature of the Too Much.'

The Steigenberger emptied and the lucky ones went on to the World Cup. 'The day after I went to fix up an appointment to see Rous again,' says Morley Myers. 'And they said, you can see him now. Normally he used to be surrounded by his allies and I went up and he was there by himself sitting at this huge round table and he was stunned. He was traumatised.

'"I'm shocked, I treated Havelange as my son and he stabbed me in the back," he said.

'I said, "No, it's politics, winners and losers." He was a very forlorn and lonely figure. My story was headlined: "LONELY KNIGHT AT THE ROUND TABLE". It was like seeing a beaten champion. I don't think Rous expected any of this, he was going on past record and he didn't expect the French, the Greeks, the Africans to turn against him and there were some people he thought were his friends and they weren't.'

Sir Stanley was given the consolation title of honorary president and lived another dozen years, making it to Mexico for the 1986 World Cup and dying two weeks after Argentina defeated Germany 3–2. By then the world of football he had led was under the control of the spivs he'd fought to keep at bay.

SEPP BLATTER, MADE BY ADIDAS

A new leader rolls off Dassler's production line

IF HAVELANGE couldn't deliver on his extravagant election promises and come up with a bigger World Cup and eight more teams in the finals he would be a one-term president, a football failure, a dead man in four years time when he met his voters in Buenos Aires on the eve of the 1978 World Cup. He needed money, lots of money, and he relied on Horst Dassler to get it for him.

For Dassler, this was going to be bigger business than selling sports kit. Football didn't know yet but it was about to be shaped into a commodity. Dassler sent John Boulter to London to run an eye over fresh-faced super-salesman Patrick Nally who was making a name for himself persuading companies to sponsor sports and pay for coaching in return for good publicity.

Dassler invited Nally to his headquarters at Landersheim in Alsace, just inside France. Forget little England, he said, throw in your lot with me and work the whole planet. Together they created a company in Monte Carlo to sell the marketing rights they'd bought from sports federations – including football rights from FIFA. The silver-tongued Nally and the charismatic Dassler pulled off a coup enticing one of the world's biggest brands, Coca-Cola, to invest heavily in Havelange's development schemes. They'd help fund coaching, new tournaments, refereeing courses, all sorts of good things. In return Coke got to plaster its logo all over the World Cup.

Once Coca-Cola had signed up, everyone wanted a piece of the action. Sponsors competed for the right to use FIFA's badge and slap the words 'World Cup' on their products. They got lots of free seats for entertaining business contacts and rewarding loyal staff. They also got to mingle with football officials and athletes. 'I told Pele over dinner last night that he always made his best moves when played a square ball,' is one-upmanship that *can* be bought.

The news of Horst Dassler's great achievement in the corridors of the airport hotel was greeted thoughtfully in the committee rooms of world sport. The era of volunteers giving up holidays, weekends and evenings to run international organisations was waning. If the brilliant Dassler could pension off the patrician Sir Stanley, what else might he achieve?

'Money like you've never known it,' he replied over long lunches. Once, he just wanted the athletes wearing the three stripes and trefoil of Adidas. Now he wanted the whole sport. A new word entered the vocabulary of sport: 'support'. Dassler deployed his team to 'support' favoured candidates. And when they'd won they returned the favour, selling him the right to market their logos, their entire sports, their athletes' achievements, to commercial sponsors. The new federation leaders got money to develop their sports with more events, more trainers and more facilities.

They were praised in industry handouts, soon reflected in the press, as wise leaders who had brilliantly brought new money into their sports.

The language of sport was rewritten and the word 'sponsors' moved aside to make room for the more friendly 'partners'. Nally spent half his life in the air wooing new partners from Japan to New York. Sugared drinks and fatty burgers were promoted by well-rewarded athletes whose own diets were carefully balanced for fitness and health. The administrators, even the ones who ran second in their elections, were comforted with first-class air travel, five-star hotels, generous expenses, honoraria and pensions all paid for by the big corporations. Dassler breathed new life – and money – into the General Assembly of International Sports Federations, a talking shop for sports leaders. And he gave them a home, a plush villa in swanky Monte Carlo.

Dassler, a man unknown to the fans, was becoming the puppet-master, controlling the leaders of world sport. Ambitious officials begged him to marshal his team behind them, organise their campaigns, bring in the votes. He was a generation ahead of his competitors. A highlight at every congress and committee meeting of most Olympic sports was the Adidas dinner in the hotel banqueting suite, fixers making nice to the officials. As elections drew near in the world's best-loved sports the big question was: 'Who's Dassler supporting?' Once in place, and so long as they behaved themselves, these winners had Dassler's protection. Only extreme old age or death could separate them from power. Eventually, presidential elections weren't held for decades at a time at track and field, the IOC and FIFA.

The fixer team grew with full-time employees and part-time agents positioned throughout the international federations. Some had responsibility for continents or ethnic and language groups, others looked after their boss's interest in specific sports. Dassler hired the petit German fencer, Thomas Bach, who rose to become a leading member of the IOC. Dassler sought out the big, blustering Anwar Chowdhry from Karachi, who scoured the East forcing athletes into Adidas strip, and with Dassler's 'support', took control of world amateur boxing in Bangkok in 1986. Olympic boxing swiftly degenerated into fight-fixing and bribery but Chowdhry survived because, as he once boasted to me, while guzzling breakfast yoghurt in his Houston hotel bedroom, 'I know many things.'

Dassler's agents worked to fix which cities got to stage the Olympics. At the heart of his network was the IOC president's top advisor, the silver-haired Yugoslav Arthur Takac. From his office in Lausanne he oiled Dassler's relationships with IOC members and his burly son Goran channelled bribes from cities keen to be hosts. Goran went into business with Russian IOC senior statesman Vitaly Smirnov.

In 2004 BBC television's *Panorama* reporters posed as businessmen keen to bring the Olympics to London in 2012. They met Goran Takac and, on camera, he explained how it was done. *Pay me the money and I'll get you the votes.* That was the end of his Olympic career.

Always the visionary, Dassler had anticipated that it was best to have journalists on your side. He sponsored the Munich-based fortnightly newsletter *Sport Intern*. Publisher Karl-Heinz Huba helpfully set the media's agenda, filling his pages with 'exclusive inside information' that freed some reporters from the bother of working to find their own stories. Huba boosted Dassler's companies. Dassler's critics, business rivals and the remaining few faint voices in sport who didn't want Coke's money were traduced. Long after Dassler's death *Sport Intern* remains alive and kicking. The sheet was a great supporter of millionaire Korean

IOC member (and secret intelligence agent) Kim Un-Yong who went to jail in 2004 for fraud.

NINETEEN SEVENTY-FOUR was the watershed year. As Havelange flew back to Rio with FIFA in his pocket, the top sports official in the dying Franco dictatorship in Spain reached out to Dassler. The sharp-faced and diminutive Juan Antonio Samaranch had met Christian Jannette at the Munich Olympics. 'Samaranch was chief of protocol of the IOC and I had to work a lot with him and we became very good friends,' Jannette told me. 'In 1974 Samaranch knew that I was working with Horst and he told me that he would be interested to meet him. He invited us to Barcelona to his home and we spent two or three days there. He was Chief of Protocol of the IOC and people often say that the chief of protocol is the next president. I knew that Samaranch would like to be president.'

That year Samaranch was a vice-president of the IOC and on 18 July in Barcelona was at the forefront of the annual parade of ageing fascist comrades, celebrating their civil war victory in 1939 and giving the right-arm salute. It was the last time he'd do this in public. His mentor and patron, the dictator General Francisco Franco, died the following year.

Samaranch made the pilgrimage to Landersheim, Dassler's HQ, played tennis with Horst, the pact was agreed and 'support' was put in place.

Next in line for the Dassler treatment was track and field. Dassler supplied athletics kit all over the world. Now he wanted the television and marketing rights to the sport. He looked around for his kind of man and found Primo Nebiolo, from Turin, malleable, greedy and eager to get on. They liked each other, and Dassler gave Primo Adidas support.

Sometimes the valuable marketing rights of the sports federations, their championships and their badges took a roundabout path on their way to the jazz 'em up departments of Coke, McDonald's and the other 'partners'. Having waved bye-bye to their owners in Zurich, Lausanne or London these contracts swirled around the Swiss Alps for a few weeks, touched down briefly in some lawyers' offices and then came to rest in the centre of the country in the beautiful little town of Sarnen, population 9,000, by the lake and under the mountains. For a while Dassler parked FIFA's multi-million dollar marketing rights with an obscure company called Rofa, owned by Bayern Munich manager Robert Schwan and the club's greatest star Franz Beckenbauer. Beckenbauer moved on to other Swiss-based business activities and the sports rights crossed the road to live with another Dassler company, also based in Sarnen.

With business booming Dassler needed money to expand. One man who had it was André Guelfi.

'I REMEMBER going from Monte Carlo on the back of this boat which was zapping along at a zillion, million miles an hour towards St Tropez where André Guelfi lived,' remembered Patrick Nally, the English super-salesman. 'I suppose there were some questions about where his money came from, but having a big yacht and big cars was very helpful for Horst because he could entertain people in style.'

Lean and muscular André Guelfi lived at high speed on land and water, and piloted his own jet planes He was one of the most stylish hustlers of the twentieth century, now in his nineties yet still sharp-eyed and quick-brained, doing business deals as fast as ever. Decades before he met Dassler the young Guelfi made his first fortune hauling sardines out of the Atlantic, raced Grand Prix cars and competed at Le Mans in 1953. Guelfi socialised with the royal family in Morocco and then, unwisely, with their thuggish opponents. He made friends with gangster actor Jean-Paul Belmondo and bought property in Paris. It was whispered that Guelfi was a bearer of grudges and if you crossed him you should forever glance over your shoulder. He was, after all, buddies with the chief of France's secret intelligence service.

In the late 1970s Guelfi acquired half of the sportswear company Le Coq Sportif and sponsored Tour de France winner Bernard Hinault and tennis player Arthur Ashe. Dassler, wanting to broaden his base away from the Adidas brand, bought the other half of Le Coq and found in Guelfi a kindred spirit with money to invest. Together they bought from the Russian communists and sold to the capitalists the marketing rights for the 1980 Olympics in Moscow. Guelfi had acquired great wealth from somewhere he wasn't talking about but a chunk of it came in handy when they had to cough up 45 million Swiss francs for the marketing rights to the 1986 World Cup in Mexico.

Dassler set up a new company to specialise in selling the rights. He called it International Sport and Leisure, forever to be known as ISL.

Energetic support from Dassler and Guelfi levered Juan Antonio Samaranch into the presidency of the IOC in 1980. He responded warmly, giving Dassler the Olympic Order, gold version, and the marketing contracts for more than a decade of Olympics. The following year Dassler and his team arranged the installation of Italy's Primo Nebiolo at track and field without the uncertainty of an election. Primo went on to rig medal results at world championships, bought steroids wholesale for Italian athletes and sold his sport's marketing rights to ISL. The new IOC president moved to live in Lausanne and so did Guelfi, choosing a lakeside villa with sublime views across the pure waters of Lac Leman to the casino dome in Evian. Guelfi enjoyed it and Samaranch coveted it, and for a mere US$4.4 million of IOC money it became the construction site for Samaranch's monument to himself, the Olympic Museum.

As Samaranch expanded his Olympic empire, recruiting the new post-Soviet nations of Central Asia, he flew by private jet, owned and piloted by Guelfi. They dropped in several times on Uzbekistan and later travelled to do business in Beijing. 'We were masters of the universe,' Guelfi told a reporter.

Dassler had built a bright, gleaming influence-building machine. Into one end went cash, favours and men with more ambition than scruple. Out of the other came sports leaders branded with the Adidas trefoil. Over time, in the marble and gilt lobbies of the upmarket hotels where sports business was now done, people asked: were these men really the leaders of their sports, representing the interests of athletes and fans? Or were they agents of influence, puppet presidents, owing their primary loyalty to Dassler?

But Dassler still hadn't got full control of the mansion up on Sunny Hill, looking down on Zurich. Blocking Dassler's way was FIFA's general secretary, the long-serving Helmut Käser with his fuddy-duddy insistence on respecting protocol and convention. In 1980 Dassler began a dirty tricks operation to drive him out. Anonymous letters stuffed with disgusting allegations and rumours of kickbacks circulated. This 'Kill Käser' campaign was put on hold when a report commissioned by the conspirators from a private detective was sent accidentally to Käser.

Käser demanded an explanation from Dassler who also said sorry. Six months later Dassler was spreading word that the general secretary's days in office were numbered. This time Käser confronted the hard-eyed Havelange who, concealing a blade in his sleeve, insisted his job was safe. It was, for several weeks. Then, in late 1980, Havelange dispatched a four-page letter to Käser with a list of instructions. If he failed to obey any one of them, he was out of the door.

JOSEPH 'SEPP' BLATTER had joined FIFA in 1975 to manage their new Coca-Cola funded schemes to produce more coaches, referees and specialist sports doctors. He'd made the headlines four years earlier when he accepted the presidency of the World Society of Friends of Suspenders, a group of 120 men from 16 countries, who 'regret women replacing suspender belts with pantyhose'.

The big money deal with Coca-Cola was signed in May 1976 and in the formal photo a miserable looking Käser sits next to a hooded-eyed Havelange and one of Coke's promotions men. Standing behind and leaning over Käser is Blatter, a youthful looking man in an immaculate cream double-breasted sportscoat with fashionable wide lapels, dark shirt and a kipper tie with a large geometrical pattern that appears to be living a vigorous life of its own. The trousers are trendily flared, as every man about-town's were in the mid-1970s, and although the hairline is already retreating, the long lock draped carefully across his brow gives him a dashing air. He leans forward and looks up from beneath his eyebrows with a sly, confident smile that says, *You know you want me, Baby . . . is that a suspender belt you're wearing?*

Blatter had trained in business administration but his skills were in public relations. In 1964 he got his dream job in his favourite sport, general secretary of the Swiss ice hockey federation. Forever after, Blatter kept a souvenir hockey stick in pride of place in his office. Dassler, looking to recruit a director of development, spotted Blatter eight years later, working for the watch and race timing company Longines. Aged 39 the handsome Blatter with the warm, open smile was hired. General Secretary Helmut Käser was not consulted about the appointment and barely saw his employee for the first six months. 'Blatter was trained at the Adidas head-quarters at Landersheim before he went off to FIFA,' recalls Patrick Nally. 'He spent his time there working alongside Horst, getting to know the Adidas operation. Horst and Blatter became very close during the months he lived in Landersheim. He was very much cemented into the relationship.'

'HORST DASSLER absolutely wanted to get rid of Helmut Käser,' recalled André Guelfi in 2004. 'So Horst said to me, "Couldn't you organise something to get rid of him? Dispense with him, but not physically?" I told Horst, "I'll deal with it."' Guelfi is still upset at suggestions that he would stoop to violence. 'Contrary to what you have heard I am not a killer,' he says. 'I succeeded in convincing Käser to hand in his resignation, I said to him, "If you don't, your life will be made a misery, and everything will be hard. They will try to make you make a mistake, to find faults, to put you in a difficult position, to sack you."'

Guelfi told Käser that he had no future in the new FIFA. 'You know when a boss wants to sack someone, he can do it. So, my advice was we try to negotiate a smart exit and reap a golden handshake. Sick at heart he agreed to resign. I don't remember anymore how much he got but it was a lot of money.'

Money wasn't the only reason Helmut Käser thought it wise to get out. Something sinister was lurking in the Zurich shadows. According to Guelfi, 'Käser said to me, "I am being followed." I said to him "I don't know if you are being followed. But, if they are having you followed it is to try to make you stumble. They will try to get you one way or another so what's the point, you are better off leaving with your dignity intact and negotiate your safety. Because the bottom line is, what's important in life, at your age, you are not going to look for another job", and I persuaded him just like that and I negotiated, although against Dassler's wishes, that he got the maximum figure.' Guelfi paused and added, 'If he was really being followed, it was Horst Dassler.'

Guelfi had done the deed. Pliant Harry Cavan was happy to complete the paperwork. Cavan was a FIFA vice-president for nearly 30 years, an Ulsterman representing the four home British associations on the FIFA executive committee. If anybody could have stood up to Havelange it was Cavan with the moral weight of the founders of the world game. But Cavan was too busy counting the money he got from Dassler as a 'shoe consultant'. Brian Glanville, doyen of British soccer commentators, says Cavan 'grovelled' to Havelange. Former Northern Ireland captain Derek Dougan noted that Cavan, once a lowly-paid trade unionist, 'did very well out of the game and had a tremendous lifestyle'.

On 3 September 1981 Cavan wrote to one of FIFA's Swiss lawyers enclosing two cheques to get rid of Käser, total value 1,597,000 Swiss francs. 'Should you wish to have any more information,' said Cavan, 'please contact Mr J S Blatter.' The IOC gave Cavan an Olympic Order. Havelange, without consulting his executive committee, announced the name of Käser's replacement. And off the production line rolled Adidas's latest product: Sepp Blatter, FIFA general secretary.

Says Guelfi, 'Thanks to Dassler, Monsieur Blatter was appointed, just like that. Dassler said to me, "We are going to put this fellow there, he's alright, he is one of us." I can tell you, Blatter was Dassler's lackey. I found Blatter really insignificant, especially next to Havelange. He was, for me, like a floor sweeper. Blatter can say whatever he likes, making you believe he has done it all on his own. The truth is he owes his job to Dassler. Blatter was really in awe of Dassler, anyone could see that, you did not need a degree to see it, how he spoke to Dassler, how he was with him. We often used to meet for lunch at Landersheim and it was as if Blatter was in the presence of God.'

In the late 1990s French magistrate Madame Eva Joly was investigating corruption at the state-owned Elf oil company. She called Guelfi in to interrogate him about allegations that he had laundered US$40 million to bribe politicians in France, Europe and Africa.

He said he couldn't remember anything so she had him locked up for five weeks. By now he was close to his 80th birthday and the experience refreshed his memory. Guelfi reportedly talked about money laundering through Olympic bank accounts, claimed to have spent US$138,000 on air tickets for Jacques Chirac (before he became President of the Republic) and that whatever he did, he was 'working for France'. That prompted IOC vice-president Vitaly Smirnov to intervene, writing to Ms Joly on his IOC-headed notepaper demanding his old friend's release. While locked up in La Sante jail Guelfi was a few cell doors away from Bernard Tapie, the owner of Marseille football club, jailed for fraud and tax evasion, who had bought the Adidas company from the Dassler family. In 2003 a Paris court fined Guelfi US$1.2 million, gave him a suspended three-year jail sentence and, aged 84 and incorrigible, he set off for Moscow to discuss investing in the national rail system. A Paris appeal court later increased his fine by US$750,000 and said he must serve 18 months jail time.

Käser's widow recalled later that despite the shabby way Havelange treated him the only time she ever found her husband weeping was two years after his dismissal. He came home distraught. He'd met a friend in the street who had been a guest at the marriage of the Käser's daughter Barbara. She'd neglected to tell her parents of the event. Who was the groom? Sepp Blatter.

Horst Dassler died of cancer in 1987, aged 51, and his businesses were inherited by his son, his daughter and four sisters. The sports officials he had promoted did their best to airbrush him out of their history. Dassler, once the most powerful and influential man in sport, who had made them rich, was an embarrassment. He didn't make it posthumously to their halls of fame because his name would always remind them of their shame. The Adidas company has changed hands – and the probity of its practices – twice since Dassler's death.

Havelange would never forget that his general secretary was Dassler's choice, 'one of us' appointed to serve the interests of his companies. Neither would Sepp Blatter, the official whose values came branded with the three stripes of Adidas.

4

_____

SEPP MAKES HIS MOVE ON HAVELANGE

... and lives to tell the tale

Estadio Monumental, Buenos Aires, 25 June 1978. Joao Havelange's friends, the gold-braided and decorated Generals and Admirals seated around him in the VIP box, were ecstatic. The electrifying Mario Kempes had scored twice, then set up the third in extra-time. Argentina had beaten the Dutch 3–1 to seize the World Cup in front of a crowd that at last had something to cheer about at home. It was the FIFA president's first championship since pensioning off Sir Stanley Rous and a triumph for him and the Argentinian military dictatorship. Under the menacing glare of the soldiers surrounding the pitch, patrolling the gangways and staking out the approaches to the stadium, Havelange smiled and said, 'The world has seen the true face of Argentina.'

Certainly it was the face that Argentina's brutal government wanted the world to see. The World Cup did for them what the

1936 Olympics had done for Adolf Hitler. Another murderous regime had exploited sport and sportsmen and basked in their reflected glory.

The true face of Argentina, was, perhaps, the brave and fearful face of the women, the mothers of the disappeared, who risked arrest and worse to parade around the capital's Plaza de Mayo every day of the World Cup, bearing pictures of their missing loved ones, victims of the junta's dirty war against their own people.

Human rights demonstrations around the world had failed to have the 1978 tournament moved to another country, any country as long as it changed governments through the ballot box. When the generals seized power two years earlier FIFA's only concern was, would this interfere with staging the event? Perhaps Havelange felt personally concerned; one of his companies in Brazil had reportedly insured the championship.

The world's newspapers reported that the generals, determined to eliminate any opposition, had ordered their critics tortured in military barracks and then disposed of. For many this meant having weights strapped to them, being bundled into air force planes and dropped, screaming behind their gags, limbs flailing, tumbling down, down to where the estuary of the River Plate met the deeper waters of the Atlantic. Havelange brushed aside these reports. What had this to do with FIFA?

They'd had 25 days of glorious football, and now that Argentina had won convincingly there'd be no more dark whisperings about how they'd managed to knock in an astonishing six goals, two more than needed to make the final, past a suddenly lacklustre team from Peru who had in the first round held Holland to a goalless draw. Why shouldn't Argentine President General Videla visit the Peruvian dressing room before the game? The Argentine junta's sudden offer to the Peruvian junta of huge grain shipments and US$50 million in loans couldn't affect what happened on the pitch, could it? Bundles of cash for the team? Just sour gossip.

And well done Admiral Lacoste, Carlos Alberto to his friend Havelange. Once he'd taken over from General Omar Actis, the money had really flowed. Actis, with his talk of tight budgets and staging the World Cup on the cheap, had been the wrong man to put in charge of the organising committee. Those allegations that dear friend Carlos Alberto had been behind the gunning down of Actis in a Buenos Aires street? Just idle talk.

President Havelange was indeed a good friend to the Admiral and cheered when he became President of Argentina, if only for 11 days, in December 1981. The following year Admiral Lacoste became a vice-president of FIFA and held the position for four years. When democracy returned and Lacoste was investigated for the surge in his wealth and the purchase of a splendid residence in the coastal resort of Punta del Este in Uruguay during the years of terror, Havelange stepped in to save his skin, and helpfully explained that he had personally lent Lacoste US$90,000.

FOR HAVELANGE, life at the top was a succession of four-yearly acclamations by the FIFA congress. Lucky to assume power in the 1970s as business got seriously interested in buying sport, he and Dassler and later ISL kept their promises and Sepp Blatter efficiently put together the FIFA coaching courses and the new youth tournaments. The Europeans, cowed by the Brazilian's icy stare and the money he was laying out around the poorer countries, didn't dare run a candidate against him at the congress at the Spanish World Cup in 1982, or in Mexico in 1986 or even in Italy in 1990. And as soon as that championship was over Havelange told a South American reporter that he would offer himself for further acclamation, for a sixth term, at the next FIFA congress in Chicago in June 1994.

So why was general secretary Sepp Blatter sidling around the corridors of the congress of African football in Tunis in January 1994, under the unsmiling portraits of President Zine El Abidine Ben Ali, whispering in delegates' ears that the old man had had a fine run, done a marvellous job for the game but now, at 78 for goodness sake, surely it was time to go? After thirteen years in the shadows Sepp had had enough. He couldn't bear to wait any longer. Churning in the guts, Sepp lusted to be President.

Havelange promised one thing and did another. 'I would like to retire,' he said one day, 'and I can see Blatter as my successor . . . we can build him up.' Sepp was about to prepare his campaign for a seamless transition when he heard the familiar voice again: 'I spend 300 days a year travelling. I sacrifice myself for the youth.' And it seemed Havelange was happy to continue sacrificing himself.

Perhaps it's true what they said in the kitchen at Sunny Hill, that the old fellow really was being injected with live cells from baby cows in his quest for eternal life, and at the same time, milking a wonderful lifestyle out of FIFA. Things looked hopeful for Blatter for a while after Havelange had a dizzy spell in Barcelona in 1992, but he rested and was soon back on the road again.

But then he went too far. They were in Las Vegas in December 1993 for the World Cup final draw, Coca-Cola produced a souvenir bottle, Daryll Hall sang the tournament anthem, and Caesars Palace had announced that Pelé, the only soccer player the Americans had heard of, was to be the star of the draw for next year's first round groups. At last FIFA was launching soccer bigtime in the world's biggest market – and then Havelange snatched the guest list and drew a line through Pelé's name. And just because Pelé had publicly attacked the Brazilian Football

Confederation, the CBF, which had been run by Havelange's son-in-law Ricardo Teixeira for the past three years.

Banning Pelé spurred *Playboy* magazine in Brazil to look into the unexplored territory of Havelange's background. They dug into his past business dealings. They also examined his father's role in the arms trade. With the generals long out of power, *Playboy* felt safe to investigate the topsy-turvey finances of the Brazilian sports confederation in 1974 when Havelange was in charge.

So Blatter was smiling and pirouetting in front of the Africans in Tunis, showing off his many talents. His aides from Zurich had their instructions: *spread the word, I'll make a great president.* Then he flew home to Zurich, put the lightweight suit in the closet, got out the thick overcoat and flew off to salty Nordwijk on the sand dunes south of Amsterdam. European soccer's top brass were gathering for their executive meeting. They had long memories, they'd never forgiven Havelange for defeating their man Rous in 1974 and they'd hoped a good European candidate would emerge. Well, here was Sepp Blatter.

'If you want to get rid of Havelange, I will stand against him,' Blatter told them. 'If you support me we can get rid of him.' It didn't go quite how he'd hoped. Ellert Schramm from Iceland came out of the meeting and told reporters, 'Blatter has proposed himself as a candidate for the presidency. He said, if you all support me, I will be the candidate. Everyone was astonished by his frankness. He was rejected. I said that we should discuss the disloyal General Secretary, not the President.'

Blatter tried to put his best gloss on it. He told reporters he had discussed the question of his candidacy with UEFA and if they believed he was 'the right man for football' . . . but then the idea had drifted into the sand.

Still hopeful, Blatter jumped into his Merc and sped off to the airport, bound for JFK. The general secretary always attended the congresses of the continental confederations and next on the schedule in the spring of 1994 was the Plaza Hotel, New York City. There would be 35 countries from the Caribbean and Central America and the Americans and Canadians, CONCA-CAF. When they voted together they could swing an election. Blatter was all set to campaign. Havelange also attended the New York congress and his burning eyes could have bored holes in Blatter's back. Havelange let it be known that he was still in charge.

'THERE IS something I have been wanting to tell you for some time,' said the President, having sent the minute-taker out of the Zurich boardroom. Havelange was alone with the presidents of his six confederations and a subdued general secretary. 'I have decided that when we go to France in four years time, there will be 32 teams in the final round.' It was what Africa and Asia and the Caribbean longed to hear. More slots for the developing world, more money from more television and more marketing. As they congratulated him on the eight more places he added, 'Did you really want to hang me because of Pelé?'

It was April and still two months to the congress in Chicago and the 1994 tournament. Blatter's ambitions were squashed. Would he survive the old man's wrath? People were already whispering about a shortlist of candidates for his job. Would he ever work again? Who would employ a man famous for trying to unseat his boss?

Perhaps it was Sepp's secretary who saved him. The Zurich officials, the general secretary's team in their smart uniforms, met in Los Angeles as the World Cup began and tall, short-haired Helen Petermann in the thick glasses nominated herself as shop steward. 'If he touches my boss we're all going on strike here, in America, with the media watching,' she declared. Havelange got the message and turned his attention to pampering the 200 guests he had invited from Brazil.

But it could only be a matter of time. The old man waited, maybe enjoying the daily fear in his disloyal general secretary's eyes. Blatter would be a meal eaten cold.

Meanwhile, Havelange exercised his president's prerogative and purged his committees. Especially pleasing was eliminating the Germans Gerhard Aigner and Horst R Schmidt who hailed from UEFA. They hadn't wanted Blatter but they had wanted the president out and now they would pay. Havelange made one special promotion, elevating his son-in-law Ricardo Teixeira to vice-chairman of the referees committee and putting him on the committee organising the next World Cup, in France.

Blatter wandered the corridors of Sunny Hill like a zombie. After Brazil beat Italy in Los Angeles he'd flown back, gone straight to his office and waited for bad news. It was six months coming. On the wintry morning of 10 January, while Blatter skulked behind his big black leather-topped desk, Erwin Schmid, acting on Havelange's orders, sacked FIFA's press officer Guido Tognoni and the director of competitions, Chilean Miguel Galan. Havelange announced he had lost confidence in them. Blatter's tale was that he had never sought to dethrone his leader and it was all a typical piece of nonsense dreamed up by journalists.

5

HAVELANGE WANTS TO GET SERIOUSLY RICH

Can he turn FIFA into a bookie's shop?

JOAO HAVELANGE ruled the wealthiest sport in the world but after twenty years in the job, it still hadn't made him seriously rich. Monarchs and dictators flattered as they led him to the best seats in their national stadiums, tycoons signed telephone number deals with him and *they* made millions – and how much was he making? When was *he* going to join the lists of the super-rich?

By the early 1990s Havelange had been a member of the IOC for 30 years, president of FIFA for nearly two decades and whatever he had made, it wasn't enough. How could sport make him as rich as he wanted to be? He looked around; where was the Big Idea?

If Havelange were to extract really, really big money from the game he'd need help. Tall, angular Jean-Marie Weber had been personal assistant to Horst Dassler and emerged as the top operator and public face of ISL after his death. It was said

39

he worshipped Horst and photographs of the great innovator decorated the walls of Jean-Marie's office overlooking Lake Lucerne. Weber had helped map the shadier corners of the football business. Weber knew how to make Havelange rich.

Some of the ace salesmen in the expanding world of sports marketing were dismissive. 'Jean-Marie's not creative,' they'd say. They mocked when his bony face was looking the other way because he didn't come up with bundled 'packages' or new events that would need sponsors and could be sold to television. But that wasn't Jean-Marie's purpose. He had to get the business in. And he did.

Colleagues noted that wherever he travelled he carried two bulky briefcases. 'The confidential agreements,' they guessed. 'Jean-Marie would never trust his documents to a safe.'

A polite man, a lover of opera and fine wine, Jean-Marie knew how to cultivate people. He 'made nice' in every crowded hotel lobby and congress hall, shook every passing hand, kissed proffered cheeks and wrapped his long arms around the shoulders of old friends. When Jean-Marie sped across a room he was a skinny, pale grey-suited long-legged stork. You couldn't miss his mane of bouffant white hair and thin-rimmed glasses bobbing above the heads in a crowd or striding up the aisle at a stadium.

Let them laugh. He controlled the rights to three of the world's greatest sports tournaments: the Olympic Games, the World Athletics Championships and the Football World Cup. For a few days a year nearly every television screen in the world showed his programmes. But he still queued at barriers, clutching his ticket, to travel on scheduled air flights. He hadn't hit the big time yet.

Like Joao, Jean-Marie was looking for the Big Idea.

*   *   *

ERCILIO MALBURG thought he had it. The Brazilian business-man went first to Helio Viana, the backroom guy who managed Pelé's business affairs. Ercilio had the biggest of big ideas. If we can bend FIFA our way, we could run the most stupendously huge betting operation off the back of the World Cup, from qualifying rounds to the Final. We'll register the business in the Caribbean and clean up. Billions of dollars would flow in every year.

'You're crazy,' said Viana, 'you'll never make it acceptable to the laws in so many different countries. They'll regulate you out of business.' Pelé was not getting involved. There's the door.

Pelé had another, personal, business manager, Celso Grellet. Ercilio Malburg went to see him. 'I've got the connections,' he said. 'I know Canedo in Mexico, he's the longest serving member of FIFA's executive committee. He's a bigshot at Televisa, he understands how to make money out of football. And here in Brazil we have his close friend Havelange. What more do we need?' Grellet showed some interest but he couldn't see how to make the project work in so many jurisdictions.

But there was a Brazilian who loved to gamble and he snapped at the idea.

Matias Machline's parents came from Russia and made their new home in the southernmost cattle town of Bagé on the pampas near the Uruguay border. In 1961, at the age of 28, Machline set up the Brazilian arm of the giant Japanese electrical goods manufacturer Sharp. He made connections with the generals who seized power in 1964 and business flourished. When mili-tary rule collapsed in 1985 his good friend José Sarney, who'd fronted for the generals, became the first civilian president in two decades.

By 1990 Machline's family-controlled company was turning over a billion dollars a year and Matias Machline was one of

Brazil's leading racehorse owners – and gamblers. When the economy turned down in the early 1990s and business slumped, he cast around for another Big Idea.

His friend Antonio Carlos Coelho had set up the Banco Vega and it was thriving. Coelho and Machline were also friends of Johnny Figueiredo whose father was the last of the military presidents. Johnny loved the new sport of 'Futevolei'– a cross between beach football and volleyball. That led the old friends to start talking with Ricardo Teixeira about Ercilio Malburg's plan to make a fortune out of FIFA.

'We had one daughter, Lucia,' said proud President Havelange, 'and she has blessed us with three grandchildren, Ricardo, Joana and Roberto.' Their father was Ricardo Teixeira and the connection worked well for him. In 1989, although the marriage had crumbled, Joao installed Ricardo as president of the Brazilian Football Confederation, the CBF. Ricardo was also excited by Malburg's gambling plan.

Joao, Jean-Marie, Matias and Antonio came together at a four-star Miami North Beach hotel in mid-July 1993 – Ricardo couldn't make it. Richard Herson, an American vice-president of the Matias Machline Group, wrote in a top-secret memo to Sepp Blatter in May 2001, 'After months of informal discussions, this project was officially initiated on 27 July at a meeting in a suite at the Sheraton Bal Harbor Hotel.' Herson explained that Machline trusted him with 'the early co-ordination of this project as his direct executive assistant'.

Herson defined the project as 'the organisation of a worldwide, FIFA-endorsed membership club and lottery system dubbed FIFA Club which would operate a worldwide soccer lottery linked to FIFA sponsored events under a FIFA trademark licence.'

'A memorandum of understanding was drafted and signed by all present, except for Mr Havelange, who preferred that his name be unrecorded. All negotiations were therefore officially conducted with Mr Jean-Marie Weber.'

Within months Herson was counting his chickens. 'In a nutshell the conservative scenario projected pre-tax revenues of US$8.75 billion after year three, which would make it one of the largest gambling/lottery operations in the world.'

This was it. The Big Idea sought for so long by Joao and Jean-Marie. *Eight billion dollars a year and rising.* Think how big the little percentages would be, the commissions, the bonuses, the consultancies. Even the expenses would be grand.

Herson told Blatter, 'I recorded all materials pertaining to the project as well as discussions in several megabytes of aide-memoirs, designed to keep regular track of the project's progress, as well as links and participation of the various individuals and entities involved.'

The American had surprising revelations about what Jean-Marie was doing in the name of FIFA. 'With ISL's knowledge and agreement during the first half of 1994 these plans were presented and discussed with a number of organisations such as Caesars World and VISA International, in an effort to drum up interest and support for the project. Extensive negotiations among the original parties mentioned above were conducted in Dallas, London and in Zurich, usually at the centrally-located hotel where Mr Havelange kept residence.'

They hammered out a franchise that ISL would give exclusively to The Machline Group. Matias would be allowed to exploit the FIFA logo and its marketing rights for 'the development and exploration of selected activities'.

WORLD CUP '94 came to America and on 16 June in Chicago Havelange was given another four years power by acclamation.

The next day Germany opened the tournament against Bolivia. A couple of weeks later the businessmen were in session again at a 'conclusive working meeting' at the luxurious Mansion on Turtle Creek Hotel, in Dallas. A final contract was drafted and signed by Weber, Coelho, Machline and Herson. The same day, 3 July, Sweden defeated Saudi Arabia 3–1 in Dallas.

They met again at the Mansion on Turtle Creek 'for an additional preparatory session' on 17 July. The World Cup Final kicked off at lunchtime 1,400 miles away in Pasadena, California, where Brazil beat Italy 3–2 on penalties, but business was business. There were unbelievable amounts of money to be made. Matias Machline staged a welcome home for the winners and at a special event organised with Ricardo Teixeira they donated a television to each player and contributed several thousand dollars to a big thank you present.

A month later the businessmen from Europe and Latin America converged on a hotel in New York. They were joined by a new colleague, a business high-flier who'd quit the top slot at American Express Brazil to become CEO of 'FIFA Club'. It was 12 August and everybody signed the final contract. 'Operations were to commence soon after. It was expected that a number of large worldwide gambling and banking organisations would join the project soon afterwards,' says Herson.

Matias Machline, now aged 61, and his 30-year-old wife Maria Araújo said goodbye to their new gambling partners and drove off to Manhattan's East 34th Street heliport. At 8.30 pm the couple boarded a chartered helicopter bound for Atlantic City where Matias planned to play the tables.

Pilot Doug Roesch had passed all his tests for flying in normal visibility. But he wasn't experienced at coping with what pilots call inadvertent meteorological conditions – suddenly flying blind in cloud and relying only on instruments. After about 15 minutes in the air Doug Roesch contacted his home base. He said he was concerned about the weather conditions. He expressed hesitation about completing the charter.

Then Doug Roesch made radio contact with his colleague Eric Mansell who was piloting a sight-seeing flight over New York. Roesch said he was going to turn back – then he changed his mind and decided he'd make one more attempt to get to Atlantic City airport. Five minutes passed and they spoke again and Mansell said later, 'Roesch had changed from being worried and stressed to being relaxed and confident.' But it was very dark and he climbed to 2,000 feet trying to avoid the low cloud rolling into his flightpath.

Ten minutes later Mansell called up Roesch to see how he was doing. The tape recorder in Mansell's cockpit recorded the brief exchange:

Roesch: Eric, I'm going inadvertent (*Distressed Voice*)
Mansell: Doug, are you kidding?
Roesch: Eric, I'm going inverted. (*Panicked Voice*)
Mansell: Doug, are you kidding? Are you kidding? Are you all right?
Roesch: Eric! (*Panicked Voice*)

A witness standing outside her home in a wooded area near Whiting, New Jersey, heard the helicopter overhead. She told investigators, 'All of a sudden, the motor noise changed to a slower sputtering sound. As I was trying to follow the noise, I saw a large orange glow begin to fill the sky.'

The wreckage impacted the ground vertically, making a crater fourteen feet in diameter and six feet deep. The skids were impaled in the ground. The subsequent inquiry attributed the accident to Doug Roesch's 'spatial disorientation'.

A FORMER PRESIDENT, leading politicians, a clutch of tycoons and his four sons and daughter attended Matias Machline's funeral. The Machline Group faltered without him at the helm and the family took the helicopter company to court claiming around a billion dollars compensation. The settlement is confidential but one source close to the case said, 'The family say that had he not been killed in this accident he would have made a giant, giant fortune on the FIFA lottery.'

Meanwhile Antonio Coelho had had another of his big ideas. He invested heavily in processing alcohol to fuel cars, lost a fortune and tried to bail out the business with money from his Banco Vega. Brazil's central bank stepped in on 15 May 1997 slapping a liquidation order on Vega.

A subsequent investigation by Brazil's Senate into corruption in Brazilian football contained six pages on the dealings between Banco Vega, the Brazilian Football Confederation and Ricardo Teixeira. Lucky Ricardo got nearly double the interest rate obtained by his federation and he just happened to withdraw all his money eight days before the bank collapsed. Despite his problems Antonio Coelho was thought by Ricardo to have such business acumen that he was appointed to the federation's finance committee.

A few days after the fatal helicopter crash Richard Herson was told he had late-stage lymphoma. Less than a month later, at the request of the heirs of Matias Machline, he travelled back to Brazil. In his memo Herson told Blatter the story of what happened. 'I met with Antonio Carlos Coelho and Ricardo Teixeira at a suite in the Holiday Inn Crowne Plaza in Sao Paulo, Brazil.

It was a very difficult and acerbic meeting, in which Mr Teixeira made it clear in no uncertain terms that he and Mr Coelho intended to pursue Mr Machline's Project, regardless of any previous agreements, to the detriment of Mr Machline's rightful heirs.'

He went on, 'At the time, in spite of our indignation, there was nothing we could do to counteract such strong-arm, unscrupulous tactics, given Mr Teixeira's connections with Mr Havelange, the project's advanced planning stage, the fact that I was about to start an uncertain fight for my own life, and the fact that Mr Machline's sons had a troubled business empire to take care of.'

Herson had intensive chemotherapy and regained his health. He says that he heard rumours that Teixeira and Coelho tried to launch the gambling business in France but it never got off the ground.

Herson ended his report to Blatter, 'The Brazilian press, eager to nail down Mr Teixeira, who has been embroiled in an endless series of allegations of misconduct, was eager to learn of the details of this huge project, but I was never interested in sharing this amazing, documented saga with the press, in deference to Mr Machline's memory.'

During the Senate corruption investigation Havelange was called to give evidence. He was asked whether he was one of those men 'who has made millions from football'.

'I challenge you to produce a document,' Havelange retorted. 'All I have done all my life is to work with dignity and respect.'

6

DASSLER'S BOYS LOSE
THE OLYMPICS

... and need football more than ever

AFTER Horst Dassler's death in 1987, the family put his sister Sigrid's husband Christoph Malms at the top of the empire as president. Malms was on the short side, trim with cropped black hair. After Harvard Business School he'd gone to work at McKinsey, the management consultants full of bright young MBA's groomed to believe that 'anything you can do we can do better'. But were Harvard and McKinsey the best background for this peculiar industry? Many of the staff at ISL had doubts. Sports marketing was a people business complicated by raging egos, corruption and sometimes, bribes. Was Christoph really suited for it?

Expansion, he decided, was the future. ISL spread around the globe. The group's confidential organogram – a great diagrammatic map of ISL's world-wide operations including some based in Grand Cayman and the British Virgin Islands – grew to list more than 60 companies. The impenetrable principality of Liechtenstein, squashed between Switzerland and Austria, played host to two more companies, Lofa Football Establishment and Lofa Establishment. Inquiries into these stopped at brass plates on lawyers' doors in the capital, Vaduz.

Malms may have had the top title but it was Jean-Marie Weber who went back to the early days of Horst Dassler and was intimate with Havelange and Blatter. His job description was 'rights acquisitions and sports relations'. He schmoozed the sports leaders and persuaded them to pass their precious marketing rights to ISL, now based at the lakeside in Lucerne. Their offices sat on top of the train station, amid the charming jumble of painted ancient stone buildings, bierkellers and churches at the water's edge.

Throughout 1995 the ISL salesmen looked again and again at football and did their calculations over and again; how could more money be wrung out of the game? They had squeezed as much as the market would bear from sponsors. Jean-Marie Weber and the Dassler family wanted more. Where could it come from?

In the past FIFA had sold the World Cup television rights to the World TV consortium of public broadcasters with the European Broadcasting Union leading the negotiations. After the 1994 World Cup in America ISL took apart the balance sheet of every broadcaster that had bought rights to screen the tournament. They added up how much money each company had earned from selling advertisements. They deducted how much had been paid to FIFA for the rights to show the games – and they gasped.

The surplus was huge. Television companies were buying the games low and selling the ads high and making vast profits screening the World Cup. Jean-Marie Weber realised that FIFA were giving the tournament away cheap. They should be charging far more. This was a job for ISL.

It would be tough for public service networks like the BBC in Britain who didn't sell advertising, didn't make profits and had a duty to the public. But it was going to be wonderful news for Jean-Marie Weber and Joao Havelange and a great comfort after the disappointment of the fatal helicopter crash in New Jersey.

IN THE early winter of 1995, with ISL staffers still crunching FIFA's numbers, tall Jean-Marie Weber and short Christoph Malms flew to Japan for a routine business meeting about Olympic rights with the IOC. This piece of business was another part of Horst Dassler's legacy, the thank you from Juan Antonio Samaranch for inserting him into the Olympic presidency in 1980.

The Dassler family had treated their exclusive right to market the Olympics as a long-term investment. They started with the games in Seoul in 1988 just after Horst died and they lost money. They were in the red again in Barcelona in 1992 but in the mid-1990s looked ready to move into profit. By December 1995, Weber and Malms were about to tell the IOC that they'd signed up US$90 million worth of business with Coca-Cola and McDonald's and were close to a deal with Motorola and Shell oil. Wouldn't the IOC be pleased with all this money coming in, less of course ISL's 25 per cent commission?

But the IOC wasn't pleased. Weber and Malms were confronted in a hotel room by the IOC's hatchet-men, Director General Francois Carrard, senior member Dick Pound and Michael Payne, the former British skier who had worked for ISL before jumping ship to the IOC. They were brusque. We don't need you any more, they said. We're taking the business in-house. Goodbye.

Malms flew back to Zurich and an emergency board meeting shortly after lunch on 7 December 1995 in a room in Badenerstrasse borrowed from auditors KPMG. Christmas decorations glittered in shop windows, carols tinkled from loudspeakers but the five directors were deep in gloom. Sacked. By the IOC, of all people.

Perhaps the most anxious was Suzanne Dassler, who'd rushed from her lakeside home near Lausanne on the far side of the country. Short and dark and strongly built like her father, Suzanne, a shy woman, was proud of Horst's legacy and angered by people she thought might be trying to exploit it. She believed he had been a great innovator and she distrusted outsiders who were doing so well out of Dad.

Jean-Marie Weber didn't attend the emergency meeting. He'd spent years assuring the family that since Horst died he'd done a great job maintaining the strong personal ties with the IOC. The Olympic contract was safe in his hands, he'd said. He was fortunate to escape the Dasslers' fury that afternoon. Even through the stilted language of the confidential minutes you can sense the heartbreak. 'We have a duty to write to Mr Samaranch and tell him we do not appreciate what he is doing to us,' insisted Suzanne. The others hushed her. No independent actions, please. This must remain confidential and we need to have a coordinated strategy.

But they knew what rankled. Her father had discovered a little Catalan in jackboots and fascist blue shirt and repackaged him as the man of peace leading the IOC. Back in the 1980s after Horst had fixed the vote, Samaranch was happy to hand him the new marketing contracts. Where was the loyalty now?

What a bad day. It wasn't just a contract. The Olympics made ISL look the best, the cleanest, the most 'Olympian' of all the marketing companies in the sports business. For months they tried to stop the bad news leaking out.

They still had the rights to the World Athletics Championships and they turned a profit. But the big one, the richest one, that was about to get richer, the best contract in the world was the exclusive marketing and television rights to football. They must not lose those. The pressure was on Jean-Marie Weber.

FIFA EXECUTIVES say that Havelange and Blatter were genuinely shocked when Jean-Marie Weber turned up at the mansion on Sunny Hill and told them, *Listen carefully, never mind losing the gambling money, you never had it anyway, get your heads around this. Would you like to double your money from the World Cup? Treble it? How about 10 times as much? We're not talking millions, football's now in the billion dollar league . . .*

When the FIFA executives had absorbed the potential value of the television rights they realised the power this torrent of money would deliver. With a bulging bank account FIFA could help out every national association with money and new facilities. This would transform the world game and inevitably have the effect of entrenching the positions of those who had delivered such unprecedented growth. But would the financial controls you would usually find in a company with a balance-sheet of this kind ever be put in place by FIFA executives?

Weber was nervous. For nearly two decades, thanks to Horst Dassler's special relationship with Havelange, ISL had received the exclusive marketing rights to every World Cup as far ahead as 1998 in France. But not beyond. FIFA would have to offer the marketing and television rights to the 2002 World Cup to anyone who wanted to bid. Rivals would do the calculations and see how valuable the tournament had become. ISL might get beaten in an auction. Or win 2002 and lose next time around.

Maybe there was a solution that would save ISL's skin. *Secure a deal for more than one World Cup at a time*. But that possibility would have to be kept secret for as long as it could.

Let the rivals crunch their numbers on incomplete information. Let them arrange bank guarantees for too little. Keep them in the dark for as long as possible. But surely, this was impossible. You simply couldn't run a fair and open tendering process like that. Could you?

7

A STRANGE FIGHT FOR
THE WORLD CUP

Referee: Sepp Blatter

THERE was someone else who wanted the World Cup very badly and thought he knew how to get it: Eric Drossart, the elegant Belgian president in Europe of IMG, the American marketing company created in 1960 by Mark McCormack to exploit Arnold Palmer's golf swing and charm.

More golfers, and then tennis players, racing drivers, skiers, rock stars and fashion models joined the client list. IMG signed up baseball and basketball, cricket and rugby. They'd brought the television rights to Wimbledon, they looked after Oxford University, the Nobel Foundation, soccer clubs and Pelé. Mark McCormack's boys usually got what they wanted, outbidding all rivals. Now they wanted the football World Cup.

Eric Drossart had negotiated a partnership between IMG and UFA, the television subsidiary of Bertelsmann, the world's biggest media conglomerate. They went to their banks and obtained the guarantee letters needed to accompany a big-number bid.

Drossart opened his campaign on 18 August 1995 with a stunning offer. 'Dear Sepp,' he faxed, 'we are offering to pay US$1 billion for the World Cup 2002.' Knowing a bit about Sepp's special relationship with ISL, Drossart copied his offer to every single member of FIFA's executive committee.

You might have thought the offer of a thousand million dollars from two gold-plated companies would have made Blatter ecstatic. Quite the opposite. He was furious. 'We have to express our surprise at the way the letter to the General Secretary of FIFA was termed "strictly confidential" but copies were sent by telefax to all the members of the FIFA Executive Committee,' complained Blatter to Drossart. 'We are not convinced that this was the most suitable method of communicating a message of a confidential nature and it might have been more appropriate to have deleted this misnomer.'

Three weeks later Blatter wrote again to Drossart in London. He requested the details of the offer for 2002 alone. Notably, given what happened subsequently, he made no mention of 2006. Blatter said he wanted the information in less than one month, by mid-October. And he assured Drossart, 'FIFA are now busy arranging the timetable for the bid procedure.'

A month after that October 1995 deadline Blatter told Drossart and his billion dollars to wait for the next few months because Jean-Marie Weber had exclusive negotiating rights until 29 February 1996. 'We must respect these priority rights,' said FIFA's general secretary.

Drossart and his team at IMG weren't idle during the cold-shoulder waiting period. They met privately with Korean FIFA Vice-President Chung Mong-Joon, a son of the founder of the Hyundai dynasty, at the Sheraton at Frankfurt airport. A few days later they met with another Vice-President, African confederation President Issa Hayatou in Paris. They learned that the five continental presidents were pressing Havelange to set up a special committee to find out what was on offer, to make him and Blatter share information. But nothing was happening.

So Drossart made another dazzling offer: 'I want you to be aware of the fact that IMG/UFA are prepared to offer the most attractive bid to FIFA for the World Cup 2002 commercial rights, irrespective of alternative proposals.' An open-ended offer to blow all competition out of the water. The date was 7 December 1995, the very day that Dassler's traumatised family were in the ISL crisis meeting discussing what on earth they should do about losing the Olympics. They badly needed Blatter's help. Would he give it to them?

Blatter wrote once more to Drossart, just before the holidays. 'Best wishes for a merry Christmas and a happy New Year.' Then there was silence. The months fell off the calendar and on 15 March 1996, two weeks after the exclusive negotiating period with ISL had expired, Blatter wrote to Drossart. They were still talking with ISL, he wrote, and, regarding television rights, they'd only recently received 'a definitive offer for 2002 and beyond'. What was this 'and beyond?' Beyond what? All the talk for the past few years had been about a deal for 2002 only. What else might be on the table?

Blatter was promising 'transparency in the marketing of the World Cups'. *Cups?* How had this plural crept in? Was it a typing error? Drossart still didn't know when FIFA would talk to him about his offer.

Drossart learned more when he read the papers a few days later. Blatter put out a press statement on 19 March 1996 revealing not only was he still having private talks with ISL, he was also negotiating with the international television consortium of public broadcasting networks – known in the trade as the CCC. They had been major purchasers from FIFA for 1990, 1994 and the upcoming 1998 tournament in France at the old prices. It was hard to see how they could match Drossart's billion. Most puzzling was Blatter's claim that FIFA was 'scrutinising the offers submitted by other interested parties'. And here was that throw-away line again, a reference to offers for the 2002 World Cup and 'beyond'. But still no firm mention of 2006.

On 29 March Drossart sent another fax. 'We do not believe that the World Cup representation question is being dealt with evenly by FIFA.' Six months earlier 'you advised us that you were busy arranging the timetable for the bid procedure. We have never been told what the bid procedure is.' He went on, 'No negotiations or any sort of dialogue is taking place with us. Is this exclusion deliberate?' he asked Blatter. And what was this about rights for more than one World Cup being offered? 'We assume this is a level playing field and all bidders will be given the same information, bid document, and opportunity for negotiation, presentation etc,' said Drossart and concluded, 'You can rest assured that we will exhaust all possibilities to ensure that this process is dealt with on an even-handed basis.'

FIFA's general secretary waited nearly three weeks and then replied on 18 April. The rights to the World Cups of 2002 and 2006 were available as one package and if Drossart wanted to bid, he'd better get his finger out and submit a bid by 15 May. That left just 27 days for IMG's bid to be costed and guaranteed.

On 26 April, even as his numbers chaps were frantically crunch-ing a new set of calculations covering two tournaments and raising another billion or more in bank guarantees, Drossart wrote to Sepp, 'I must admit that I am amazed by the content of your letter of 18 April. Whilst I welcome the apparent invitation from FIFA to be involved in the bid process for World Cup rights, there are glaring inconsistencies in your letters to us concerning the basis on which the rights are being made available and such obviously preferential treatment being given to other parties such as the CCC and ISL, that as of today it is difficult to believe that FIFA genuinely wish to consider our offer on a properly competitive basis.'

Near the end of this lengthy letter Drossart said bluntly, 'Sepp, it is very difficult to conclude anything other than there being two sets of rules in operation here . . . and your responses to our efforts are merely a cosmetic exercise designed to protect FIFA from future accusations of unfair and improper competitive conduct.'

The bidding moved into the final phase. ISL had difficulties persuading their banks to underwrite their bid. Reluctantly they went to see Leo Kirch, the reclusive German television entrepreneur who had built up one of the biggest film libraries outside Hollywood and also had the rights to screen the best of German football.

The banks liked Leo and couldn't lend him enough. He had only one condition. 'I must have the World Cup rights for Germany,' said Leo and although it was one of the most prized territories, Jean-Marie had to agree. Leo pondered their request for a few minutes and then with the steely nerve that had made him a billionaire, the mogul from Munich said yes and ISL were back on track.

All bids were submitted on 15 May and Blatter locked them in his safe. Revised bids were submitted a month later and the executive committee would decide who got the business. But not all of the members appeared to know when the crucial meeting would be. UEFA president Lennart Johansson urged that FIFA's auditors should supervise the process.

The committee met on 5 July 1996, and on the agenda was what appeared to be a routine update for members on the television and marketing contracts. It was listed at point 3.1 as

'Report to the finance committee about award of the TV rights.' Havelange from the chair proposed that the rights for both 2002 and 2006 should go to the ISL and Leo Kirch consortium. He demanded that members make up their minds immediately. Havelange turned first to Russia's Viacheslav Koloskov. 'Are you not of the opinion we should accept the offer, my friend?' He blinked and said yes.

As Havelange went around the table, eyeballing member after member, Blatter kept count. Nine members agreed with Havelange, six voted against and three abstained. Absent from the meeting was the ageing billionaire Henry Fok from Hong Kong and Gerhard Mayer-Vorfelder. The German said later that he hadn't known such an important item was on the agenda.

Had Mayer-Vorfelder attended and voted against Jean-Marie Weber and Leo Kirch their bid would have died. Seven against plus the three abstentions would have outnumbered the nine favourable votes.

In July 1996, with all the bids in, the financial terms of the ISL/Kirch offer proved superior to those submitted by all other bidders. There was a further 18 months of negotiations on the marketing rights. In early September 1997 Jean-Marie Weber reported to his board that because of the 'delicate political situation' and to avoid a split in FIFA's executive committee the news that ISL had definitely won the marketing contract would be delayed while members could ask any questions. There was nothing to worry about. 'The members of the FIFA Executive Committees can ask questions, but cannot prevent the conclusion of the contract with ISL,' he reported gleefully. The minutes of the meeting record Christoph Malms congratulating Weber and his team.

*　　*　　*

THE SHOCKING statement from the bank that arrived in the basement mailroom at FIFA headquarters up on Sunny Hill that chilly winter morning in 1998 revealing the transfer of one million Swiss francs to a senior football official caused more than short-term consternation in the general secretary's corner office. Everybody in the finance department heard about it the same day. Word later spread through the building. It was a cock-up of mammoth proportions. But how had it happened?

A source familiar with the transaction explained to me later: 'It was a mistake by an ISL clerk who had been told to make a black payment to a senior football official who had helped them win the contract. Instead of sending the money direct to him, it went accidentally to FIFA. Before the end of the day the money had been forwarded to the football official.'

Five years later Eric Drossart told *Businessweek* magazine, 'The whole process was never explained, and when I made an offer, I would only receive vague answers.'

For this book I asked Drossart if he would care to say more. 'As you know, timing is of the utmost importance in life, and I believe the time when I would have been prepared to talk about the subjects you raise is long behind us,' he mused, 'and, as we say in French, it would now be considered *moutarde après le diner*. I am now looking forward to helping my company secure new substantial deals (and more accessible!) across the board of the sports spectrum.'

8

EXIT HAVELANGE,
FOOT IN MOUTH

Blatter moves into position

Nigeria, 8 November 1995. President Havelange took tea with
Nigerian President Sani Abacha in his palace at Abuja. Havelange
had a diplomatic problem. The World Youth Soccer Championships were soon to be held in Nigeria. That made Sani Abacha
very glad. But there'd been outbreaks of cholera and meningitis.
There was no way FIFA could fly teams of youths into Nigeria,
and Sani Abacha felt sad about that. Havelange wanted to make
him happy again. So he'd come to Nigeria for four days to ooze
charm at the murderous, thieving dictator.

   The world beyond the palace and the police state that Nigeria
had become was concerned about something greater than Sani
Abacha's disappointment over a football tournament. In Port
Harcourt jail on Nigeria's coast, the executioners prepared the
scaffold. It would need to be in tip-top condition for the killing of
Ken Saro-Wiwa, a man who'd been bold enough to accuse the

Shell Oil company of waging 'ecological war' in the Niger River delta, homeland of his Ogoni people. He'd led non-violent protests against Shell and against Abacha's theft of the nation's oil wealth. Saro-Wiwa would die for his courage along with eight other dissenters unless someone could change Sani Abacha's mind.

Across the world decent people clamoured to stop the executions of men who'd become known as the 'Ogoni Nine'. The trials had been rigged, the men had been beaten. This was murder. Nelson Mandela had led the protests for months. Ambassadors were withdrawn. Plans were announced to suspend Nigeria from the British Commonwealth, trade sanctions were prepared, last-ditch appeals for mercy arrived from writers, artists, celebrities, from ordinary people all over the world. The executioners admired their work. The scaffold looked ready for action.

Inside the Abuja Palace, President Havelange and Sani Abacha sipped their tea and smiled. Havelange agreed that Nigeria could host the World Youth Soccer Championships in 1997. Sani Abacha was happy again. So happy that he appointed Havelange an honorary tribal chieftain. Havelange left the meeting and told the press, 'I feel honoured to be received and I am happy his Excellency has reiterated his desire to see the 1997 competition take place in Nigeria.'

Two days later the executioners rose early. Acting on Sani Abacha's orders they tied Ken Saro-Wiwa's hands behind his back and tightened the noose at his throat. Then they bungled it. It took five attempts but finally they snapped the bolt cleanly and Ken Saro-Wiwa's body dropped down, down, and came up sharply, neck broken, voice of dissent forever crushed. Next. It was a hard morning's work murdering the Ogoni Nine.

In one of his last, moving statements, Ken Saro-Wiwa had told the court, 'I am not one of those who shy away from protesting injustice and oppression, arguing that they are expected of a military regime. The military do not act alone. They are supported by a gaggle of politicians, lawyers, judges, academics and businessmen, all of them hiding under the claim that they are only doing their duty.'

He might have added, they are supported by the FIFA president too.

Cornered in Prague two days after the hangings Havelange said defiantly, 'I will not let politics affect my promise to award the 1997 World Youth Soccer Championships to Nigeria. Sport and politics should not be mixed.'

In London *The Sunday Times* accused Havelange of 'a one-man campaign to bring world football into disrepute ... while shock and anger have been expressed over the hangings, the FIFA president was sucking up to their military leaders.'

Two months later at the African Nations Cup in South Africa angry fans waved posters mourning the Ogoni Nine and damning Abacha. Their fury found no echo inside FIFA. For this was Planet Havelange. A world he had created in his image. It had a different scale of values. Still, Havelange had slipped up. He'd shown a lack of judgement. It was a matter of presentation. He'd made FIFA look bad, embracing Abacha so warmly. His position was weakened. Havelange should take care not to trip again.

He tripped again. And this time it mattered hugely to football. Havelange had allowed Japan and Korea to compete to stage the 2002 World Cup. Didn't he realise the depth of bitterness among Koreans? Japan had occupied their country for the first half of the twentieth century. As winter gave way to spring in 1996 the bickering between Japan and Korea was getting nasty. And FIFA was coming in for the blame. How could they be foolish enough to set up a contest in which one of these proud nations had to lose face?

In his arrogant way, Havelange had assured the Japanese that he could deliver the vote for them at FIFA's executive committee. But Korea was determined to win and they had a lot of backing on the committee. The bidding war surged aggressively. As spring gave way to summer the rumours of bribery took shape when FIFA vice-president David Will said he didn't want to be offered any more gifts. Will, a reserved lawyer from Scotland's chilly north-east, said he'd been offered everything except cash. You don't offer cash to David Will. That's not to say a few others weren't better off by the end of the campaign. One said of another, 'I know he takes bribes. I've had to pay him myself.'

Havelange was the last one to surrender to the obvious. FIFA couldn't wind the clock back. Only giving the tournament to both nations, permitting what FIFA had always said they didn't want, co-hosting, could prevent missiles flying across the Sea of Japan. It would be an organisational nightmare and his inept leadership was going to cost them a fortune. They'd need to pay for two of everything from now on.

Things just weren't going Havelange's way. And there was bitterness in the executive committee, especially among the Europeans, about the way Havelange and Blatter were handling the bidding for the rights to the World Cup of 2002 and 2006. IMG's Eric Drossart copied his furious letters to Blatter to every member of the committee.

Havelange and Blatter ignored Drossart and cold-shouldered the European members who took his side. They weren't happy and they took a little revenge. Denmark's Poul Hyldgaard was a Havelange man on the finance committee and he worked with Blatter supervising the war of the contracts. At their regional congress the European members savagely voted Hyldgaard out of his seat. Knifing Hyldgaard sent a message to Havelange.

Having seemed infallible for twenty years, Havelange's

dictatorial reign was disintegrating. He liked to make his own decisions, have them rubberstamped by the committee. They weren't going to do that anymore. He celebrated his 80th birthday on 29 May 1996. He knew it was time to go.

A SEAT ON FIFA's executive committee is among the most prized and best-rewarded positions in world sport and some soccer administrators will do anything in the hope of squeezing their bottoms on to one. It's a golden club and there are just 24 members.

It's not just the lavish expenses, the salary, first-class flights and swanky hotels to be enjoyed for the rest of their lives – even when they leave they'll get honorary membership, seats on committees and tickets for the World Cup, guaranteed all the way to the morgue. It's the power. Wealthy nations dropping to their knees begging to be given the World Cup tournament, the youth cups and the women's championships. So many people who have no other aim in life than be nice to you.

As FIFA's decision often hinges on which way a couple of votes will swing, you're a guest for every big match in the royal box or the president's stand. The big Merc whisks you through the hordes of fans trudging the last mile to the stadium. There've been so many objections to the extraordinary self-indulgence at the IOC yet few have noticed the holidays, gifts and all the goodies on offer to FIFA's magnificent 24.

In July 1996 FIFA held its two-yearly congress, in Zurich. On the agenda, a proposal to increase the size of the committee. There was huge excitement in the ranks. More seats meant more power. And there was one man in particular who was hungry for power.

You can hardly kick a ball against a wall between Georgetown,

Guyana, and the Arctic Circle without Jack Warner's permission and he'll expect a cut of the ticket and TV sales. He's a short, muscular man with a surprisingly squeaky, lisping voice. But when he speaks, people jump.

From the office in Port of Spain, Trinidad, that he owns and rents back to CONCACAF, the regional football confederation he controls, Warner fondly regards his thick wedge of the global soccer cake, stretching from the Atlantic to the Pacific. It gives him, automatically, a seat in FIFA's golden club, the executive committee. Most of his members come from tiny Caribbean islands, where the only professional soccer is beamed in by satellite from Europe. There's so many islands that his confederation qualifies for three executive committee seats.

Zurich, Kongresshaus, 4 July 1996. It wasn't easy getting through from Port au Prince but finally Dr Jean-Marie Kyss, president of Haiti's football association, got a connection to Caribbean football officials who'd already arrived in Zurich for the congress. 'I won't be coming,' he told them. 'The post is so slow, the invitation has just arrived, we're short of money and we've got a Cuban team visiting so, what with one thing and another, we'll pass.'

Damn doctor Kyss! There goes a precious vote. The delegate has to be there. But then, who knows Dr Kyss? He's just a doctor in the Port au Prince slums. No-one outside Jack Warner's obedient continental federation would recognise Kyss. Let's find someone to vote in his place.

It couldn't be a European, an Asian or an Arab. And every available African was already wearing credentials. Warner hadn't brought any spare Caribbean men with him. They'd all been named and listed. He could hardly send one of his retinue back into the lobby stuttering, 'Sorry, I was drunk when I arrived, I

66

got my name wrong. Actually I'm a soccer official from Haiti –
bonjour – can I have my accreditation please?' Even the gaggle of
cowed Blatter staffers handing out delegate badges couldn't let
that pass.

And then clickety-clack, the required dark skin, all heels and
no-accreditation person – the wrong sex, but who cares? – came
shimmying through the crowds. Yes, she'd do fine, Vincy Jalal,
the girlfriend of Jamaica's football president Horace Burrell.
She'd come along for the fun of a trip to Europe, a few nights'
rumpy-pumpy in a five-star bed, some boutique hopping and a
glimpse of the Alps. They called Horace the Captain, because he'd
been an officer in the Jamaican Defence Force, he loved his rank
and the image that went with it. Yes, the Captain's lady would
be perfect.

A quick call to FIFA's head of credentials. Dr Kyss had
dropped out long ago, Haiti's sent a replacement, V Jalal, and
Jack had got his vote back. Who cared that she was one of only
half a dozen women amongst a thousand men? Hadn't general
secretary Blatter said that women were the future of football?
She took her place near the centre of the hall at Haiti's table, in
time for the roll-call. FIFA seats its delegations in alphabetical
order, Albania and Angola at the front, Uganda and Ukraine at
the rear. Seated next to Vincy Jalal was Guyana, represented by
Jack's close ally Colin Klass, and a few tables away was Jamaica
from where the good Captain Horace could toss billets-doux,
blow kisses and whisper words of advice to this novice in FIFA
procedures.

There were 44 delegates in the hall from Jack and Horace's
region, the Confederation of North, Central America and
Caribbean Association Football and they'd all been together three
months earlier in Guadalajara in Mexico for their own congress.
Most knew the men from Haiti but not one of them wondered

aloud how the place of the quietly spoken and reserved grey-haired, bespectacled Dr Kyss had been taken by an eye-catching babe.

General secretary Sepp Blatter started the roll-call. Vincy's an English speaker but when 'Haiti?' was called, she did her best to deliver a firm 'Oui'. The voters were welcomed to Zurich by Marcel Mathier, president of the Swiss FA, chairman of FIFA's Disciplinary Commission and the guardian of football's morals.

When the resolution that could give Jack Warner another seat for his continent came up for debate, the vote was called and Vincy got up from her seat, click-clacked to the front, showed her credentials, took Haiti's voting slip, went to the booth and, behind the curtains, voted the way Burrell told her to. Vincy's attendance proved to be a waste of time. Jack didn't get his extra seat.

IOC president Juan Antonio Samaranch graciously accepted FIFA's Congress Gold Medal and praised his hosts. 'Examples set in the deliberations taking place would be closely watched and emulated by other sports federations,' he said. FIFA's Order of Merit was awarded to businessman Robert Louis-Dreyfus who'd bought Adidas, Doug Ivester of fellow sponsors Coke and Henry Kissinger.

As he came to the end of a speech examining his 22 years in power, and finding his conduct nothing less than admirable, Havelange sprang his great surprise. Happy days were just around the corner. Every one of the national associations would from 1999 be given a million dollars every four years, thanks to ISL, 'our partners and friends'.

Where would this cash windfall come from? Television networks were going to pay more than ever before to screen the World Cup. Everybody was going get rich.

The record of the meeting was checked and approved by five

FIFA member countries, including Jamaica and Switzerland. That official record will show forever, near the bottom right-hand corner of page six, that although Dr Kyss stayed at home, Haiti did have a delegate whose name, misspelt, was 'Julal Vincy'. After the Captain and his lady had retired for the night and the rum began to flow there were a few laughs at her expense among some of the braver Caribbean delegates. Ever since, but only when Jack and Horace aren't in earshot, Ms Vincy Jalal has been known as 'Ms Oui'.

AT THE END of 1996, in the first week of December, Havelange wrote to every member of the committee, reminding them of the special dinner they had given for him and his wife Anna Marie on his birthday. 'That evening will remain unforgettable for me,' he said, 'since it symbolises the warmth of your friendship.' FIFA and its continents were in a blessed state of unity and, 'convinced that I have fulfilled my mission' he would not run again in 1998. Who would replace him?

LENNART JOHANSSON started work at the bottom of a large industrial flooring company and rose to the top. He made his way from the grassroots of Swedish soccer to lead the national federation. He climbed upwards through UEFA and when they made him president in 1990 he automatically became a FIFA vice-president. Johansson was a man moulded by sport rather than politics. His Scandinavian low-church upbringing gave him an allegiance to democracy and openness that set him apart from trefoil-branded politicos like Havelange and Blatter.

Politely, when Havelange announced his retirement, he waited for nine months and then in September 1997, surrounded by

European soccer leaders in Helsinki, Johansson said he would run for the presidency. That left another nine months until the Paris congress in June 1998, on the eve of the next World Cup.

Johansson, at 69, a big lumbering, jowly bear of a man with greying hair produced a reform programme. He promised democracy, solidarity and transparency. But that wasn't good news to some people. In his solid, thoughtful, choose-every-word-carefully manner, Johansson said that if elected, 'I will push for an independent accountant to examine FIFA's business practices.'

Johansson produced a campaign brochure and in it he claimed the support of IOC President Juan Antonio Samaranch, Pelé, Sir Bobby Charlton and Franz Beckenbauer. It was all very impressive but none of them had a vote.

Johansson's Mr Clean campaign needled Havelange. How dare he call for independent investigations? Havelange had no affection for Blatter; hadn't the man tried to unseat him? But there was one thing going for Sepp. He might call for transparency but there was no danger that he'd actually open the shutters and let some light in. So Havelange's secrets might stay safe in a FIFA ruled by President Blatter.

Meanwhile Blatter sat tight up on Sunny Hill talking, talking all the time on the phone to football officials around the world. He could have spoken firmly to more than half of the national associations, and demand they repaid loans outstanding to Zurich – but he didn't. Given the chance, they'd want to thank him for this, they could see what kind of friendly president he would make.

In early December FIFA and the coaches and journalists from the 32 countries that had qualified for the French World Cup met in Marseille for the final draw. Havelange mentioned casually that Blatter had 'all the qualities to be the president'. But Blatter wasn't running. At least, not openly.

Christmas passed, election year commenced and Blatter rarely left his office. After 17 years as chief bureaucrat in Zurich he knew when old friendships could be profitably renewed and new friends made. One frantic period was at the beginning of a World Cup year. In 1998 the magic date was 15 January, the closing day for FIFA insiders to place orders for tickets, ahead of them going on general sale.

It was a time when the venal would whack in vast orders for resale to touts, brokers and package tour operators. Perhaps the scoundrels believed Blatter would be disinclined to say 'No' to anybody this year. Some general secretaries of national associations ordered tickets.

Chet Greene from tiny Antigua faxed his order direct to 'The General Secretary, FIFA House, Switzerland', although it's not known whether the General Secretary himself ever saw it. His demand came in the name of the Antigua and Barbuda FA. Attached to his covering letter were three sheets listing every one of the 64 matches between the first round and the Final. He wanted 47 tickets for the Brazil–Scotland opening game, hundreds more for other games and 147 tickets for the final. Chet Greene's total order was for 2,964 tickets.

Havelange made another carefully timed interjection that he thought Blatter would make an 'outstanding' president.

Blatter had nothing to gain from openly declaring his candidacy. The longer he procrastinated, the longer he could continue as general secretary in the control room of the sprawling organisation, manipulating the power and patronage at his disposal. Johansson was the challenger, Blatter was effectively the heir apparent.

He put it about that he hadn't made up his mind. 'However, if one or several federations wish to nominate me then I will make up my mind,' he said. 'You're not credible,' taunted Italian vice-president Antonio Matarrese, Johansson's first lieutenant and UEFA's attack dog.

Despite the ticket rackets and debt forgiveness, courtesy of Blatter, Johansson was making solid gains. In February he pitched his reforms to a meeting of the leaders of the African Football Confederation in little Burkina Faso, sandwiched between Mali and Ghana. They promised that the votes of all Africa's 44 nations would be cast in one block for him. As president of UEFA, Johansson could expect nearly 50 European votes automatically and with Africa and the promises from East Asia he was confident of the support of more than half of the 200 or so national associations.

The election was drawing closer and still Blatter hadn't declared. The weeks were ticking down and with no announcement, no campaign and no rival programme to attack, Johansson was frustrated. His allies on the executive committee forced a meeting in mid-March in Zurich with one topic on the agenda: What were Blatter's intentions?

They simply couldn't allow him to be an undeclared candidate using his general secretary's power and influence to win votes. This time they figured they had him cornered. *Here are the options. Announce your candidacy and resign your job. Or tell us you're not running for president. If you equivocate, we'll suspend you.*

Blatter could expect 14 of the 24 voters to be hostile to him when the meeting began on the morning of 13 March under the gilt and chandeliers of a salon in the Dolder Grand Hotel. Havelange tried to seize the initiative, proposing that it was acceptable for Blatter to continue as general secretary, as long as he operated under certain unspecified constraints.

Member after member tried to extract from Blatter a clear statement of intent. *Speak up, no more prevaricating, are you or are you not a candidate?* Each time Blatter inspected his finger-nails, shuffled his pens, adjusted his tie, gazed out of the window. Time and again Havelange squashed the questioner. After four exhausting hours the Europeans had had enough. *Let's put it to vote*, they said. For the first time in 24 years of chairing FIFA's executive committee Havelange was going to suffer a defeat. He'd never been outvoted. What would he do?

'Everybody was stunned,' Scotland's David Will said later, in the hotel lobby. He's a moderate man, a silver-haired lawyer, but there was fury in his quiet clipped tones. 'A majority of the executive committee wanted Blatter to resign. At that point Dr Havelange and Mr Blatter walked out of the meeting and we were prevented from taking a vote.'

Havelange compounded the Europeans' fury by summoning the press and claiming that he had adjourned the meeting because they couldn't agree. 'I have to abide by the laws of this country,' he said bafflingly, 'and if there was a doubt, there was no point in proceeding.' Having bullied, baffled and bamboozled, Havelange turned on the charm. 'Many general secretaries have followed their presidents into office, why should it be so different at FIFA?'

THE KING IS DEAD,
LONG LIVE THE KING

Blatter delivers the money

Paris, 30 March 1998. Blatter delayed two more weeks, out of sight and range of Johansson's artillery, then chose Paris on a Monday to announce that he'd been begged to run by several national associations including Australia, Brazil, Saudi Arabia, Jamaica, Trinidad, the USA and France. 'I am a servant of football and I will try to be as good a servant to football in the future,' he told the press. At his side was Michel Platini, now as hungry for success in football politics as he had been hungry for goals for France and Juventus. All curls and charisma, Platini was Blatter's choice to fill a new position, FIFA's Director of Sport. Blatter planned to be both president and continue as chief executive.

Platini, taking time off from his day job organising the World Cup, just weeks away, told journalists that he did not believe

FIFA was run democratically and feared that if Johansson won the election there would be no change. 'I have absolutely no personal interest,' he added. 'I'm a man of conviction and if I do this it's because I think I'm the only person who can get FIFA to change course because I was a player and a coach.'

Blatter promised to expand the executive committee. Places would be guaranteed for women. For referees. For players. Anybody who might get him a headline. When he won he would have to be paid but his salary would, and here emerged a word that he would often return to, be 'transparent'.

As well as being utterly transparent Blatter was going to protect soccer from 'exploitation by commercial and political forces'. An aide posted on Blatter's internet site the assertion: 'The success and standing of football in the world today can to a large degree be attributed to Joseph Blatter.'

Johansson braced himself for a dirty campaign. 'I am afraid that what has transpired until now will continue,' he said, 'that one will be confronted with things that are not acceptable from an ethical, moral and legal standpoint.'

Kigali, 5 April 1998. Havelange touched down in Rwanda, ostensibly to honour the nearly one million people slaughtered in the genocide four years before. Once that was out of the way, there was important work to be done. Havelange used the occasion to buttonhole officials who'd come from 17 East and Central African football associations to join the anniversary gathering. The crucial message: *Blatter is the man to support.*

Back in Zurich, Havelange wasted no time. He dictated a letter to his secretary, Marie-Madeleine Urlacher. The recipient, a Somali official. 'I should like to tell you how happy I was to see you in Kigali where you were able to expound your Federation's point of view,' smoothed Havelange. He said he was looking forward to greeting two Somali officials at the coming Paris congress, one funded by FIFA, 'and the other, as I promised you, will be my responsibility, as well as the cost of accommodation'. Football in East Africa was so dear to his heart that 'As to your national association, I have had a meeting with the FIFA Deputy General Secretary, Michel Zen-Ruffinen, concerning your development.' He promised technical seminars for referees, doctors and administrators. And he'd fly two lucky officials to Brazil for more courses.

Coincidentally, postmen and delivery drivers in Nairobi, Khartoum and Kampala were suddenly laden with gifts for the region's football decision makers, signed, with warm regards, from their dear friend Joao. Fax machines and photocopiers were wrapped and despatched to offices across Africa. Every nation represented at Kigali got one. In case that wasn't enough to swing the votes of the region Havelange instructed finance director Erwin Schmid to send one regional official a cheque for US$50,000. All Erwin needed was the name and number of a bank account. Havelange didn't bother to get approval from the finance committee. Why should he? He was the president.

Another letter went to the fabulous Fok family of Hong Kong. It was addressed to the billionaire Timothy, president of the local football association, a man with strong influence in Asian sport and soon to join the International Olympic Committee. Tim's dad Henry, who made one of his fortunes out of gambling in Macau, was scheduled to receive FIFA's Order of Merit in Paris. 'My dear friend President Timothy,' cooed the FIFA president, 'I seek your support for Mr Blatter.' Could Timothy deliver the votes of Hong Kong, Macau, China and North Korea? Havelange was especially concerned because he knew that Johansson was at that moment lobbying in China and the fabulous Foks, well-connected in Beijing, were the best hope of chopping him down.

Dublin, 30 April 1998. Havelange was in the enemy's camp. The season of the continental congresses had begun and the Europeans met at Jury's Hotel. The day was all about boosting Johansson. Blatter, the rival candidate, had not made the trip. This was not the time and place to drive a wedge through Europe. Havelange sat in the gloom of the auditorium's front row, peering up to the brightly lit stage where they celebrated Lennart Johansson, the man they hoped would replace him in six weeks time at the pinnacle of world football. The tributes went on and on.

At last they called Havelange to the platform and a UEFA official clipped their diamond pin of merit to his lapel. They said it was for his services to football but in truth it was a goodbye-and-good-riddance award.

Europe's treasurer was the amiable German, Egidius Braun. Chirruping like a happy sparrow at the podium, he reminded everyone of UEFA's financial aid to Eastern Europe (are you new guys at the back listening? Remember kindly Mr Johansson when you go to the ballot box in Paris). Havelange chewed on a piece of gum. When the two big screens above the stage flashed alive with Braun's financial report featuring lots of lovely Swiss francs Havelange perked up. Not for long. Having caught the old man's attention, Mr Braun chided that in the new world of honesty after the FIFA Congress, 'there must be no second cashbox – as they say in Switzerland!'

There was another ambush coming. The big screens lit up with Pelé, Johansson's number one fan and enemy of Havelange. He made a political speech with cheeky smiles. 'I have met many

Kings and Queens, presidents and stars in my travels around the world,' he beamed into the camera. 'But I have never met anyone who cares more for the honesty and transparency of the sport of football as my friend Johansson. I hope deeply in my heart that he becomes the next president of FIFA.'

The congress closed with a last burst of applause for Johansson, Havelange rocketed out of his seat and, more sprightly than any 82-year-old should be, he moved through the delegates to the back of the hall. He saw an old friend and paused. They muttered briefly and then he was off down the corridor, moving relentlessly through the crowds. Breathless, I scrambled my way through the melée, I nearly caught him in the hotel lobby but he was out in the car park already, climbing into Dublin's biggest rental Mercedes and speeding away into the late afternoon spring sunshine up Pembroke Road.

THE RIVALS circled the globe, their wingtips nearly touching as they tried to filch each other's support. Another two weeks on and Blatter and Johansson were in Kuala Lumpur for the congress of the Asian federation. Blatter told them that Europe and Africa were divided and that he would win. Johansson said he had received written pledges of support from 50 of the 51 European associations, at least 60 more worldwide, and he called Blatter's claim wishful thinking.

Blatter has the raw energy and instinct of a professional survivor, scanning a room in seconds to beam friendly glances to faces he knows, even if there's no love lost between them. Johansson is from a more gentlemanly background; football is a family and you shouldn't be rude about a cousin, even if they have spent the last six months trying to shaft you.

He nearly let himself go in Kuala Lumpur. 'Havelange is not

neutral. He even puts words in my mouth, which is wrong. He is not using truth, and this is very alarming to me.' Then Johansson pulled himself up, half-ashamed. 'I have tried to keep quiet about it, but sometimes it becomes too much.' Was this the first time his aides saw the possibility of defeat, suspected Lennart wasn't ruthless enough? Was he naïve to trust that all those written pledges would turn into votes?

Nairobi, 20 May 1998. It began as a dot in the sky but in less than a minute it took the shape of a small charter jet coming towards them from the south, from the Golden City. The eager football officials at the airport shaded their eyes in the African May morning sunshine. They made their way to the tarmac as the jet taxied towards the Nairobi terminal building. The engines stopped, the door opened and here he was, Mr Blatter, fresh in from Jo'burg, all waves and warm smiles, confident he could remember the names that his onboard briefers said would be ready to greet, shake hands, hug and think again about the precious votes they had promised to his rival.

Blatter flew in with joy in his heart. He'd had meetings with officials from South Africa, Mozambique, Angola, Lesotho and Namibia, five votes. He'd promised them that with his backing South Africa would host the World Cup in 2006. If he won he'd pump even more money into the continent. His audience liked what they heard from him in public and in private. That was five votes wrested from Johansson who was backing Germany for 2006. In Kigali Havelange had begun picking apart the block vote promised by African football's leadership back in February. Blatter was picking off more. Africa was splitting.

Coming off the plane behind Blatter were his persuaders, the tight, ruthless team determined to change minds in Africa. Right behind Blatter was his daughter Corinne. Next was Emmanuel Maradas, a big shaven-headed man from sub-Saharan Chad. Emmanuel was Blatter's occasional press spokesman. He was based in North London, married to Nim Caswell, sports editor of the *Financial Times*, and together they published the monthly *African Soccer Magazine*.

Jean-Marie Weber's ISL company bought pages of expensive advertisements in the magazine and the couple were familiar guests on the well-padded FIFA circuit. Blatter and Havelange were frequently the targets of attacks in newspapers around the world but Nim and Emmanuel tended to take a kinder view. In his luggage Emmanuel was carting copies of *African Soccer Magazine* and its May editorial 'Divided Loyalties' giving comfort to those who might want to vote for Blatter.

Last down the steps was the young Swiss lawyer Flavio Battaini. This was odd. Shouldn't he have been behind his FIFA desk in Zurich? What was he doing, risking his lawyerly reputation for neutrality by being seen in one of the rival camps? When Blatter finally declared he was a candidate he was forced to retreat from Sunny Hill and run his campaign from his spacious top-floor apartment in Zollikon with its views over Lake Zurich. He had given his word he would not take advantage of the organisation's funds, equipment or personnel. But his ever-loyal secretary Helen Petermann, from her office, next to Blatter's now empty one on the first floor, had drafted and dispatched the fax calling today's Nairobi meeting.

There'd been allegations that Blatter was improperly using FIFA's money and resources for his campaign and that was a lie and he wanted to squash it, urgently, immediately he landed in Nairobi. Blatter summoned the local reporters waiting at the airport, looked them in the eye, and, as one of them wrote, *vehemently* insisted, 'No travelling expenses, faxing, couriers, cell phone. Not a penny! All I have from FIFA is moral support!'

Now it was time to lobby the officials from Kenya, Uganda, Tanzania, Zanzibar, Somalia, Ethiopia and Sudan, the East and Central region of Africa.

The African officials were too canny to endorse Blatter immediately. They wanted to see what more Johansson might offer. Even so, Blatter said, 'I feel tremendously positive' and a dozen hours after he landed at Jomo Kenyatta airport, he was up in the air again, on the way back to Sunny Hill. The next day the headline in the *East African Standard* summed up Blatter's visit: 'BIG MONEY PROMISED.'

So, how was the now unemployed Mr Blatter paying for his costly campaign, hiring charter jets to hop around the world, entertaining at classy hotels, promising free trips to Paris, rarely off his cell-phone? His rival Johansson was given US$534,000 by UEFA and he told reporters, 'The executive committee approved this. All the details are open, they are all public, there is nothing to hide.'

Blatter told one reporter he had only US$135,000 to spend, then he informed another that actually his budget was US$300,000. Later, in a throwaway line, Blatter mentioned he had 'a few minor sponsors', the seriously rich Mohamed Bin Hammam from the fabulously wealthy oil and gas statelet of Qatar, for one. A few days before the election Blatter said, 'I have nearly run out of money. Michel Platini has graciously said he will foot the bill for the few drinks and refreshments we are going to have this morning.'

Platini took up the theme. 'What does FIFA mean to today's players? Nothing. The people they see are figureheads, staying in five-star hotels and eating in expensive restaurants. We want to change that.' Platini was talking with a reporter from the Associated Press who noted, deadpan, 'Platini's organising committee paid for the news conference, held in a meeting room of a four-star hotel and offering champagne and ritzy hors d'oeurves afterwards.'

'THEY OFFERED me US$100,000 to switch my vote from Johansson to Blatter ... Half in cash and the rest in football equipment for my country!' Once the lean man from Mogadishu in his white skull cap and gold-rimmed glasses started talking about the 1998 election he didn't stop for an hour. He was Farah Addo, Vice-President of African football. 'When I said no, I will not change my vote, they said OK, but we want you to influence the others. They thought I was stupid.'

Suddenly it was worth the two-day wait in the pink-dusty heat of Mali, watching the big trucks rumbling out in the cooler night to Timbuktu. It seemed that nearly every official at the African Nations Cup in January 2002 wanted an appointment with Farah Addo, once an international referee and now an influential football politician, and I was at the back of the queue. Addo held court in a sparsely furnished whitewashed office in a squat two-storey building in Bamako, across the road from the broad, slow-moving Niger.

Addo, flanked by officials in flowing robes from around the continent, made his points with vigour, his thin moustache flying up and down. He told how he took a call in his Cairo office from a former Somalian ambassador. It was troubling. The man was calling from a Gulf country. He was acting as a middleman. He was offering a bribe, US$100,000, if Addo would vote for Blatter. They especially wanted to get Addo aboard Sepp's campaign because he was also president of the Central and East African confederation and might influence more than a dozen votes.

Addo sent them packing and thought little more about it until he got to Paris and received a shock. 'When I reached the Montparnasse hotel my name was not there as President of the Somali Football Federation. It was not at the counter where you got credentials. But I had a copy of my original application for accreditation.' Addo lobbied the leaders of African and European football. 'They went to the leadership of FIFA, telling them they would make a scandal if my right to vote was not restored.' He got his vote back. Addo makes it clear that he has no proof that Blatter was involved in or had any knowledge of the attempt to bribe him or of the attempt to remove his vote.

Addo's claims that he was offered a massive bribe to sway votes to Blatter were amplified by former Somali officials who claimed they had been given a mixture of cash, air tickets and expenses to go to Paris. Some said the man behind the induce-ments was Mohamed Bin Hammam.

Bin Hammam is a small, slim man in his mid-fifties with a receding cap of flat, tight curls. He's quick to smile and quick to order coffee when we meet but come a point of disagreement his eyes suddenly narrow and his thin moustache twists as he curls his upper lip in disdain. Perhaps he's not used to being argued with, accustomed as he is to the respect of his half-a-pace-behind-him-eyes-averted entourage of bag carriers and bill settlers. His clothes are conservative and whether close-fitting dark suits or white silk jalabiyyas, look as if they engrossed a tailor for many months of delicate stitching.

He's not just rich. He is one of a select band of 35 men who sit on Qatar's Advisory Council, handpicked by absolute monarch Emir Hamad bin Khalifa Al Thani. A member of FIFA's cabinet since 1996, Bin Hammam is one of the Emir's favourites. His high profile in world football politics brings sporting status to a tiny country that pays big money to ageing foreign stars to play out the twilight of their careers in the local league. Out of season Qatar pays fortunes to young African runners to switch nationality and win medals for their new country.

When the bribery allegations began to fly, Bin Hammam produced a lengthy rebuttal. He didn't think anything wrong had happened in 1998. 'It is regrettable to see what we believed to be a fair contest and duel between knights, has now changed to a dirty war: I helped Mr Blatter immensely in his campaign in the 1998 election and some even claimed that I was the major reason for his victory not because I bribed people but because we planned the battle. We were right in the field while the others were sitting behind their desk.'

Bin Hammam revealed the personal cost of backing Blatter. 'We were in Paris and were planning a trip to South Africa in a commercial flight, not belonging to or financed by HRH the Emir of Qatar. The night before we travelled I received a frantic call from my wife with the shocking sad news that my son aged 22 years had met with a very serious accident and was fighting for his life and his condition was more towards death and was lying in the intensive care unit in a coma. I should immediately return to Doha. I regretted and apologised to my wife, and told her that my son doesn't need me but needs the blessing of God and help of doctors while it is Mr Blatter who is in need of my help now. So I sacrificed seeing my son maybe for the last time.'

Lennart Johansson and Michel Zen-Ruffinen, then FIFA general secretary, confirmed to me that Addo's 1998 congress registration documents had been altered to exclude him from voting, although they did not say by whom. They said they had insisted his accreditation was returned to him. Addo later asserted that at least 18 African officials, although publicly committed to Johansson, had sold their country's votes to supporters of Blatter. That would be enough to swing the result. If claims by Addo and others are true, then Blatter is an illegitimate president and Johansson was robbed.

At the end of 1998 Blatter was confronted by a Swiss reporter with the allegation that Qatar had provided the money for his expensive campaign. This he denied, retorting, 'The Emir gave me his plane only once for a flight from Paris to Dakar.' Blatter insisted that he had paid all his own election expenses.

Some time later in 2003, after I had asked Bin Hammam about the specific allegations, he invited me on an all-expenses paid trip to Qatar as his personal guest. 'I hope that you will accept my invitation,' he wrote, 'so I can send the air ticket to your address.'

For a moment I imagined life as it might be for a foot-soldier in the world of FIFA politics. A super-rich and famous man likes me. He wants to take me on a trip. He'll send tickets to my home. Kind hospitality. Sumptuous hotels. Perhaps he'll give me pocket money.

I pinched myself and politely declined his invitation.

DAYLIGHT ROBBERY *AGAIN*

How they stole the vote in Paris

DR JEAN-MARIE KYSS completes the morning's obstetric consultations for the impoverished women who come to the single-storey Centre Médical O. Durand in the pungent downtown streets of Port au Prince. Then from behind his desk overflowing with patients' files, he tells me about the problems he'd had trying to attend FIFA congresses. 'Soccer is big in Haiti,' he explains, 'and in the 1990s it generated a lot of cash at the turnstiles of our national stadium. First of all the government tried to steal it by imposing its own people on our federation. When that didn't work they tried to seize the stadium itself. The Secretary for Sport sent police and security men. Come and see it for yourself.'

Four years earlier in June 1998 as FIFA slithered towards its congress, the money was flowing again into the Stade Sylvio Cator. Closed for five years during another of Haiti's periods of violent upheaval it had recently reopened with a morale-boosting 3–0 trouncing of Martinique by the home team. For the poorest nation in the Western hemisphere, any kind of victory was sublime. So was the rattle of the cashbox to the crooks in the government.

Now, in the spring of 2002, grey-haired Kyss, in his neatly pressed but threadbare dark suit, was no longer president of the Haitian federation. He still didn't know what had happened at that FIFA congress back in 1996 in Zurich. Nobody had ever had the courage to tell him that his vote had been stolen by a gorgeous stand-in. But he *thought* he knew what happened in 1998.

We picked our way along half a dozen hot, crowded streets, around the market women, the motorbikes and piles of garbage, through the stadium gates, the tunnel and onto the brown pitch. Kyss is a well-loved man; there were smiles and waves from the ground staff. 'The clubs were behind me in 1998,' he said. As for the crooks in the government, 'eventually we beat them in the parliament and in the courts. So it seemed a good time to go to the congress in Paris.' But the thieves kept up the pressure.

'I and my wife Nicole went to the airport but when we got to the immigration control somebody told me, "The Doctor is not supposed to leave the country." I asked, "Have I committed any crime, have I violated any law?" They said it was the order of the Secretary of Sport. We had to stay in Haiti because there was no way we could get on the plane.'

Kyss had fought a brave battle to protect football in his own country but he couldn't argue with the gunmen at the airport. He put his passport in his pocket and walked away.

Kyss went back to his consulting rooms and started calling Paris, trying to reach officials of CONCACAF, the Caribbean and North American soccer confederation. 'I spoke to secretary Chuck Blazer and president Jack Warner. I explained to Mr Warner what had happened and told him that Haiti would not be represented at the FIFA congress. FIFA's rules do not allow proxy voting but

I would not want to mandate anyone to sit in our seat in Paris. That empty chair symbolised the interference of our government in our sport. It was our gesture of defiance. That empty chair sent a powerful message to the world.'

Sadly for Kyss, Jack Warner had other plans.

Paris, 8 June 1998. Football's parliament, the Congress, met to elect its new president. This was FIFA's most important day in 24 years, the first presidential election since Havelange outwitted Rous at the Frankfurt Kongresshalle. It was a sunny morning on the south side of the city and Lennart Johansson and half a dozen aides strolled along a narrow tree-lined street through crowds of reporters and cameramen to the Salle Equinoxe, an austere metal-clad assembly hall in an ugly exhibition complex. The reporters called to him and Johansson smiled back. He looked to have recovered from the late betrayal of the English. They'd switched their vote to Blatter in the hope that he'd bring the 2006 World Cup to England.

Blatter had been delighted, saying, 'The fact that England, the motherland of football, has come out so strongly to back me has touched me like nothing else in my campaign.' Johansson, glum, said 'a week ago the chairman of the English FA, Mr Keith Wiseman, told me they would be voting for me. Clearly they can no longer be trusted.' After the Heysel stadium disaster when 39 Juventus fans died, England had been banned from Europe and it was Johansson who'd got them back in. How soon they'd forgotten.

Johansson's worry had to be, who else would break ranks in Europe, his power base? First the French, now the English. His prediction of a lead on the first round followed by victory in the run-off was looking shakier.

Here was someone who must be important. Gliding up to the kerb was an extra-long Merc, flanked by running men in suits with government haircuts, curly wires coming out of their ears, and bulky lumps under their jackets.

A glimpse of robes in the back; it was Prince Faisal of Saudi Arabia. Prince Faisal was a member of the International Olympic Committee but he habitually missed their meetings and Games. Any other member would be cautioned, then expelled. Not a Saudi prince. So why had he and his sharp-eyed bodyguards made the journey here this Monday morning?

The Prince was going to cast a vote. Something no-one is allowed to do back home in undemocratic Saudi. Bring up that topic over sugared mint tea in the souk and your next public appearance may be in Riyadh's Chop Square. But the wealthy Prince was a great supporter of Blatter and keen to help lever him into power. It would be risking death by a dozen bullets to get near enough to ask him a question but one African official, Mr 'Bomba' Mthethwa, had told the *Swaziland Times* that his expenses had been paid by someone from the Middle East. He declined to name them, saying it might have 'a negative impact'.

Havelange conducted his final congress with his usual grace. The charisma that charmed enough voters to eject Sir Stanley Rous all those years ago had not dimmed, only matured. He still had that noble bearing. His penetrating eyes were sharp as ever. But they were set deeper in their sockets and looked darker; from some angles there was something of the night about him. Henry Fok stepped up to get his Order of Merit, a South African diplomat stood in for Mandela, England's Sir Bert Millichip got his. Then Havelange, well practiced at his own valedictories, delivered over the past couple of years, described himself as an 'idealist and visionary' and took credit for thinking up the idea of selling marketing and television rights.

He talked wistfully of his sponsors, the good people who made him what he was today: 'The collaboration of Coca-Cola and Adidas in the youth development programme and in youth competitions stems solely from a mutual desire to invest in youth and to create personal contacts and exchange of ideas beneficial to the "Planet Football".' Elsewhere on his planet, football was in trouble.

Havelange sat down to the applause he expected, the congress dealt with a few procedural matters and then moved to the election. Tension rose. The candidates, according to protocol, left the hall before the ballot. Johansson looked confident. For all Blatter's posturing, enough voters, especially the Africans, had looked Lennart in the eye and promised their support. Never mind the defectors, he'd still win by at least 10 votes. One by one, delegates cast their votes, Albania first, then Algeria and all the way to voter number 191, Zimbabwe's Leo Mugabe, nephew of his president.

But surely there'd only be 190 votes. One country wasn't voting. Had anyone noticed Kyss's eloquent gesture of defiance? Had anyone asked, why Haiti's empty seat? No-one had and here's why.

Jack Warner had put someone in Kyss's seat. Not a woman, this time. Too risky. A woman is a rarity in football's parliament, the place was swarming with reporters who might notice. No, it had to be a man. A black man who could be relied upon to keep his mouth shut. Warner knew just the fellow.

It was Neville Ferguson, a friend of Warner's since they'd trained together at Mausica teacher's college in Trinidad back in the sixties. Neville was a fan. When interviewed about his famous friend, Neville said that Jack 'liked to have a good time with the ladies and I was amazed he could find the energy to go to church every Sunday morning. He knew that there was a Force far stronger than he was capable of controlling that was running his life.'

And Neville was on the payroll. Jack had made Neville deputy general secretary of the Caribbean Football Union, a job involving lots of international jaunts at football's expense. And Neville had Jack to thank for the fees he earned as an international match commissioner. He'd come to Paris as one of Jack's personal assistants. Suddenly he found himself promoted to delegate with proper plastic accreditation around his neck. Not quite proper, Neville was just a pretend delegate and he wasn't even a citizen of Haiti.

So, sitting in Kyss's seat was Neville Ferguson. Did anyone speak up about the difference? Not Guyana's Colin Klass, who'd failed to spot Vincy Jalal last time. Certainly not Jamaica's Captain Horace Burrell, General Secretary Horace Reid, and almost within touching distance many of the Caribbean Football Union's 30 national associations and several dozen officials. Perhaps FIFA should get a group booking for an eye test.

And while they're at it, perhaps they should have their hearing checked too, because at the roll-call Haiti's man didn't speak French, but said in unmistakeable Caribbean English, 'present'. When Neville cast 'his' vote – you can see him do it on the official FIFA video – a scrutineer looked sharply at him, looked again, but the moment of doubt passed. And Neville's vote was counted along with all the others.

Johansson was stunned. He hadn't won the first round. He'd lost it badly. Blatter had got 111 votes to his 80, not quite enough for a two-thirds victory so they began the second round. But Johansson knew he'd lost it. All that campaigning, all that self-restraint, all that trying to pretend it was a contest between gentlemen, a football family matter. All that trust shattered. He stopped the ballot and, with tears in his eyes, lifted Blatter's hand.

Later, he said with heavy emphasis, 'I was astonished that people I talked to told me they would vote for me and then a lot of them didn't. I've learned a lesson.'

Corinne Blatter spoke the truth when she gushed, 'The vote was won in Africa.' Jack Warner crowed, 'We played a pivotal role in Blatter's victory and we shall be benefiting in both financial and technical areas very shortly.'

At Blatter's victory press conference a German reporter, Jens Weinreich, asked him about allegations that his campaign had been funded from the Gulf. He replied, 'The match is over. The players have already gone to the dressing room, I will not respond.'

It was alleged that US$50,000 bundles had been handed out to African delegates in the Meridien Hotel, supposedly advance payments for development projects in their countries but perhaps unsurprisingly seeming to others like inducements. People talked about bags of cash arriving from the Gulf. In response a Blatter spokesman said, 'Mr Blatter vehemently refutes the allegations and will investigate the source of such malicious reports ... He stresses he reserves the right to take legal action against the seekers to defame him.'

Graham Kelly, chief executive of the English FA, said after Blatter's victory, 'We are delighted he has won, he was the best man for the job.' England's World Cup campaign leader Alec McGivan said, 'If I was German I would be very worried. In the last year their campaign has been ineffective.' Actually, it was the English who should have been worrying, because a week later Blatter said the 2006 tournament should go to Africa and two years later, it went to Germany.

I told Lennart Johansson in April 2002 about the theft of Haiti's vote. He was shocked. He wrote to Blatter, 'I find this revelation very disturbing and must ask you to investigate this urgently.' Blatter did nothing.

I asked CONCACAF Secretary Chuck Blazer about this matter. He responded with a one-line email: 'I am not familiar with the allegations you are making.' I asked CONCACAF vice-president Alan Rothenberg, who'd been sitting towards the back of the hall with his US Soccer delegation. He told me, 'I have no interest in talking to a biased hatchet-man. If you had a shred of impartiality you would recognise the incredible contribution made to the enormous growth of soccer on and off the field by Sepp Blatter, Jack Warner and Chuck Blazer.'

I rang Neville Ferguson. He didn't want to elaborate on the day he became a delegate for a foreign country at the Salle Equinoxe. He hung up and switched on his answering machine.

I tried Jack Warner. He referred my questions to Karen Piper of Trinidad, one of his many lawyers. She told me to stop 'harassing' him or she would take 'appropriate action'. I asked Blatter and his Zurich press minders. They didn't reply to my questions but accidentally copied to me an email Blatter sent to his Caribbean ally: 'Dear Jack, this is part of a never-ending story until we both will be re-elected. Good luck and especially patience. Sepp.'

I flew to Miami in late April 2002 to attend Warner's regional congress, hoping to ask some questions at his press conference. I bumped into him in the lobby of the delightful art deco Loews hotel on South Beach. I said Hello, held out my hand. He declined to shake hands and said, emphatically, in his familiar squeaky lisp, 'You smell!' He was so taken with his own eloquence that he's said it again each time we've met.

Strolling towards the press conference in Loews, I was surprised to find my way blocked by a gentleman much bigger than me. 'Would you be Mr Andrew Jennings?' he asked. 'Yes,' I said, 'Why do you want to know?'

'Mr Blazer says you are not permitted to attend the press conference. You can't go in.' I looked at the accreditation hung around his neck and said, 'So you are Mr Melvin Brennan from Jack and Chuck's New York office. You're an American citizen and you're against freedom of speech?' Melvin, broad as a barn door and nearly as high, looked a bit embarrassed. Still, he wouldn't let me in.

So, Jack didn't like my fragrance and Chuck didn't like my attitude. I felt a bit crest-fallen. I wouldn't be in there to ask Warner about his vote-rigging. I had to make do with reading Warner's unchallenged claim that ran on the news wires later. 'The delegates did not see what all the hullabaloo was about. There is no Haitian problem. The delegate who did not vote gave permission for his vote to be mandated.'

Four years later when I told Kyss what happened to his vote, he was stunned. 'This is the first I've heard of this. I was never sent any information about what happened in Paris. I feel bad about it.' And he looked really sick.

PRESIDENT BLATTER AND THE GOLDEN GOOSE

Leafing through Sepp's expenses

Sunny Hill, 9 June 1998.

Bringg

Bringg

Hello, FIFA House? Oh yes, Good morning Mr Blatter.

I'm sorry, forgive me, yes I saw the news on the TV last night. Congratulations and Good Morning President Blatter. How is the weather in Paris?

You wish the sign saying President to be moved immediately so it points to your office? Certainly.

And, I beg your pardon Sir, did you say scrap the headed notepaper. What, all of it? Of course. Immediately.

New notepaper to be headed, 'President Joseph S. Blatter.' Right away.

And a sheaf of blank expenses forms to be put on your desk. Yes, Sir. Will that be all? Hello?

Sunny Hill, 13 July 1998. The new president turned his gaze back from the distant Alps, shimmering in the summer heat, to the pile of receipts, bills and invoices littering his desk. Campaigning to become FIFA president was an expensive business, especially when you had to work from home and weren't supposed to use the office facilities. Now, what have we got here? DHL couriers.

Yes, there were some very valuable packages to be moved around the world. Faxing. Yes. And the cell phone. That took a hammering, and look at what they charge. Outrageous. He wrote on the claim form, 'Campagne Présidentielle: Natel, fax, DHL. Nearly thirteen thousand francs; 12,527.70, to be precise.

Then, the travel expenses. It would take forever to itemise them. Better to write down the total and bang it in. 'Frais de voyage Campagne Présidentielle.' 56,032 francs.

Johansson would have a fit if he saw this. But he would never see them. Blatter's expenses were none of his business. In fact they were nobody's business. He didn't have to run them by anybody.

Every member of FIFA's leadership has a private account locked away in the finance department. Their travel expenses, hospitality bills, sometimes private spending on themselves, World Cup ticket purchases, it can all end up in their secret numbered account. Sepp Blatter's isn't quite as secret as it might be. The records show that it was his Golden Goose.

The pages covering the period from December 1997 when Blatter was general secretary, through to December 1999, when he had been president for 18 months, make for curious reading. One day, Blatter puts in a bill for champagne, the next day he's shopping at the Co-op, then he's picking up trainers from Adidas (with FIFA discount) and paying for his personal laundry. The Golden Goose lays eggs, sometimes golden and bejewelled – timepieces from Cartier and Longines. The Golden Goose lays a clutch of tickets for an England v Poland game. In Seoul she lays a weighty load of clothing – handmade suits, most likely, and a big, big, here it comes . . . generous purchase from 'Jeweller to the Stars' Harry Winston of Geneva.

The Golden Goose clucked around Sepp's family and friends as well. When Sepp's brother stayed at the Dolder Grand Hotel, who picked up the tab? Sepp's Golden Goose. When Blatter's daughter, Corinne, went off to live in Chuck Blazer's luxury apartment in Trump Tower on Fifth Avenue, back came the bills from the Precision Limousine company of New York to Dad's Golden Goose. To remind her of home, the Goose laid a subscription to the family's local paper, the *Walliser Bote,* and more shoes from Adidas. It was like a fairy tale. All thanks to Daddy's access to FIFA's bottomless purse.

Sepp's girlfriends, asked how they travelled, could chorus 'I fly FIFA!' The Golden Goose laid eggs for them and showed a talent for tact and logistics. She laid air-tickets so they could spend time with him around the world, and the flights were specially scheduled to avoid unfortunate meetings between rival girlfriends en route.

But the Golden Goose sometimes needs to be fed, even by the man who believes himself the most important in world football. President Blatter had made occasional repayments to FIFA for some personal items but by 30 December 1999 he still hadn't paid back all he should have done. The accountancy firm KPMG was taking over the audit of FIFA's books. On the president's desk was a request from the finance department for 44, 751.95 francs. He took out his chequebook and filled in the numbers on a cheque drawn on his personal account and handed it to accounts clerk Guy-Philippe Mathieu.

Before he sent it off to the bank, Guy-Philippe did a curious thing. He photocopied the cheque on to a sheet of A4 paper, then he scribbled a calculation beneath the image. He rounded Blatter's repayment down to a more manageable 44,000 francs and converted it into US dollars: $27,500 of them.

Then Guy-Philippe did a second calculation; he divided the $27,500 by $500 – the amount President Blatter is entitled to claim for every day he spends outside Switzerland on FIFA business and wrote the answer in German, '55 tags' – 55 days. To emphasise the importance of these 55 days he drew thick penstrokes above and below. So the 44,751.95 francs that Blatter *owed* FIFA had apparently been recast as the number of days he would have to *claim* in expenses in order to be square!

I wrote to Guy-Philippe asking why he did this curious thing and wrote '55 days' on a photocopy of Blatter's cheque. He didn't reply. But in a statement to a Zurich investigating magistrate looking into these transactions and documents in July 2002 Guy-Philippe confirmed that he had written the calculation, adding, 'There was never any cash payment made or any advance of the amount.'

I put the same question to Blatter. He did reply, briefly. 'The handwritten note has nothing to do with this repayment and is of no relevance,' he wrote to me. Blatter insisted that over the next two years after receiving this statement, he repaid to FIFA the money he owed it. Following the conclusion of the Zurich magistrate's investigation, he claimed, 'All the allegations that had been made were dismissed.'

SEPP PATTED his pocket, retrieved the precious envelope that he'd been guarding since his last, taut, meeting with Havelange in Paris and picked up his phone. 'Yes, Sepp?' breathed Helen in the next room. 'Send up Erwin,' said the boss.

The Finance Director's heart must have beaten a little faster as he walked around the corridor to what he, like the others, must now learn to call the President's Office. This was their first formal meeting since Paris. Did he still have the boss's confidence? Was the man he called his best friend, JSB, still his friend? What did he want? Helen hadn't said. Erwin knocked. 'Enter.' 'Sepp?' Blatter welcomed Erwin warmly. It wasn't the sack, today.

He presented Erwin with a most important envelope. Erwin went back to his office, closed the door on Guy-Philippe and the secretaries and opened the envelope. It was a memo from the office of Joao Havelange – the very last memo he'd written before leaving the presidency. Above Havelange's signature was an instruction to pay Joseph S. Blatter a six-figure loyalty bonus, a *prime de fidelité*, every 1 July. For good measure, it was back-dated to July 1997. So, Sepp was in for two year's bonus. And a very handsome windfall every July for the rest of his years at the top. Erwin placed Havelange's order in the red, confidential salaries file to which he alone had access.

THEY WERE the troika that knew everything and disclosed the minimum about FIFA's finances. Sepp Blatter, Julio Grondona and Erwin Schmid. Grondona had the self-confidence of a man who had survived more than two decades presiding over football in Argentina. Havelange knew him well from their years in Latin America and put him in charge of FIFA's finance committee in 1996.

Grondona was now Blatter's senior vice-president and the second most important man in world football, but he had a knack of making his big, rounded frame seem insignificant. At the occasional press conference they shared, all eyes would turn to the articulate, gesticulating Blatter. Grondona, sitting silent to one side, listening to translation of the reporters' questions through his headphones, would slowly slump, eyes hooded, looking down at the desk, not seeking contact.

Grondona had done all he could to help get Blatter elected. Now, in this new era, FIFA awash with cash, it was time for Blatter to improve the rewards for the people at the top. He began with a handsome salary of US$50,000 a year for all 23 volunteer members of the executive committee, FIFA's cabinet. Announcing this to the press in September 1998 the President thanked Grondona, cooing, 'The Finance Committee has been very gracious and generous.'

That wasn't the full story. There was more they didn't announce.

Sepp and Grondona instructed FIFA's advisors to negotiate a favourable tax deal with the Swiss authorities and in March 2000 the advisors wrote to say they had got one. Because the cabinet members were foreigners the Zurich cantonal authorities would settle for a 10 per cent deduction instead of the usual 25 per cent for residents.

Better still, FIFA paid the tax for them, so every six months each member receives a cheque for US$25,000 and a note to show their local tax inspector that tax has been paid.

When committee members go on the road all their expenses are met, as you'd expect. Taxis, trains and planes, hotels and restaurants are all paid for by FIFA. These men tend to have expensive tastes – a hotel with less than five stars is hardly a hotel – and for everything, FIFA foots the bill.

On top of all that, each member is encouraged to claim an extra 'allowance' of US$500 a day whenever he travels on FIFA business. As there are few one-day trips, the allowances soon mount up.

The flow of cash into other people's pockets grew as Blatter created more committees. He now has in his gift more than 300 committee positions, all distributing expenses and allowances. His nominees have to go before the executive committee for approval and the sound of rubber stamps echoes through the Alps.

Just as the president has his Golden Goose, so every member of the executive committee can have a Silver Goose, an expense account where he can accumulate the various payments. According to records I have seen, at least one member stashes tens of thousands of dollars in Zurich. From time to time the money is withdrawn in cash and shipped home. When the drug police began to crack down on travellers carrying more than US$10,000 in cash at least one member began sending girlfriends to Switzerland at FIFA's expense to suitcase a share of the money home.

Sunny Hill, 18 December 2000. 'My apologies for disturbing you for the third time on this matter,' wrote accounts clerk Guy-Philippe Mathieu despairingly to general secretary, Michel Zen-Ruffinen. To emphasise his concern, his desire to be relieved of an unpleasant burden, he copied it to FIFA's new finance chief, Urs Linsi. Among Guy-Philippe's tasks was the unenviable chore of processing expense claims submitted by his employers, the executive committee.

Uniquely, FIFA's top dogs have given themselves permission to submit expense claims without attaching any evidence that they actually spent the money. They don't have to bother collecting receipts, hotel and restaurant bills, taxi chits, credit card slips, airline invoices. They can, if they wish, bang in a demand for any amount of money they think they can get away with.

Honest members scrupulously document every claim they make. Others don't and Guy-Philippe has to make judgements. On this occasion he had had enough. One member had recently pocketed US$44,000 for his involvement in a modest FIFA tournament. Now the same man wanted US$27,420 in 'settlement of his mission last week in Acapulco'.

That wasn't all. He wanted a further US$13,717 for a trip from his home to Zurich. He'd transited through London, stayed two nights in a hotel at a cost of US$700, and getting around town had cost another US$150. He did not produce a scrap of paper to justify his demands.

In his grey-walled office overlooking the car park Guy-Philippe, the mildest of men, blew his top. He scribbled on the claim, 'Last year he defrauded us.' If that wasn't clear enough Guy-Philippe added, 'Ripped off.'

I WANTED to give Blatter a chance to tell his side of the story. I sent him detailed questions about how FIFA's money was spent. It didn't take him long to work out I'd been leaked a copy of his expense account. He banned me from his press conferences. Why did he ban me? Was it a punishment? Was he worried that I might, in front of the world's press, start waving documents that might shed some light on the truth?

Sadly I couldn't ask him to his face about the Golden Goose and the eggs it laid for him. A colleague did me a favour, went along to a press conference in April 2003 and asked him if he had charged any of his presidential campaign expenses to FIFA. 'Absolute nonsense,' he insisted. After the vehement denials in 1998, he couldn't really say anything else.

Another colleague emailed Blatter's new spokesman, the youthful Markus Siegler, asking him to explain why Blatter put in the claim for nearly 70,000 francs he'd spent on travel couriers, faxes and cell-phones during his presidential campaign.

'It is clear to us that in the course of your self-appointed status as watchdog over the wellbeing of FIFA, you are running out of material of any relevance whatsoever,' replied Markus, 'and therefore resort to ever more meaningless bits of "information" obtained unlawfully, be it by theft committed by third parties or other means that shed an even more dubious light on some of your sources and/or contributors.'

Markus raged on, 'But feel free to publish yet another lie, yet another fabrication which we shall simply add to the list of charges that are presently being prepared.' It was all rather illogical. I didn't like to explain to Markus; he's bright enough to see it for himself. If these bits of information were indeed the real thing, however they'd been obtained, then they were the basis, not of a lie, but of the simple truth.

I think Markus must have regretted his crossness because when I emailed him asking why members don't have to produce receipts when they claim their expenses, he was all sweetness though not a lot of light. 'As a matter of principle lack of documentation is not fatal to a proper claim for expenses,' he told me, 'provided proper procedures are followed which is FIFA's practice.' But how can you have a 'proper procedure' without receipts?

I asked Markus, 'Is it true there are problems with claims from other members?' He said, 'That question is impertinent.'

IN MAY 2000, before they set off for the Olympics in Sydney there was sad news for FIFA's cabinet members. General Secretary Michel Zen-Ruffinen sent them a memo, saying, 'We shall try to accommodate you in keeping with our standards but the number of junior suites has been restricted to an absolute minimum and cannot be guaranteed.'

The news got worse. 'Unfortunately it will not be possible to give you personally assigned cars.' To make up for the disappointment President Blatter authorised a new category of expenses that didn't have to be documented or accounted for. 'As regards the person (wife/partner) accompanying you, we are pleased to inform you that she will receive a daily allowance of US$200 – and the travel costs reimbursed.' This was on top of the US$500 a day the member was charging for attending the Olympics, all expenses paid.

'MR PRESIDENT, HOW MUCH DOES FIFA PAY YOU?'

'Er . . .'

IN THE CORPORATE world it is standard practice for company reports to include details of directors' salaries, perks and pension packages. It's a matter of transparency, so shareholders can see what these people are doing with their money.

What happens when you ask FIFA about the rewards paid to its administrators? Can stakeholders and fans find out what slice of the billions of dollars generated by the World Cup is pocketed by its senior officials? What does Sepp Blatter earn?

Urs Linsi, Blatter's finance director is the man to ask. And he trumpets his commitment to transparency. In January 2003 he granted a no-holds-barred, ask-me-anything-you-damn-well-like exclusive interview to . . . a press officer he employs at fifa.com. It was headlined, 'We have to be as transparent as possible.'

He insisted that 'FIFA is a healthy, clean and transparent organisation with nothing to hide.' Then, in more reflective mood

Mr Linsi noted, 'We should always remember to let the media and the public know what we are doing. There is huge public interest in FIFA, therefore we have to be as transparent as possible. We will try to communicate in a more open way concerning football matters so the world can believe us and be proud of their federation.'

I emailed Urs Linsi and asked him if he would tell me what the president earns in salary, pension contributions, cars, bonuses and any other perks.

He didn't reply.

Instead, FIFA spokesman Markus Siegler wrote to me: 'Dear Mr Jennings, We can answer your question as follows: The matter of the compensation (not salary!) of the President for this term was dealt with and decided unanimously at the Finance Committee (in the presence of all members) at its meeting on 15 December 2002 in Madrid. The respective minutes have been ratified by the Executive Committee at its last meeting on 6/7 March 2003 here in Zurich. Thanks for your understanding.'

I emailed back to Siegler. Actually, no, I didn't understand.

Why were he and Linsi refusing to reveal even one fact, one sum of money, not even the tiniest clue about Blatter's rewards package? 'We must abide by internal rules and cultural traditions,' Siegler explained. 'In Switzerland, salaries or income are simply not published. Also, you must not question FIFA's dedication to transparency.'

Markus, a former journalist asked me, a journalist, 'Who would like to know Mr Blatter's salary, as a matter of interest?'

Well, the public, Mr Siegler. Remember them?

Vice-President Chung Mong-Joon from Korea tried to find out in 2002. He wrote to Jack Warner and pointed out that when vice-president Lennart Johansson asked how much Blatter trousered he was told, 'The remuneration of the President was fixed by the finance committee at the same time as the indemnity to the executive committee was ratified.'

Mr Chung noted, 'This is an example of the arrogance of the FIFA President. Why do you think I cannot get a straight answer for this legitimate question?' Chung asked Warner, how much is Blatter paid?

Warner replied to Chung, his fellow committee member, 'Dear MJ, I vacillated for some time on whether I should dignify your letter to me with a reply or not. And then, today, I decided to reply to you if only because I did not want to leave you with the false impression that your perfidious letter is worth the paper on which it has been written.'

He concluded, 'I judge myself by such universal virtues as honesty, integrity, loyalty and friendship.'

Blatter's salary remains a secret. Inside FIFA they say 4 million francs (about £1.7 million) sounds about right. And his secret employment contract is said to contain a poison pill. Sack Blatter and FIFA must pay him 24 million francs. That's nearly £11 million. The allowance paid towards the cost of his rooftop apartment in Zollikon is said to cost FIFA 8,000 francs a month (almost £1,000 a week), then there's the top-of-the-line Mercedes.

And the pension? Another secret matter. On top of all that, the bonuses. But how many? He always received a bonus from his earliest days as general secretary. Was Havelange's farewell, backdated present a second one? Could there be any more, extracted from any of his other responsibilities at FIFA?

Whatever Blatter's friends on the finance committee pay him, it's not enough. It can't be, because Blatter still needs to claim that US$500 a day pocket money.

Whenever he's in your country, or making a speech or receiving an award anywhere outside Switzerland, he's pocketing US$500 a day, as Guy-Philippe Mathieu acknowledged when processing Blatter's expenses repayment. He usually spends at least 150 days on the road and that's worth US$75,000. In his busier years he can hope to claim as much as US$125,000 on top of his salary and other perks – just for going to work, first class with red carpets waiting at the airport.

The Honorary President, a title Havelange accepted from his last congress in Paris in 1998, gets a pension but FIFA won't say how much. They won't say anything about what the Brazilian has trousered in the past and continues to take. It is believed that from 1994 he was paid US$125,000 annually. He travels extensively and expensively on what FIFA calls 'representational duties' and can charge for a companion. His driver shows up with a Mercedes when required, anywhere in the world from Bamako to Salt Lake City. Havelange retains his FIFA credit card.

SEPP BLATTER has lived in Zurich since 1975, but registered his tax affairs on the other side of the country in Valais, the canton where he grew up and which has lower rates.

Then he discovered the tax-avoider's paradise. Eighty kilometres east of Zurich is the tiny canton of Appenzell, only 15,000 people living in six villages. A rural community with not much to raise taxes on, the canton had gone into the business of doing tax deals with wealthy people. The local politicians reckoned that some money was better than none at all and if other cantons lost out, too bad. They advertise that their canton is a product and the tax office is a sales office and welcome people to come and negotiate their own secret deal. They say to rich Swiss and foreigners, 'You will never walk alone, you will always find friends who are on your side and support you.'

The burghers of Appenzell are notorious in secretive Switzerland for their dislike of transparency in public affairs. Their local dialect word, *heimlichfeiss,* that translates roughly as 'clandestine', sums up their opposition to openness. Blatter registered his tax affairs in Appenzell and told the Zurich authorities that he was a *Wochenaufenthalter* – he lived in Zurich only during the week.

Life was sweet. Then in the autumn of 1995 the Swiss tabloid *Blick* came knocking at Blatter's Zurich address with some questions. Could he tell them the address where he was registered in Appenzell? Blatter tried and got it wrong. Then he tried again and still got it wrong. Eventually the *Blick* reporters had to tell him. They estimated that Blatter was saving at least 250,000 Swiss francs (£110,000) a year on his tax bill and in time-honoured tabloid style, they delivered their dossier to the Zurich Canton tax inspectors.

Blatter volunteered his version of the story to a local paper from his home canton of Valais, the *Walliser Bote.* First, he asked his old friends and neighbours to believe him – there was no story. A successful man like himself was always going to be a target for the jealous and the sensationalist press. It was nothing more than the prejudice of city slickers in Zurich looking down their noses at a country boy who had done well for himself. It might also be the case that he was being targeted in what was really a clandestine attack on Havelange.

Talk of an investigation by the Zurich authorities into his tax affairs was incorrect, he said. There was some checking going on but merely a clarification of his address. He said he couldn't reveal any more information because he had transferred his tax registration to Appenzell for very private reasons to do with his emotional life.

What Blatter didn't tell the reporters from Valais or from *Blick* or indeed anybody else outside FIFA's finance office is that he doesn't pay tax on his earnings. FIFA pays it for him.

IN THE LATE Spring of 2000, the Zurich tax inspectors gave FIFA a month's warning that they were coming to conduct an audit of their tax files. The KPMG team that took over the auditing of FIFA's books in 2000 was led by Fredy Luthiger, a partner from their Zurich office. Fredy, long, slim, bespectacled, occasionally running his delicate fingers through his white hair, seems like a man who's never happier than when he's spending his days reading spreadsheets.

When challenged about some of the far from transparent financial procedures at FIFA, the president, his mouthpieces and his lawyers can bellow from the same hymn sheet, 'It's been audited by KPMG!' and claim that gives them an absolute justification to refuse to answer more questions.

I wrote to Fredy asking him why members can claim expenses without receipts. Fredy replied that his professional code of ethics prevents him discussing his client's business. One specific thing Fredy couldn't talk about was the confidential Management Letter he submitted to FIFA in 2000 and the warning he gave, that FIFA had not been obeying its duties under taxation processes.

Fredy clearly spelled out his message. 'There exists a risk of being held accountable because of non-compliance.' If Fredy had used the language of the street criminal he might have warned, 'If you don't get this sorted fast, guv, you'll be nicked.'

In his Management Letter for 2001 that he submitted to FIFA the following year, Fredy had to point to more embarrassing problems. He had been examining the individual accounts that every one of the 200 or so national associations and the six regional confederations has with FIFA. They list payments, debts, loans, development funds and secret purchases of huge quantities of World Cup tickets. What a mess they were.

During Blatter's years as general secretary FIFA hadn't always chased up debts. Seventy-five per cent of the accounts – that's around 150 of the 200 associations – had lingering debts.

Why hadn't FIFA made the associations pay their debts? They're not saying. Fredy said that this 'was not satisfactory'. Then he talked as tough as most accountants who have just picked up a big, prestigious piece of business. 'We recommend taking action against such associations.'

FROM CARROTS AND STICKS . . .

Blatter builds his citadel

LIFE CAN BE TOUGH for powerful men. Sometimes they have to sacrifice their friends on the altar of their ambition. As new president, Sepp Blatter regarded with fresh eyes his friend Michel Zen-Ruffinen. For years as general secretary Sepp had been proud to call his deputy 'my protégé'. They both grew up in the canton of Valais in the south. Blatter studied in Lausanne, Zen-Ruffinen graduated in law from the university in Geneva, further along the lakeside.

Blatter hired Zen-Ruffinen in 1986 to take charge of refereeing and work in FIFA's legal department. Tall, dark, lean and hand-some he was the youngest referee to control first division games in Switzerland and in 1993 he passed his exams and qualified to be an international class referee. He gave up the hobby in 1995 when Blatter made him deputy general secretary. And when Sepp was forced to stand down to campaign for the presidency, Michel stepped into his shoes. Now, aged 39, Zen-Ruffinen was poised to receive his mentor's blessing and become the new general secretary.

But Blatter knew how dangerous general secretaries could be. Hadn't he tried to oust Havelange? A strong general secretary might be death to Blatter's ambition. He had lived a long time in sports politics and he had learned how to survive. Just look at that marvellous survivor, Juan Antonio Samaranch. He'd dismissed his director general, made himself executive president and micro-managed every aspect of the organisation.

Primo Nebiolo, another Dassler placeman, had done the same at track and field. They were survivors, they took control, and Sepp Blatter was going to take control, he was going to make the world's most popular game dance to his tune.

Blatter set in motion his plan to take total control of FIFA. Some of the employees up on Sunny Hill thought they knew why. It wasn't just about money, the secret tax-paid remuneration and perks-package. Some said his firm hold on FIFA and its international empire gave him the security he lacked in a life littered with the wreckage of failed marriages and countless meaningless relationships.

So Blatter moved to have Michel Zen-Ruffinen sidelined. There was another Michel in Sepp's life. France's Michel Platini, three times a World Cup hero. He hadn't lost his good looks and his charisma could light up a room. A fabulous goal-scorer, three times European Footballer of the Year, and World Footballer of the Year in 1985, Platini had gone from French team manager to chair the organising committee for the 1998 World Cup in France. He too had ambitions to rise up FIFA.

Blatter's plan was to reconstruct FIFA so that he was Executive President. In his office at 7am each day he'd receive reports from his top two lieutenants. Michel Platini would take charge of football affairs – 'my sporting conscience' Blatter was already calling him – and Michel Zen-Ruffinen would be head of administration, a paper shuffler, lacking power. Blatter would immerse himself in marketing and money, the areas of his empire where the real power lay.

But FIFA's executive committee, more than half of them still smarting from Blatter's manipulations during his election campaign, were in no mood to create a super-president. Meeting in Zurich on 3 December 1998 they insisted that the office of general secretary must be maintained. Teeth clenched, the president welcomed Zen-Ruffinen's promotion.

But it was still early days in Blatter's reign. It takes time to build citadels. So, Blatter had to accept Zen-Ruffinen as general secretary. So what? He could manoeuvre to rob the man of power. When the executive committee met again on 11 March 1999 around the boardroom table in the new concrete and glass building next to the mansion on Sunny Hill, Blatter gestured warmly to the best-known face at the table, the only face there that said football.

'A warm welcome please to Michel Platini, a household name who really needs no introduction, he will be an advisor to the President and also please meet, I'm sure many of you remember him from last year, Jerome Champagne, in the new post of my personal advisor. His past experience as head of protocol for France '98 and in the French diplomatic corps aptly qualify him for this post.' Did anyone guess that this was the start of Blatter's parallel administration, an outfit that would split FIFA's soul?

Blatter surveyed his executive committee, a mix of men who were in his debt, men who could be bought, good men who had been put firmly in their place or soundly beaten. And men who were biding their time, building their own power bases, who might some day strike Blatter down if they could. Looking around the table it was clear, this wasn't about football, it was about power. Some of these people had been put there by continental federations, they didn't all see things Blatter's way. Not yet, but he could work on it. For now, Blatter had to keep friend and foe, in the room and around the world of football, busy. Fortunately, he had the power to nominate more than 300 lucky officials to seats on committees. They would rack up the kind of expenses and allowances that after a while they'd find hard to live without.

Just a few feet away from the president sat vice-president Lennart Johansson. In the hours after the Paris vote his aides at UEFA had quietly briefed reporters that they would not accept the result. Then it dawned on them that there was nothing they could do, Havelange and Blatter had outwitted them. Johansson, asked if bribes had been paid by Blatter's camp, said stiffly, 'I have no proof of this and I refuse to speculate. I do not want to appear a bad loser and I congratulate Mr Blatter on his success.'

Johansson went back to lick his wounds in European football's headquarters in South Switzerland, presiding over the UEFA Cup and the Champions' League. Johansson was a rare one; he wasn't there for the expense account and some people respected him for that. He was capable, too. So Blatter showed a little respect to Johansson and the European nations he represented, and put him in charge of the committee organising the next World Cup in 2002. That would keep his mind off the African bribery rumours. He'd have to work hard to bring harmony to the tournament in Korea, a country that had spent the first half of the previous century under the boot of the other joint host, Japan. So Johansson was busy, and these days his health wasn't the best and, just in case he should think to stir trouble again, Blatter installed his own man, the loyal Julio Grondona, to be his deputy.

Grondona was more than the senior vice-president, he was chairman of the finance committee, the one that mattered most to Blatter. He also chaired the marketing and television board.

Grondona's deputy at finance was Jack Warner, they took the key money decisions and the minutes of such meetings were never published. Grondona had some distasteful opinions – he didn't think much of Jews – but despite expressing his views on television that didn't harm his career at FIFA.

Jack Warner was a protégé of Havelange. He was a great man to have on your side, a fiercely loyal supporter. His association with FIFA had made him a fortune. It was a matter of prestige to be on the World Cup committee and no vice-president could be left off. He also controlled two of the potentially most lucrative committees in international football, the ones organising youth tournaments.

Jack was the man who could give the thumbs up – or down – to countries vying to host these championships, staged every two years. Sure, they weren't the big ones but some countries, like the oil and gas-rich potentates of the Gulf, who could only dream of hosting the World Cup, badly wanted the youth tournaments.

Warner complained about slights real and imagined, but really his life was good. He once told a Trinidad reporter that he was a multi-millionaire, thanks to world football. 'I began buying properties across Trinidad from the salary and allowances I received from FIFA. I have had one or two good fortunes. I get ultra-fantastic paycheques.' The former schoolteacher loved to flaunt his wealth and show off the solid-gold paper knife given to him by King Fahd of Saudi Arabia.

Jack's side-kick, Chuck Blazer, his general secretary who ran CONCACAF from their New York office, was the only member of the executive committee who wasn't elected by the rank and file. He was Jack's personal appointee. When Jack looked his regional confederation in the eye and told them that Chuck would take the FIFA seat, not one mouse roared.

Chuck was into money as much as Jack was and he kept

a close eye on the stock markets. Like some other Americans who rose to the top of world football, he'd never played the game, only stumbled across it and spotted a lucrative business opportunity.

You could see why Blatter chose Chuck to head the media committee. Chuck knew how to hold a door tight shut against enquiries and he had an astonishing way of giving off hostility without any discernable effort, as if by perspiration alone. And he could switch on the charm when it was needed. Chuck was a favourite in Zurich and so was his talented daughter Marci Blazer, who got a seat on FIFA's legal committee. Few lawyers in the world could claim membership of world football's 'Commission de Questions Juridiques.'

Mohamed Bin Hammam from Qatar looked younger than his mid-50s. He'd sat at this boardroom table for two years and deserved a reward for his fine work during the election campaign that left Johansson in tears. Blatter gave him the top job at the new Goal Bureau. The Bureau had a whacking US$100 million to spend at Bin Hammam's discretion, and that was on top of the US$1 million that each national association would get from the new television money.

Bin Hammam's Goal Bureau would entertain applications from national associations who wanted new offices, pitches and equipment. The president called this 'tailor-made solutions' and he would be travelling the world frenetically in the next three years as the great benefactor.

Sometimes Bin Hammam travelled with Blatter to the ribbon-cutting ceremonies but he made as many trips alone, with his personal entourage, descending from the skies, graciously receiving flowery speeches of gratitude. And who wouldn't defer to a man who can influence an Emir, a ruler endowed with deep deposits of natural gas, one of the richest men in the world?

The man with the money from Qatar was a rising star, popping up everywhere on the committees that mattered. He helped Grondona and Warner at the finance committee. He chaired the technical committee. A seat on the national associations committee gave him more contact with the grassroots, handing out money. Bin Hammam was gluing together his own band of officials who felt personal loyalty to him, not yet a parallel empire but in time he might threaten the president. Bin Hammam had helped put Blatter up there and in time, Bin Hammam might take Blatter down.

Blatter rewarded the silver-haired Russian Viacheslav Koloskov with chair of the national associations committee. In the old Soviet days he'd kept Eastern Europe solidly in line behind the Zurich establishment. When that disintegrating bloc lost its vice-presidency Koloskov found himself out in the cold. As Blatter came in as president, Koloskov had the bad luck to leave the executive committee at the very moment when members were awarded a tax-free US$50,000 dollars a year.

Never mind, Blatter paid him US$100,000 anyway. When this payment came to light in 2002, Blatter said maybe he should have told the Finance Committee about it, but he also emphasised that Koloskov had been doing wonderful work for football in Eastern Europe. 'There was no corruption on my part,' said Blatter. 'To claim so is tantamount to slander.'

Havelange wasn't actually in Sepp's boardroom, but he might as well have been. His nominee was there. Son-in-law Ricardo Teixeira, whose wheeling and dealing in Brazil had hit the headlines, represented the minority sulking tendency. Havelange had never wanted to go and his Brazilian entourage resented their loss of power over FIFA's money. Ricardo harboured dreams that if his national team went on winning the World Cup he could bid to oust Blatter. He was one of the babies at the table, born in 1947 – eleven years younger than the new president, two years younger than Bin Hammam. Ricardo had time on his side.

Blatter needed to keep Ricardo busy in a job that had no influence. Step forward Ricardo Teixeira, chair of the Futsal committee, master of indoor soccer. Blatter cast about for another position short on political power and influence and made him deputy chair of the referees' committee in late 1999. It was an unlikely job for a man facing allegations of corruption at home in Brazil.

Further round the table, David Will, the Scottish vice-president nominated by the four British associations, wasn't going to lead any revolutions but he could be sticky on points of principle. So Blatter gave him FIFA's legal committee to run and issue tickets for the World Cup. That's almost two full-time jobs. Something always goes wrong with the tickets and inevitably he'd be deluged with noisy complaints just as the president's re-election campaign peaked in the weeks before a World Cup tournament.

The biggest potential threat for now was the Korean, Chung Mong-Joon. He was probably the richest man in the room, a member of the Hyundai family. A vice-president from Asia, he took a dim view of the shabbiness at FIFA and would come into greater prominence as the 2002 World Cup was held in his country. He spoke English and German, was a Trustee at Johns Hopkins University in Baltimore and a FIFA youngster – born as recently as 1951. If he didn't decide to run for the presidency of Korea he might go after FIFA's top job. From Blatter's viewpoint, Chung was dangerous: very bright and, with his boyish smile, worryingly good looking.

Fortunately he was kept busy in Seoul and he accepted Blatter's offer to chair the almost invisible protocol committee. The other threat in sight was Issa Hayatou from Cameroon, a FIFA vice-president and president of the African confederation. Hayatou and his large continent had to be shown some respect. So Blatter gave him a couple of committees – Olympic football, a lot of hard work, and the Confederations Cup tournament which sounds important and costs a lot, but nobody takes it seriously.

It was hard work filling the hundreds of positions on FIFA's ever-growing list of committees, weighing up who had a powerful backer, who'd like the allowances and expenses, who would pledge their vote for a seat. Then there was the delicacy needed for appointments to the Football Committee where living legends like Franz Beckenbauer, Sir Bobby Charlton, Pelé, Eusebio and George Weah came up with suggestions about the future of the game that were widely reported and then, more often than not, sidelined. The legends were useful props to put beside a smiling Sepp in happy snaps that were swiftly posted on fifa.com.

And what were all these important men, gathered at vast expense, here to do? Were there vital decisions to be made for the good of football? Not really, the decisions that mattered were made in private among Blatter's inner clique.

On Blatter's executive committee table were piles of reports, reports on the Confederations Cup and the World Youth Championship. They all lost money but gave less powerful soccer nations opportunities to compete internationally and more administrators a chance to share in Sepp Blatter's largesse.

The executive committee listened politely while Blatter prepared to offer an apology. A while back Blatter, dreaming aloud, had blurted out to a news reporter that he was thinking of holding the World Cup every two years.

The football press were outraged. It would wreck the world game. Football's finest players would be permanently tied up in round after round of qualifying games. It would be death to the leagues. Clubs and fans would hardly ever see their stars, always absent travelling, training, playing and picking up injuries with their national squads.

Fans in Europe's top leagues would have to make do with watching reserve teams doing their best. If you wanted to destroy football, this would be a brilliant strategy. But there was one good thing in it. A World Cup every two years would mean double the money: twice the television fees, twice as much from McDonald's and Coca-Cola.

Members of the executive were furious. A change so momentous should be discussed first by them before a whiff of it reached the press. Blatter told the members: 'I feel I owe you an explanation. I unwittingly mentioned the idea of a World Cup every two years at a press interview, never suspecting that it would be construed as revolutionary and unleash a storm of emotion. It was only when some members had expressed annoyance at finding this out through the media that I realised I should have informed them before allowing my enthusiasm to run away with me. I therefore ask you to accept my apologies and in future I will avoid such a situation arising. Thank you.'

It was the same patter that powerful men everywhere, prime ministers, presidents, corporate chiefs, tend to offer, when they forget for a moment that they owe a duty to some kind of democratic process and start making up policy on the hoof. And it was just as sincerely meant.

14

DIVIDE AND RULE

FIFA's civil war

IT DIDN'T take long for the FIFA workforce to figure out that Jerome Champagne was something more than an advisor to Blatter. Michel Zen-Ruffinen might have had the general secretary's title but big, brooding Jerome had got the job. He'd got the flash new Mercedes too, and 23,000 Swiss francs (£10,000) a month, the highest salary in the building after Blatter, and an apartment high up near the Sunny Hill mansion. His hiring had been handled with the utmost discretion and when he'd arrived in January 1999, he preferred a low profile, describing his new job as 'A little like a principal private secretary, I organise the calendar, the communications and the travels of the president.'

Jerome's description of himself suggested the kind of modesty you'd expect of a man schooled in diplomacy's black arts. Two decades earlier he'd spent too many of his student days freelancing at a French football magazine, neglected his studies and failed to complete his course at the National School of Administration which admits only the brightest of the bright, but that didn't hold him back. Champagne studied Oriental languages – he speaks English, Spanish, German, Portuguese, Chinese and Arabic – then political science, before joining France's ministry of foreign affairs and, aged 25, was posted as a cultural attaché to Oman. After a spell in Cuba he moved to Los Angeles where he was appointed consul-general and met his American wife.

In July 1994, three days before the Brazil–Italy World Cup Final at the Los Angeles Rose Bowl, consul-general Champagne staged a garden party in Beverley Hills for members of the France '98 Organising Committee. Three years later Champagne was number two in the embassy in Brasilia, renewing an acquaintanceship with Michel Platini who was President Jacques Chirac's sidekick on a goodwill tour of Latin America. By 1998 the French government bought Jerome home and put him in charge of state protocol at the World Cup, where he struck up a relationship with Sepp Blatter.

Blatter saw a man he could use, a collaborator, a bodyguard, a campaign manager for the next FIFA presidential elections in three years time but not a man equipped to replace him. A perfect shadow general secretary. And a brilliant advance man with a turn of phrase that made his boss look good. 'We live in an individualistic and uneven world in which the short term becomes the rule,' Jerome told *France Football*. 'It is necessary to restore values like solidarity and universality. I would not be where I am today if I did not share these ideals with Joseph Blatter.'

After FIFA's executive committee blocked Blatter's re-organisation plans, Michel Platini established his own office in Paris with his secretary Odile Lanceau and press officer Alain Leiblang. Platini's staff were paid nearly 18,000 francs (£8,000) a month, more than most salaries up on Sunny Hill.

As the new, parallel FIFA management team grew, so the

people who thought they were running FIFA found themselves out of favour, and sometimes out of work. Blatter evicted his old friend Erwin Schmid in mid-1999 and out the door went an unrivalled encyclopaedic knowledge of the Blatter years. Erwin knew everything about FIFA's bank records and the expenses and bonuses available to Blatter and Havelange. Erwin took legal action to secure a bigger pay-off and won.

Blatter could now choose the money man he wanted for his new regime and the strong belief up on Sunny Hill was that the recommendation came from a senior executive at marketing agents ISL.

Urs Linsi had just turned 50 and spent most of his working life in the leasing department of the Credit Suisse bank. Immaculately dressed, and with his domed head and cautious manner, Linsi looked like a banker but a tough heart beat beneath the conservative clothes. A world-class triathlete, he started the FIFA endurance race as finance director. His colleagues were impressed by his work rate in his first few months, staying so late at night in the office. 'He obviously found what he was looking for,' said a colleague sourly after Blatter confirmed him in his job.

'He looks like Tom Cruise,' giggled the secretaries when the handsome Flavio Battaini joined as a junior lawyer in 1996. He'd been on Blatter's campaign plane in Africa and his name was on the new appointments roster in January 1999, as Director of Marketing. Flavio had no record in marketing beyond reading contracts in FIFA's legal department. Perhaps appointing Flavio with his limited experience might leave Blatter free to continue his dealings with Jean-Marie Weber without interference.

The president personally hired his new personnel chief, a key figure in FIFA's reorganisation. Michael Schallhart, in his late 30s, was an international ice hockey referee who'd worked for the Samaritans. Blatter recruited his own personal propaganda man, a direct link to the media that would circumnavigate FIFA's communications department run by Englishman Keith Cooper. Blatter chose Markus Siegler, a tall and good-looking former local reporter who had been freelancing for FIFA. His boyish charm and warm smile helped him sell the president's positive messages.

The president's plans to divide and rule were working. FIFA had an administration run in theory by General Secretary Michel Zen-Ruffinen and a parallel and challenging administration led by shadow General Secretary Jerome Champagne. The house was divided. Bitterness and distrust festered. The people who did all the work felt betrayed. Their bosses didn't seem to be in charge any more. Who were they working for? Blatter and his tight little team seemed to be making all the decisions. Sometimes Zen-Ruffinen sat in on the inner-circle's meetings but he wasn't made welcome. They seemed to be snatching power from right under his feet.

Blatter had a name for his new parallel administration, the *Führungscrew*, the 'F-Crew' or 'Leadership Crew'. People on the staff felt it was an insult to Zen-Ruffinen and, by extension, an insult to them. Blatter claimed, 'The F-crew is a consultative body that aims to promote internal communication and accelerate problem solving.'

It was having the opposite effect. Staff morale was in terrible shape. Even Blatter could see that all was not well. He turned to Norwegian Bjorn Johansson, who runs a small but classy head-hunting consultancy for top executives from his top-floor offices by the lakeside in Zurich. Bjorn advised him to try to heal FIFA's wounds.

Bjorn knew a bit about unhappy organisations. He felt that time apart sometimes helped. And so in February 2000 he took FIFA's senior managers – without Sepp or his clique – off up Lake Constance to the health spa of Bad Ragaz, a haven of thermal baths and ski slopes, that promised 'year round caressing for souls and bodies'. After all the acrimony, FIFA people needed some caressing. Bjorn encouraged them to talk and he listened.

The managers begged for improvements in internal communications. They wanted problems to be solved and open, honest and fair discussions. They wanted closer co-operation with the President and wanted to know where FIFA was heading.

They complained that FIFA was in one terrible mess. FIFA's most important job, its reason for being, was staging the football World Cup, and the other competitions for women and youngsters. Yet with just 18 months left before the World Cup, they hadn't even got a director of competitions. And too many of the junior managers didn't know what they're doing. They weren't convinced that decisions were being made for the good of the game, and were concerned that staff in the development department were not being consulted about how the money was spent.

After the counselling sessions had finished for the day, Sepp Blatter turned up from Zurich for the formal dinner, like an errant husband crashing in late on the dysfunctional family therapy session, hoping a big box of fancy chocolates would set everything right. He handed out his brochure *The House of FIFA, Vision and Aspirations*.

Blatter assured them his heart and soul was in football and FIFA, and his vision was to make the game better and take it to the world. Then he told them their priorities were the next congress, the World Cup – and getting him re-elected!

As Blatter's limousine swept away, the team talked freely again. They agreed that the open and honest atmosphere of the meetings changed during the dinner thrown by the President. They felt it had been right to exclude the President from their discussions. You just couldn't speak freely with Blatter around.

*　　*　　*

EVEN BLATTER could see that his *Führungscrew* plan wasn't working. Setting up a parallel administration had been intended to destabilise general secretary Zen-Ruffinen, not enrage and depress all the senior managers. Blatter pondered on the problem and came up with a solution.

They needed re-educating. He did what autocrats throughout the business world had done before him. He summoned McKinsey, the management consultants. By sheer coincidence, McKinsey's head of European Sports Practice was Philippe Blatter, nephew of the FIFA president. According to FIFA spokesman Andreas Herren, Philippe 'supported the McKinsey team as an expert . . . however he is not in charge of the work at FIFA'.

FIFA people who don't have a photo of Philippe in the family album could look him up on McKinsey's website. He's handsome, athletic and beside his picture is one of those McKinsey mission-blurbs they seem to like so much. Philippe asks, 'What is the point of getting up in the morning if you can't believe that something extraordinary will happen to you?'

Philippe did triathlons, played tennis and spent a vacation driving through the deserts of Yemen. He'd recently worked in Argentina and Brazil and now he'd head a team that worked on 'a client service mission' to encourage Uncle's managers to new heights of efficiency. Philippe didn't spend a lot of time on site but his youthful five-strong team were given offices in the 'chicken house', a building that had once housed a miniature zoo belonging to the city of Zurich. According to McKinsey, these were 'team-rooms often used at the client's site to optimise work efficiency'. Disgruntled FIFA staffers immediately labelled them 'the green-horns'.

First they looked at jazzing up Blatter's US$100 million scheme to build offices and training pitches for the poorer national associations. This was called the Goal Bureau project, and it was chaired by Qatar's Mohamed Bin Hammam. The greenhorns got to work, deploying the language of management-speak that was soon echoing around the corridors of Sunny Hill and in the bars after work as staff tried to puzzle out what was going on.

It was all rather comical. FIFA was rent with bitterness, conspiracies and back-stabbing, there was a seismic power struggle between the President and his chief executive, and the greenhorns, oblivious in the chicken house to the grinding of football's tectonic plates beneath their feet, enthused about 'aspiration-setting workshops'.

At the end of every month Dr Jens Abend, boss of McKinsey's Zurich office, sent in his bill. Come Christmas 2000, Abend popped in one for a couple of months' consulting fees, plus 20 per cent in expenses, and the bottom line said 903,000 francs (almost £400,000). That was a lot of money, even by FIFA's standards. It was way above the maximum grant to any of the poorer countries FIFA was supposed to be helping.

Month after month jargon rolled out of the chicken house and Dr Abend's big bills rolled in. To pay McKinsey's mounting fees FIFA had to tighten some belts. Not Sepp's, though. Staffers had their working away from home allowance slashed by half to US$100 a day. Then the greenhorns knocked 5 million francs off the refereeing budget and cut FIFA's donations to charity by 550,000 francs.

FIFA workers, who'd had their tools updated, their aspirations reset and their allowances slashed, puzzled over the greenhorns' strenuous efforts and dubious results. They may perhaps have thought that McKinsey were being used unknowingly to undermine Zen-Ruffinen, by showing him how 'innovative' he should have been. If all the gobbledygook had any meaning it seemed to be saying, 'You haven't been running this place the right way, Michel. You're inefficient, incapable, out of touch with modern management techniques. We are the cutting edge of business science, we are the massed ranks of the McKinsey MBAs. We know best!'

One frosty night McKinsey's greenhorns swept FIFA's workers out of Sunny Hill and off to the curling rink at Ruti. The greenhorns split them into two teams and told them to slip into special shoes, then had them hurling lumps of granite across the ice and danced in their path with sweeping brushes. Greenhorns made careful notes on everybody's performance. Zen-Ruffinen was dragged along and people noticed that he seemed to feel the night's chill.

No sooner had their curling aches and pains faded than the poor FIFA people were off again to a country hotel 20 km from Zurich. They were split into two groups, led to identical rooms and given two minutes to look at a pile of wooden beams and planks – something like Lego for grownups. Then they were pulled out.

'You have seen the materials,' a greenhorn told the baffled football administrators. 'Now you will appoint a project leader from your ranks. You have 15 minutes to design a bridge from what we have shown you. Then you must build it.' The team led by Zen-Ruffinen did well and the other didn't, the greenhorns took more notes and Dr Abend sent another bill for the good of the game. Blatter later praised their work, saying it was of the highest quality and of tremendous benefit to FIFA. McKinsey don't come cheap, and in total, FIFA paid them at least £2 million.

MCKINSEY BOAST that they're not scared to confront clients with unpalatable truths. If the boss is leading a business in the wrong direction, McKinsey will tell him. They claim they've even told bosses to quit, for the good of their company.

I asked McKinsey's London office, was Philippe working for

Sepp or for FIFA? Did Philippe get any bonuses for bringing in £2 million worth of fees? McKinsey's spokesman, Tony Danker, gushed, 'I am glad we could work together on this!' Then he told me the work was confidential and he was unable to comment.

15

A MESSIAH FOR TRINIDAD

The rise and rise of Jack Warner

'JACK WARNER is a wonderful and loyal friend. He is very competent and I just have to say that Jack is one of the top personalities in the world of football.'

Ask around the twin islands of Trinidad and Tobago and few people share Sepp's opinion of Jack. Many say he's a dictator who's built his power climbing up on other people's backs, a man who's become richer as he's climbed up the FIFA ladder.

But why the hostility? Why should people feel so passionate about Sepp's loyal friend, a man who has taken tea with the Queen at Buckingham Palace – and chided her that British companies were failing to spend their sponsorship money on football in Trinidad & Tobago?

We've met Jack already, levering an attractive babe into Haitian Dr Kyss's seat to vote in more power for Jack in Zurich in 1996. And we met him again, levering his friend Neville Ferguson into poor old Dr Kyss's seat to vote for Sepp Blatter in 1998.

Warner's a mover, a shaker, a fixer, a manipulator, he's the man whose entrepreneurialism and cheek tells us so much about Blatter's FIFA. And he's the man who, unchecked, could find himself FIFA president within the decade.

At home in Trinidad & Tobago he says he owns shopping malls, hotels, offices and warehouses. He claims to have 'a few businesses' in the United States, purchased, he told a reporter, 'with the salary and allowances I received from FIFA. I have had one or two good fortunes'. He says that as a FIFA vice-president, he receives 'ultra-fantastic paycheques'. Estimates of his wealth range between £10 million and £20 million.

When not the centre of attention Warner looks a bit sulky. He tends to slump in his chair, slide his short legs forward, throw his head back. He's an image of brightly flowered ties, crisp white shirts, blue suits and glossily polished shoes. Jack looks studious in his large-framed gold-rimmed glasses. On one wrist he wears a chunky gold bangle, on the other a chunky gold watch. He wears, one, two, three fat gold rings. At play, Jack wears a brightly patterned shirt, open at the neck to display a thick gold chain.

He's been a favourite of Trinidad's corruption-prone UNC party led by Baseo Panday. In government they gave him a special diplomatic passport. Flexing his muscles at FIFA underlings back in 2001 he made this astonishing assertion: 'I am a senior member in the Gov't of T&T and, effective from this Thursday 15 August, Chairman of the Airports Authority.' Neither claim was true, though he certainly gave Panday's discredited regime a lot of support and a lot of money, much of it from football.

When Panday's government fell Warner went on the stump for the UNC, describing political opponents as 'Taliban'. He told voters in the constituency of La Brea that on a recent trip to New York he had obtained TT$2.5 million from FIFA to build a sports centre in La Brea. There was one condition. They had to vote in UNC man Norris Ferguson. 'If he don't win, no sports, simple as that,' said Warner.

A hung parliament followed and Panday's crew rewarded Warner by nominating him as Speaker, although he wasn't an MP. The nomination failed. Even some of Panday's supporters shunned him.

OUR JACK Warner story starts in January 1943. Warner was born, in his own words, 'a poor black boy' in Rio Claro in the south of the island of Trinidad, a church-loving child with a passion for the movies, an unpopular boy who knew unhappy times at school. Fellow pupils treated him as an outsider and dirtied his school uniform.

Jack and some other lanky youths queued up outside St James's Barracks in 1961 to sign up as police cadets. What a different life he might have led. A life of contentment shaking down speeding motorists for a handful of crinkly notes and setting about the citizenry with his night stick after closing time.

It wasn't to be. Jack's mum and his parish priest pounded up, grabbed Jack by the collar and marched him home. No, Jack was going to be a teacher. And that was that.

Jack trained as a teacher (though when his mum wasn't looking he signed up for the Special Reserve Police, known to the island's wags as Something Resembling Police). He soon learned that power was something he enjoyed. He agitated briefly in Trinidad's Black Power movement, and then spotted a bigger opportunity: football.

The first black man to run football in Trinidad was Eric James who took the secretary's seat in 1942. For nearly three decades James earned a reputation as a decent man, a man of principle who, like his brother CLR James, the celebrated cricket writer and political thinker, served his people and sport unselfishly as Trinidad found its post-colonial feet.

Getting rich out of sport was furthest from their minds. Within months of Eric James's retirement Warner had taken over the association and was running it in a whole new way. He created new organisations that seemed to have no clear purpose and could exercise voting rights should his position come under threat. According to Jack, he and his friends were lending large sums of money to the association but, with endearing modesty, not all of them wished to be named.

The press attacked him. He's running a dictatorship, they said. Jack himself joked that he had 'one set of books for the clubs, one for the public and one for the Sports Minister'.

Jack is, by his own account, close to God. In the biography he commissioned for himself in 1998 from Tino Singh, sports editor of the Trinidad *Guardian*, Jack's sister recalls his brilliance as a child, always able to defeat her at checkers. He loved Sundays because 'there was always something to learn from the sermons'. And he learned, 'never to try and fool God'.

'My husband would never have achieved any of the things he did if he was dishonest . . . he is close to his Creator,' says his wife Maureen, whose credit card is said to have one of the highest limits in Trinidad.

Jack had planned to call his biography *A Prophet Without Honour* to suggest his messianic qualities in a country where he endures widespread loathing. But he stumbled across a better title, *Upwards Through the Night*, from the poet Henry Longfellow: '*The heights by great men reached and kept were not attained by sudden flight, but they, while their companions slept, were toiling upward in the night.*'

It's true, there was a little sleepiness, a lack of vigilance, around Trinidad where people had become accustomed to sports administrators from the James brothers mould.

One of Eric James's achievements was setting up the Caribbean Football Union but it was Warner who saw that the Union offered a stepping stone to greater power. In 1983 he ran successfully for the presidency and that gave him an automatic seat on FIFA's executive committee. Biographer Tino Singh, recorded this was 'a step that created major revenue earning opportunities'.

President Havelange, nine years in power, recognised Warner's qualities, and promoted him. For the next six years Warner learned to say what the Gulf billionaires wanted to hear, attended the Olympics as an honoured guest and lived the lifestyle he had dreamed.

FEW THINGS unite a little country like success in world sport. The streets of Trinidad & Tobago were alive with happiness. Calypsos blared from bars and sound trucks. People walked tall and smiled. Trinidad was one game away from qualifying for the 1990 World Cup. Little Trinidad! They were On the Road to Rome. All they had to do was draw with the Americans at the national stadium on 19 November 1989 and they'd be off to Italy.

Coach Gally Cummings, one of Trinidad's most respected former players, who'd turned out for the New York Cosmos, took his team away from the ceaseless drumming, the interfaith services of hope and the overflowing rum shops and mentored them quietly at their camp at Fyzabad in Trinidad's oil belt, 50 miles from Port of Spain.

These were fantastic days for the squad. Their whole nation was behind them. And, they felt, the whole world. Who could resist the happy notion of this little island defeating the super-power?

As the Trinidad team trained, Jack Warner, secretary still of the association, made preparations of his own. He printed thousands of extra tickets for the match and drove a coach and horses through the rules forbidding alcohol sales at the stadium.

Jack seemed to have gone from having God close by, to being God himself: *Let the multitudes come! Let the fans drink! Turn orange squash into beer! Let the profits roll in!*

Come the day excitement in Trinidad was explosive. It seemed the entire country was going to the game. It seemed like that thanks to Jack's decision to print all those extra tickets. Tens of thousands of fans swathed in red and waving their precious tickets surrounded the stadium, far more than it could possibly accommodate. Match stewards, fearful for fans' safety, opened the gates early. Soon every aisle was blocked with fans standing. The stadium bulged. The bar opened. People started drinking. Meanwhile, outside, thousands of people who'd spent their hard-earned cash on Trinidad's biggest match in living memory found they couldn't get near the stadium. And they were angry.

As Jack Warner enjoyed pre-match drinks in the VIP lounge with Horace Burrell from Jamaica and Colin Klass from Guyana, fans chanted curses against him. Through the melée glided the air-conditioned luxury coach bearing the US squad. Trinidad's little minibus couldn't get through the angry crowd. Eventually Trinidad's finest footballers were manhandled over the heads of the crowd and into the stadium.

It wasn't, perhaps, the best preparation for the game. The Americans scored a single goal and were off to Italy. Trinidad was devastated.

According to Warner's biography, Havelange and Blatter were downcast. They'd been silently backing the underdogs, said Warner, and felt so bad that they gave Trinidad a fair play award in an effort to console them. As for Warner himself, he was so upset, he claimed, that tears streamed down his face. He felt suicidal. He threw himself down on his secretary's couch and sobbed his heart out.

The local press meanwhile accused Warner of 'massive fraud'. According to the Trinidad *Guardian*, 45,000 tickets had been printed for the game, even though the stadium would hold only 28,500 fans. It went on to say, '35,000 patrons jammed into the stadium before midday when the gates were closed . . . Such was the overcrowding that several persons fainted from the heat and had to be treated. Fire officials said that the situation was high risk.'

Warner stonewalled. The media wouldn't let up and after four days he finally decided to call a press conference. National association president Peter O'Connor sat to one side, arms folded on the tabletop, looking as if his proximity to Warner was giving him piles. General Secretary Warner was the passionate one, both hands pressed flat to his bosom as he leaned forward and begged the hacks to believe him.

Warner initially told FIFA that he had sold 43,000 tickets in total – 10,000 to corporate Trinidad & Tobago to enable the association to pay off its debt (although he had not told colleagues about his plan), 28,000 on the open market, and 5,000 reserved for 'emergency use'. Now at this press briefing he claimed that the association had printed and sold only 28,500 tickets and argued that the stadium's figure of 34,834 tickets was wrong. *At least 6,000 of the tickets were bogus!*

The government appointed a retired QC to lead a commission of inquiry into the scandal. Lionel Seemungal, reading through some papers about the breaches of safety rules, pondered aloud: 'Did Warner believe he was God or merely think he was running the country?' Warner leapt on the comment, and went to court to have Seemungal removed. He failed but the inquiry eventually ground to a halt, leaving Warner claiming he wasn't able to tell his side of the story.

He did his best in his approved biography with it's glowing introduction from Havelange – he offers it for sale at US$20 a time from his office in Port of Spain. Printing the extra tickets and then initially denying it had to be confronted. Biographer Tino Singh explained, 'Warner's later credibility would be undermined by this single action. What had in fact been a series of critical errors of judgement – to sell more tickets than the stadium could properly accommodate, to hold even more tickets to meet a "special" demand, and, worst of all, to keep his executive completely out of the picture – was now complicated by a fabrication, a denial and an attempt to create a smokescreen around what had really transpired. By compounding his initial error, Warner now made any later explantion or clarification further fodder for the gristmill of innuendo, rumour and overt hostility.'

Singh went on to say: 'The public perception was that Warner had personally pocketed the proceeds from the sale of the extra tickets. This was of course not true – the audit performed on the accounts of the game afterwards by Ernst & Young revealed that all the tickets had been properly accounted for, including the 5,000 "extra" tickets Warner had reserved. But by the time that audit became public, no one seemed to care. Warner's name had already been irreversibly besmirched.'

Surely a prophet was never so unwelcome in his own country as Jack Warner. His disillusionment culminated in his resignation as Secretary of the association shortly afterwards. But there was good news. The day after the match, according to Jack's biography, he heard a knock on his door. In walked the immensely round, shirt-button popping figure of Charles Gordon Blazer, forever known as Chuck, a vice-president of the US soccer federation, Commissioner of the American Soccer League, and believed to have a 24/7 full service McDonald's built into his bedroom closet. They'd got to know each other on the CONCACAF circuit and Chuck brought glad tidings.

'Jack, you have done enough for your country,' proclaimed the American. 'But they have never accepted you. CONCACAF is in the doldrums. Use your skills to help build it up.'

Football was never to be the same again. On the horizon was the next CONCACAF election. If Chuck and Jack could prise the presidency from the longtime grasp of Mexico's ageing Joaquin Soria Terrazas and turn the region's 35 votes into a solid voting block at FIFA, they would be among the most powerful men in the world game.

Whoever replaced Terrazas would need the virtues of 'a Gandhi or a Martin Luther King', reflected Blazer. Warner, he was sure, had these qualities in abundance. Jack the Messiah had found his John the Baptist.

BEHOLD! I SEND MY MESSENGER

Chuck the Baptist

JACK AND CHUCK made a fabulous team. Chuck made it his business to go ahead of Jack, hailing his greatness, 'If he wants to, I believe he can head FIFA one day,' said Chuck. 'If he decided that that was the way he wanted to go, you will find that there will be a tremendous amount of support for him.' Chuck went ahead of Jack in 1990, managing his campaign to win control of CONCACAF. Standing in their way was ageing president Joaquin Soria Terrazas.

Jack and Chuck looked at the voting numbers and realised this election would be hard to lose. Warner already had the islands of the Caribbean Football Union tied up and they held the majority of the votes. They knew that many people felt slighted by Terrazas, they felt he'd failed to consult them, they couldn't afford to travel to his congresses and he had allowed the confederation to become moribund. A couple of inspired hustlers might stimulate more football, more money – and more jobs for the boys.

Warner worked his rocky outcrops in the Caribbean, and won the crucial support in Central America of wealthy Costa Rican Isaac Sasso. In April 1990 the Warner bandwagon drew up at the Sheraton Conquistador in Guatemala City, where CONCACAF's national associations would vote for their new president. Present as guest of honour and to make sure the congress reached the right decisions was President Havelange and a fixer from the Adidas team.

The mood in Guatemala City was 'frightening' claimed Blazer. 'Security with machine guns were checking credentials ... Warner's supporters were being targeted ... Jack was being called with threats of execution and other terrible possibilities. He was determined to go through even if it meant losing his life.' The congress began at 10.35 am and 13 bitter hours later it closed. It started on a sour note. There were attempts to prevent Warner from standing but his people got that overturned and Trinidad was back in.

When it came to the presidential vote Terrazas, realising that Warner had his troops well organised, withdrew. Rival candidates from America and Canada pulled out, leaving Jack the sole candidate. Still they held a ballot. Warner won 16 votes and the presidency; ten were cast against him.

Warner immediately named Chuck Blazer as CONCACAF's new general secretary. Then he appointed the unambitious, un-threatening 64-year-old Isaac Sasso to replace Terrazas on FIFA's executive committee, alongside Warner and Mexican television magnate Guillermo Canedo.

A week later Warner sent a private fax to FIFA general secretary Blatter in Zurich. 'The whole procedure was a very sordid affair with several of the past officials ... conducting a smear campaign against me,' he reported.

'Finally, let me place on record my sincere thanks to you and

FIFA for your support and understanding over the last few months. I shall always remain eternally grateful and permanently indebted to you and I do wish to give the assurance that in all our deliberations and actions loyalty to you, to our president Dr Havelange and to the organisation of FIFA itself, shall always be paramount.' And off Warner went to the World Cup, the only happy Trinidadian in Rome.

Chuck Blazer got a deal with New York property magnate Donald Trump and the confederation moved its headquarters into the 17th floor of Trump Tower on Fifth Avenue with its pink marble walls and indoor fountain. An impressive address. How was it achieved? He has an explanation. 'I knew of Jack's closeness with God,' said Chuck. 'We didn't get Trump Tower by accident . . . it had to come from some divine intervention. Every so often I would look at Jack and say that we are good at what we do. But I am also mindful that there appeared to be some spiritual force looking after us.'

God helped Chuck get himself an apartment on the 49th floor. Visitors say that his office overlooking Fifth Avenue is dominated by his pet parrot, Max. Blazer is said to have a beach house at Paradise Island in the Bahamas. That's close to the confederation's business registration filed in Nassau.

CHUCK set up a new venture in the year 2000 in the Centre Point tower that dominates London's Oxford Street. Called Global Interactive Gaming (GIG), the company's ambition was to generate more gambling on sports television. 'We enhance the experience of watching a sporting event by attaching a financial component to arouse the viewer's interest,' they claimed. 'Our revolutionary approach offers an order of magnitude paradigm shift in this expanding marketplace.' It sounded just the way Chuck talks.

Fans watching their favourite sport on interactive television would be invited to place bets: Which team would score next? Who would have the next throw-in? Would a penalty whiz past the keeper?

It wasn't that revolutionary. As in any form of gambling, the only consistent winner was going to be the gambling company. I called a GIG executive and asked, would they be taking bets on the 2002 World Cup? He said, 'Most likely, yes.'

Blazer kept his part in the new project under wraps – there were no announcements on the FIFA website. His partner in the venture was the Kirch group. And they, together with ISL, were paying FIFA more than a billion dollars for the television rights to the next two World Cups. Events on which Chuck's new global betting shop was expecting to take bets – and make money.

Blazer was a member of FIFA's executive committee that had voted the contract to Kirch. He had a responsibility to scrutinise the company's performance and might at any time have to penalise them if they failed to honour their promises. Now he had gone into partnership with them, stood to profit personally from business that would most likely involve the tournament that FIFA owned and Kirch had bought. I emailed Blazer: Was there any conflict of interest?

'There is absolutely no conflict of interest,' he replied. 'Individual members of the executive committee have actually no functional or supervisory relationship with Kirch and its subsidiaries.'

He went on, 'I trust that when you have a total picture of our accomplishment you will applaud it for being the natural extension of people who are entreneurian [sic] by nature and have found a unique niche in which we are the first ones to develop a plan to facilitate interactive gaming.'

Instead I filed a story for the *Daily Mail* about the 'FIFA boss who wants to take your bets on the World Cup'. The morning we published, 18 December 2001, Chuck was due at a meeting of the executive committee, but he cancelled his flight and emailed his excuses to the president: 'I have caught laryngitis which has me sounding something like a frog. Maybe a Prince, sounding like a frog and just waiting to be kissed.'

After the meeting, Blatter held a press conference. He seemed shaken. 'We need to establish a code of conduct to avoid such situations for members of the executive committee,' he said. 'This is the game of the world and the youth of the world and we cannot afford to have in our committee people who do not totally deserve a reputation for ethics and morals. Just give me some time. I need to look into this. Please believe I will do it.'

He added, 'Blazer has nothing to do with World Cup rights and he had explained this to me in a telephone call.' Blatter said Chuck called from New York early in the morning before the committee began its four-hour meeting. Asked about Blazer's activities, he replied: 'I am not happy about it. I am not happy at being telephoned at three in the morning New York time by Blazer. I will go into all this and I say just give me time to do it and I will do it.'

Blazer reminded colleagues that eighteen months earlier he had written to general secretary Michel Zen-Ruffinen informing of his joint business with Kirch and assuring him that where necessary, 'I am prepared to recuse myself from voting on such issues.'

And he had recused himself. Earlier in the year the executive committee had met in Buenos Aires and voted on Kirch taking over the World Cup television rights surrendered when ISL went bust. All the committee voted – except for Blazer who disclosed his relationship and abstained.

So, it turned out, Blatter and FIFA's entire committee had known about Blazer's plan for personal enrichment with Kirch. And that wasn't a problem. Chuck didn't have to make a choice between serving FIFA and serving himself an extra helping from the FIFA pie.

'ALL I LIVE FOR is to give back to my communities,' Jack Warner once told a local newspaper, 'because I believe I am a beneficiary from the community.'

Some Trinidadians might be puzzled by the first part of that statement. No-one could argue with the second. Jack Warner has been a beneficiary of international football and of the Caribbean in a stunning and most audacious way. They've even built a palace for him. It's called the Dr Joao Havelange Centre of Excellence in Trinidad. Its purpose, according to Jack, is to raise football standards throughout CONCACAF.

If the region had really needed a football centre and if there had been a fair and open and accountable planning process, they might have put it near the middle of the region, somewhere like Jamaica or Cuba, so players and officials could get there easily.

But none of these things came to pass and, far from being in the middle, it's in Trinidad, well south of most of Jack's regional football community. The Dr Joao Havelange Centre of Excellence is set back from the road at Macoya, between the airport and Port of Spain. It's a 6,000-seat football stadium with three practice fields, a swimming pool, offices, a conference hall and the 50-bed Sportel Inn for visiting officials.

Back at what passed for the planning stage, Warner calculated that he'd need US$16 million to build his centre. But FIFA's total development budget for the years 1999 to 2002, for the entire region, came to US$10 million. So, US$16 million for one small Caribbean Island. Impossible!

Not for Jack. There were presidential elections on FIFA's horizon and Jack controlled 35 votes. Nobody, least of all Blatter, wanted to disappoint him. And so it was that the entire region's development budget, US$10 million, went to Jack, along with a US$6 million UBS loan, guaranteed by FIFA.

In one of his last official duties President Havelange opened the Centre in May 1998. He told the regional officials: 'Vote for Blatter'. He spoke warmly of Jack, calling him, 'My brother'.

Eighteen months after the grand opening Julio Grondona, chairman of the finance committee, and President Blatter sent a formal letter to Warner reminding him that he hadn't repaid a cent of the US$6 million loan. What tough action did they propose? 'FIFA is contemplating reimbursing the loan of US$6 million made . . . on your behalf, since it appears unfeasible that your confederation will find the means to do so.' So they let him off the hook, and said they would raise the money themselves.

At about the same time, Bin Hammam, who chairs the Goal Bureau, agreed that Warner could have a US$400,000 Goal project in Trinidad. What did the McKinsey team in the chicken house, who were being so ruthless with less powerful applicants for Goal money, think of all that money pouring into Warner's empire? That's another of their client confidences.

When in Zurich Jack likes to drop by the finance department. After one such visit Hans Ulrich Schneider, who controls the purse strings for FIFA's development budget, agreed that Warner could delay repaying tens of thousands of dollars of debt. He bravely stated that this was 'not intended as a precedent for the future'.

However much money FIFA handed over to Warner he always asked for more. They'd paid for the Centre and they'd have to pay again to use it. In August 2001, Warner hit on Blatter direct, no intermediaries, demanding US$77,000 for a four-day refereeing seminar, at Macoya and in Mexico City, in October 2001.

Warner, saying he could chip in US$28,000 'from our meagre resources', attached his budget for the Macoya Centre. FIFA would have to pay US$3,000 – that's US$750 a day – to rent the conference room it had built. The 32 participants would need to eat and that would cost FIFA another US$15,000 or US$468 per head. Accommodation expenses of US$16,000 sounded about right to Jack, US$500 for each trainee – in the hotel FIFA paid to build.

The list wound on down the page. Renting audio-visual equipment? That would be US$12,000. 'Other' equipment? Another US$3,000. Advertising and promoting the course would cost US$2,500 and certificates, a snip at US$50 apiece. Then Jack tagged on 'Miscellaneous US$4,000' on the end.

President Blatter passed Warner's request to Bin Hammam's Goal Bureau. No way would they agree to Warner's demand for US$77,000. He must be given more! Two days after Warner faxed his request and 'budget', Urs Zanitti, head of the Goal department, faxed back that they wanted to give him the whole US$105,500 cost of the course. Zanitti effused, 'We congratulate you on taking the initiative to organise such useful courses.'

Seven months later Warner was at it again, telling Zurich that he intended to recruit Pelé, Sir Bobby Charlton, Carlos Alberto Parreira and Gerard Houllier for a coaches' course in autumn 2002. What a stunning line-up. But it turned out they were busy, all of them. Instead Warner signed up FIFA's head of development Jean-Paul Brigger and Ghana's Abedi Pelé but FIFA paid up anyway.

*   *   *

GOAL'S Mr Zanitti might have been less impressed with Warner if he'd known how little the FIFA-funded Centre was used for regional coaching and football development. In 2001 it was just 36 days of the year. The following year, just 35 days. By 2003, there was only three weeks of courses at the centre. It was hard to see what all those millions of dollars were doing for the great world family of football.

One family was certainly benefiting, though. Daryan Warner, son of Jack, owned the high-priced restaurant that fed football and other visitors. The Centre had barely been open a year when Warner decided it was the place to stage the 1999 Miss Universe Pageant. 'The Miss Universe offices are in the same building as my offices in New York,' he said and that was the last anybody heard of it.

Jack had another fantasy for his football palace. He'd create his own personal football club, they'd play in the World Club Championships, and he'd make a fortune.

Here's how he explained it on his website. 'Back in 1996 whilst Trinidad and Tobago mourned the early exit of the National Senior Team from the qualifying tournament for the 1998 World Cup, patriot and committed servant Austin Jack Warner was plotting the next step forward to take this country to the 2002 World Cup finals. Out of the bowels of this disappointment, the Joe Public Football Club was formed.'

The club directors were family, wife Maureen, son Daryan and old college pal Harold Taylor who was regularly recycled through positions with the local association, the Caribbean Football Union and CONCACAF.

Warner hoped to cash in on selling his best players abroad. One of his sons would become a registered agent and 'no transfers could be done without his approval'.

His team won the 1998 Caribbean Club Championship and

Warner announced, 'Joe Public FC is fast becoming the Manchester United of the Caribbean.' He predicted that his club would reach the finals of the World Club Championships. They didn't. Joe Public slipped down the rankings and in January 2004 Warner abandoned the dream.

HURRAY FOR YOUTH SPORT

. . . and the Warner family piggybank

Port of Spain, 12 June 2001: 'I have served the FIFA faithfully and well these last 18 years. I have seen mortals of less loyalty and service as well as their off-spring enjoy benefits from FIFA,' emailed Jack Warner to Sepp Blatter. 'Having been promised that my son's firm will share in the fruits of FIFA's e-Strategy, this is the result.'

Jack wasn't getting what he wanted. FIFA had been manipulated into staging its Under-17 World Championship in his island and now a tasty contract was being denied to his son. Warner had promised his family they'd get their share of the tournament spoils but the faraway Zurich bureaucrats – damn them, his own employees – were dragging their feet.

'The FIFA family can only survive and remain intact if its children genuinely believe that there is a place in the House of FIFA for them,' Jack rumbled. 'But regrettably, while the FIFA House may have a place for everyone, I guess, everyone should know his place, and, apparently, I do not know mine. Regards, Jack Warner.'

Warner was chairman of the FIFA youth committee that gave the Under-17 Championship to Trinidad for September 2001. There would be lots of contracts, millions of dollars of government and FIFA money to be allocated. Four new stadiums to be built, an existing one renovated, lots of expensive infrastructure and plenty of associated business to be snapped up.

He set up a planning committee with his friend Ameer Edoo, later to become chairman of Trinidad's airport authority. They got funding from the Minister of Works and Transport, Sadiq Baksh and Finance Minister Brian Kuei Tung, members of the UNC party that Warner supported with influence and cash. In May 2004, with six other politicians and businessmen, Edoo, Baksh and Tung were arrested and charged with corruption during the construction of the new national airport at Piarco. The case continues to drag on in Trinidad's courts.

'I make no apologies for doing what I did for us to win the bid,' chuckled Warner, recalling how he had outmanoeuvred his colleagues at FIFA. 'Several other countries including Peru, Japan, Finland, Scotland also made bids. I singlehandedly fought them and won. When they lost, there was talk about insider trading and conflict of interest and unfair advantage.'

Warner appointed himself chairman of the tournament organising committee and drew up a budget. That was approved by FIFA's six-man finance committee (deputy chairman Jack Warner) and rubberstamped by the executive committee of which he was a vice-president.

There was unhappiness at the way all those stadium contracts were being awarded. The local Contractors Association wrote to Prime Minister Panday complaining about how 340 million Trinidad dollars of public money was being spent. They claimed that the tendering laws were being 'violated'. The process wasn't transparent and it was 'highly irregular'. Despite requests, Warner has refused to respond to these allegations.

Warner thanked finance director Urs Linsi for FIFA's goodwill and the prompt financial assistance received towards the FIFA Under-17 World Youth Championships scheduled for 2001.

In early 2001 broadcasters sent a technical team to report on the new stadiums. It was led by a man called Keith Thomas. He discovered, to his horror, that little thought had been given to the location of power supplies and television cables and cameras. Roof beams and dangling cables would obscure shots of the field. When Thomas tried to ask questions he was 'castigated' by FIFA bureaucrat Walter Gagg.

'It is obvious TV issues cannot be discussed on site and information has to be obtained by myself questioning tradesmen and labourers,' said Thomas. 'The planning and organisation of the inspection visit was poor.' He stated, without comment, that Warner and his business associates on the organising committee were involved in the management of the construction.

The fast food and beverage contract at all five stadiums went to the restaurant business run by Warner's son Daryan. The organising committee's chief executive Sandra Bachir told a local radio station, 'I think that at times, yes, we should be concerned about these things. But we need to grow up and get over these things and look at the broader picture. We spend sometimes too much time dwelling on little things which we cannot change.'

Another thing that couldn't be changed was Warner's power to influence how Blatter awarded FIFA contracts. The 15 visiting teams – players, coaches, doctors, support staff and officials – would be flying in from as far away as Europe, Asia, Africa and Australia. Around 500 tickets had to be paid for. Normally these flights would be organised by FIFA's travel office in Zurich. Not this time. This time it's a good piece of business for the lucky travel agents.

FIFA's Barbara Eggler circulated a memo telling all the participants that 'In accordance with the wishes of Jack Warner, and after agreement with the FIFA President, the travel arrangements for the U17-Tour will be organised by a local organising committee travel agency called Simpaul's Travel service (a family-owned travel agency).'

Simpaul, based in Port of Spain, is part of what Jack calls 'the Warner group of companies' and it does very well out of football, internationally and regionally. Warner himself, forever jetting around the world, invariably books himself and his entourage with Simpaul.

FOR THE 2002 World Cup FIFA were investing heavily in internet software and intranet systems. They wanted fans in hotel lobbies and meeting points to be able to access instant match reports and tournament news. Trinidad's Under-17 tournament would provide a test run. A big Dallas company was the lead contractor. Semtor, a software company based in Weston, Florida wanted sub-contracts but weren't making much progress.

Jack Warner put in a word for Semtor at FIFA: 'I thought I should send this email to you so that you can see what the developments are to date, re my son.' Daryll Warner was a Semtor project manager. Time to conclude a contract was getting short. Jack emailed again, 'I look forward now with some anxiety over the discussion involving my son, Daryll and his firm, Semtor.'

In June 2001 Daryll Warner emailed his Dad: 'Like you I am very confused since we were told that the regional website would involve Semtor Inc. In addition I am TOTALLY dumbfounded as to who is the decision-maker at FIFA.'

Jack replied, 'Look, Son, don't you worry too much, just stick to what you and Semtor have to do and nothing else ... The decision-maker at FIFA concerning this matter is the General Secretary, Michel Zen-Ruffinen, and he has repeatedly told me (supported by both the FIFA President and also by Urs Linsi) that there will be a role for Semtor at the FIFA and I take them at their word.'

Daryll wrote again to Dad, this time addressing him by his rank, President of CONCACAF. 'Dear Mr Warner; I would like to thank you for your vote of confidence concerning Semtor Inc. Unfortunately, your FIFA colleagues do not share your sentiments or aspirations.' This saddened Daryll.

'I am disappointed with FIFA,' Daryll informed his daddy. 'From where I am, it seems that today's FIFA is not the same FIFA that you joined so many years ago. Where were the ethics, morals, honesty, in dealing with Semtor? As a child I wanted to become part of FIFA because of FIFA's golden values. Unfortunately, today it seems that that hope is fading fast.'

Semtor kept up the pressure, sending FIFA a draft contract that only needed a signature. Semtor would develop a dozen or so 'kiosks' that would go into hotel lobbies and other places where fans gathered. That would cost just over US$1 million. Semtor would supply the content for another US$362,500 and provide Internet audio for US$320,000.

On-line video production would rack up another US$75,000 but this wasn't just for Trinidad 2001. The scheme was 'designed to create a model and paradigm that will continue through World Cup 2002'. If Semtor could pull that one off in Japan and Korea, they were going to be making a whole lot more money. But just for now and bringing the total bill for Trinidad alone to just under US$2 million was a final clause. Daryll Warner would act as 'management liaison between all web initiative consultants' for a fee of US$60,000.

Dad sent the draft contract high over the heads of the people usually responsible for such matters and direct to Blatter and finance director Urs Linsi. Two weeks later, keeping up the pressure, Warner emailed Linsi. 'Re: Semtor's contract. I know you guys are very busy but, notwithstanding that I still do need your confirmation of the contract I sent to you both by email last Thursday.' Jack was in Argentina for a FIFA congress. 'I have the hard copy here in Buenos Aires for your signatures on arrival. I await your response with some anxiety.'

Jack got what he wanted. The contract was signed. But that wasn't the end of it. Daryll wanted to feature FIFA sponsors in his output. He wanted FIFA's marketing department to sort it out. Dad stepped in again, 'Daryll pls advise me specifically what you wish of the FIFA Marketing AG or any other agency or person and I shall use my office to assist.' Then Dad emailed Zurich, 'Can anyone in FIFA, anyone, assist Semtor?'

Not soon enough, they couldn't and it drove Warner crazy. At the end of July 2001 he emailed Blatter and both his secretaries, Helen and Christine, general secretary Michel Zen-Ruffinen and his secretary Doris, finance director Urs Linsi, marketing advisor Guido Tognoni and presidential advisor Jerome Champagne.

'I'm confused, Sepp, and do beg for your help. Sepp, I tried my best not to bother you but, after having explored all other possibilities I remain as confused and distressed as ever. The under mentioned mail from my son is self-explanatory. I've made every effort to get some response from some persons, even going so far as to sign my official title in my mails but to no avail.' Daryll had been complaining again. Apparently someone in FIFA's marketing department had told him they'd never heard of Semtor.

The pressure from Dad helped the boy again. Daryll was just a project manager for a hopeful little company seeking a tiny contract from an organisation that struck deals with global corporations. And the president was taking a personal interest. On 2 August Sepp Blatter emailed. 'Dear Jack, There is good news! The General Secretary and project manager will inform you accordingly. I will be on holiday until 11 August and will be back in office with full batteries and power! Best regards, Sepp.'

Semtor went ahead and placed their kiosks. Daryll Warner got his money and Jack got his, because the tournament news that went out through Daryll's kiosks was provided by a British company called Team Talk – whose consultant was Jack Warner.

FIVE DAYS into the FIFA World Under-17 youth tournament, Jack Warner faxed Sepp Blatter. 'My dear President and Friend, Due to the [9/11] tragedy in USA last Tuesday many airlines and freight companies are not accepting cargo owing to increased security concerns. As a result, it makes perfect business sense to delay ANY shipment of kiosks until this matter has been rectified.'

The kiosks were brilliant, Jack told the trade press after the tournament, 'They are helping to revolutionise the entire sport. Semtor's important contribution to the 2001 FIFA Under-17 World Championship enabled football fans around the world to join with local fans in the enjoyment of this unique celebration of the football and flavours of Trinidad & Tobago.' And it was reported Semtor hoped to sell a further 300 kiosks to FIFA for the next World Cup.

Immediately after the tournament Daryll love-bombed 23 FIFA officials in Zurich with emails thanking them for their help and welcoming 'the opportunity to continue assisting FIFA where applicable'. In the new year he emailed Jack, copied to Sepp: 'Dad: I will give you a draft of items that I think I can assist FIFA with for the fiscal year 2002/03 and make both the executive committee and president Blatter look like winners in the eyes of their many critics (media and otherwise).'

In February 2002 Daryll emailed Urs Linsi, slugging his message 'High' importance. 'I would like to share some thoughts/ideas that I think would be beneficial for FIFA . . . if possible, please feel free to share this with the powers that be within FIFA (notably the general secretary, exco/finance committee, and FIFA IT). If need be, I am more than willing to elaborate on ALL points where appropriate at your earliest convenience.' Linsi obediently copied Daryll's email to his colleagues and told them, 'In my opinion it would be worthwhile to examine alternatives like proposed in Daryll's mail.' He copied his approval back to Daryll.

THE TRINIDAD Under-17 tournament itself proved disappointing to some young players. The Australian team arrived at their hotel late at night. Team manager Les Avory was incandescent. 'There was no night porter so the team had to unload 86 pieces of luggage. No night manager either. There was no hot water in some rooms, the tiling was dirty and some showerheads missing. Some toilets wouldn't flush and anyway, it was already in a smelly location. Another team refused to stay there and moved somewhere better. I got hold of Warner but he refused to move us. He said, "I've paid US$59,000 in advance."'

The Aussies, drawn in the same first round group as Trinidad, soon learned more about hospitality and fair play Warner-style. 'Our training ground was at Arima,' said Les. 'One and a quarter hours' travel each way and we were expected to do that twice a day. We asked if we could use an alternative pitch and that was rejected. So we went to that huge public space in the city, the savannah, which might be fine for Carnival but better for dirt-track racing than practising set-pieces for international games.' A local school took pity and invited the Aussies to share their pitch but the kids still needed it some of the time.

'A FIFA doctor had told us we should avoid playing between 11.00 and 16.00,' says Les Avory. It was dangerously hot under the Caribbean sun. The Aussies' matches against Brazil and Croatia were duly scheduled for the evenings. But when they came to play the local Trinidad team, the rules were different. Jack arranged the match at lunchtime when the sun was at its highest. And there was something else that made it harder for the Aussies. Les Avory said, 'We should have been given a 72-hour break after the Brazil game but this was only 41 hours.'

Despite filthy accommodation, hours on the road, shabby training facilities, lack of rest and the hot, hot sun, the Aussies beat Trinidad 1–0.

Avory said, 'Afterwards I demanded a meeting with Warner and told him, bluntly, "This is gamesmanship." He didn't like the way it was going so he called in a secretary to take minutes. That was pure intimidation.' As far as we know, Warner has never responded to this allegation.

Avory's youngsters won through to the quarter-finals but lost 5–1 to Nigeria, eventually the losing finalists. Trinidad, scoring no points, had gone out in the first round. The final day of the tournament coincided with FIFA's 'Fifth Fair Play Day Worldwide'.

As the tournament costs soared Trinidad's *Express* warned, 'We must be careful that Trinidad & Tobago is not used simply to further Mr Warner's business interests at the expense of the taxpayer. Teams have been staying at Mr Warner's hotels and guesthouses and his restaurants have been supplying meals.' The editorial said, 'Mr Warner seems to be enjoying the lion's share of the benefits ... We need to ensure that the major beneficiaries extend beyond simply Mr Warner and his family.'

Sepp Blatter happened to be swinging through the Caribbean on a meet 'n' greet 'n' build-the-vote tour. He dropped in on Trinidad and assured the *Express* that 'Jack Warner is a wonderful and loyal friend. He is very competent.'

One of Blatter's senior officials, Walter Gagg, asked, 'Why do people still have to ask the questions about what happened and why this happened? Without Jack Warner, I don't really think we would have been able to host this Championship and we have to be very, very happy to have him in the organisation.'

Still, some of the Trinidad press carried on attacking Warner. And he believed FIFA insiders were supplying the ammo. He didn't realise the dislike for him in some areas of FIFA had been so deep.

PRESIDENT BLATTER, sitting beneath a banner with FIFA's slogan 'For the good of the game' was going pale beneath his tan. The boss of world soccer was entertaining reporters at the Hilton Port of Spain press conference with imitations of a goldfish. I'd asked him about all those Warner family contracts. Was there a conflict of interest? Blatter fiddled with his glasses. He adjusted his microphone.

'If I have to give you an answer, I need to give it in writing when I return to Zurich next week. The FIFA president was not in charge in the organisation of this Under-17 tournament,' he said, referring to himself in the third person. He added, 'I will go back and inform you ... because I'm going to work for transparency.'

Other reporters chipped in with similar questions. Blatter did his goldfish thing. Then someone lobbed in a question from the back of the room. Calypso and steel bands had been terrific at this tournament, would they now become the preferred music at FIFA events world-wide? The mood changed. Blatter was out of danger. All thanks to a quick-thinking member of Warner's organising committee.

After the press conference the president's spokesman Markus Siegler came to see me in my room at the Hilton and what a pleasant fellow he was. He shared his Gaulloises and assured me that, as a former newspaperman, if he thought there was anything hooky going on in Sepp's empire, he'd head straight for the door. 'I'd walk out,' he announced, round-eyed at his own daring. We took afternoon tea, we shook hands and he left.

A little later my phone rang and a friend whispered that Markus was telling the FIFA team elsewhere in the hotel that he had taken care of me and I 'wouldn't be a problem any more'.

Blatter had promised to get back to me, had promised transparency. So, I wrote asking him to comment on each of the numerous contracts the Warner family had gained from this FIFA tournament. Weren't there conflicts of interest?

His response landed 17 days later and 800 words long. About the Semtor contract, his answer rambled through projects in Estonia, Armenia and Cameroon and through internet and extranet pilot projects. Daryll and his US$60,000 fee didn't rate a mention. Nor did those three little words: Conflict of interest.

Regarding the allocation of the Under-17 tournament, he says, 'FIFA awards the tournament to a national association, which then has control, subject to its budget being approved by FIFA.' Then here's a bit of Blatter-speak about the Warner family contracts: 'Whether or not the outsourced services are profitable to the respective companies is left up to them as they are obliged to

provide these services within the agreed contractual framework.'
Pardon? Read it again if you like; it still doesn't make sense. It's
President Blatter being transparent.

Trinidad's newspapers kept up the attacks on Warner and
his family's contracts. When the press keep chewing away at a
story like a dog with a juicy bone, there's a public relations trick
that sometimes works. Throw the dog another bone. Warner and
Blatter concocted an exchange of mutually supportive letters,
copied to the local media.

Warner wrote affectionately to Sepp, 'I am pleased to advise
that all member federations of CONCACAF are fully supportive
of your re-nomination as President of FIFA for a second term just
as they were for your election in 1998.'

Quoting Warner would take up an awful lot of space in the
newspaper because he went on, 'Such overwhelming support indi-
cates in no uncertain manner the immense satisfaction with which
we have all viewed the discharge of your functions during your
current term in office. As such therefore it is firmly believed that
you should be given the opportunity to continue the good work
for the advancement of FIFA and for this my entire Confederation
has given its commitment. Please be guided accordingly.'

Sepp was touched and he too could fill columns in the paper.
'Dear friend Jack,' he publicly replied. 'It is with an immense
pleasure that I received your letter dated 5 October expressing the
unanimous support of the national Associations of CONCACAF
and of the CONCACAF president himself. As you know I have
dedicated my life to football and to FIFA with a strongly determined policy to advance the universality of our game in the spirit
of solidarity and democracy among the members of the world
football family. More than ever after the recent qualification
of countries such as China to the FIFA World Cup 2002, I am
convinced that this path is the right one.

'Your letter is an encouragement for me as well as a very strong incentive to pursue this action for the sake of the 204 National Associations and for all the lovers of football around our planet.'

Blatter swiftly followed up with another letter stating that Trinidad would get a special award from FIFA for being such marvellous soccer fans. He praised Warner for the tournament's success. Obligingly, Warner made this public too.

In private the correspondence was less cheerful. Three weeks after the French team flew home with the Under-17 trophy Warner emailed Blatter, 'The accounts do show a deficit. On receipt of the same and, in view of the presently orchestrated antagonisms against me through the local and foreign media, including but not limited to Andrew Jennings of the *Daily Mail*, I trust that the accounts, when submitted, will remain the business of FIFA only. I thank you for your usual understanding in this regard. With kindest regards, Jack.'

In late November 2001 Jack wrote again to Zurich. 'I have since checked and rechecked my submission to FIFA and the (deficit) is US$1,529,723. I should therefore be grateful if the error could be corrected and we can bring some closure to this matter for which I do thank you in advance.'

Then Warner set out to do it all over again. He urged the Trinidad & Tobago government to splash out T&T $30 million on hosting another youth championship. But some things had changed in Trinidad. There'd been an election, his friends were out of office.

The new sports ministry didn't want another FIFA tournament. They were still figuring out where all the money had gone in the last one. Warner, they said, 'did not fulfill the Ministry's request for a report on the 2001 FIFA World Under-17 Championship'. The Ministry added, 'We also wanted to know what the tendering process would be and what were the benefits for Trinidad & Tobago.'

For all his international success, Jack Warner has kept up his interest in youth football in Trinidad. In September 2002 the country's original Under-17 coach for the tournament was sacked without warning or explanation. Speculation grew that this may have been connected to his omission from the final squad of Jamal Warner, Jack's 16-year-old son, who was immediately reinstated by the new coach (formerly of Warner's Joe Public team).

BIGGER, BIGGER AND BIGGER...

Weber puffs up the ISL bubble

AFTER THE devastating loss of the Olympics Jean-Marie Weber had to build ISL up again. In July 1996 they clinched the FIFA deal, with two World Cups in the bag. Hurrah! But within months there was nothing to cheer about. Before the end of the year three of ISL's top men walked out of the door and into the arms of Leo Kirch, the German media mogul who'd helped ISL raise the money to back the World Cup deal. So Weber found himself short of three brilliant rights men in a market where people and contacts are everything. And Kirch had turned from Weber's backer into a powerful rival.

And there was more to be glum about. After all the jubilation over the World Cup deal, it was dawning on ISL that they'd made a mistake. Kirch had guaranteed bank loans in return for the rights to screen the World Cup in Germany, and he'd named his price, 120 million francs, which now looked like a fantastic deal for Leo and a bad blunder by Weber and his team. One

ISL executive wrote in a confidential memo in April 1997 that 'Germany is the world's No 1 market for Soccer television rights sales. The serious loss here,' the executive warned, 'will leave us struggling everywhere.' He thought they should have held out for 300 million francs.

Then, another blow. Sepp Blatter wasn't happy. The three star executives who'd walked out, Steven Dixon, Peter Sprogis and Thomas Hipkiss, had been crucial to ISL's and FIFA's hopes of selling the World Cup rights for big money. The most valuable marketplace was Europe and in mid-1997 Blatter insisted that Weber surrender these to Leo's new hot team. Weber still had almost half the World Cup business, but losing Europe really hurt. If he was going to turn ISL into a public company, it would have to be bigger then this.

Jean-Marie Weber went shopping for rights. He'd already snapped up, back in the Spring, the World Volleyball Championships and World Swimming. Next came gymnastics, followed by a chunk of London-based Copyright Promotions that exploited cartoon, movie and television characters, *Star Wars, Mr Men* and *Dennis the Menace* along with the Cricket World Cup.

Meanwhile Weber wanted to make the most of the rights he had, and worked on plans to exploit FIFA's 'brand values'. There would be FIFA Shops, FIFA Cafes, FIFA Prime Licensing. 'Many advertising agencies would dream of that!' said a confidential report to ISL's board of directors in November 1997.

Then *vroom, vroom,* in June 1998, Weber raced across the Atlantic and spent US$300 million on Championship Auto Racing – CART – the race series that wasn't Indycar. 'CART is not only a core element of ISL's North American business but also an important component of ISL's global growth strategy,' said the company, but a lot of people wondered why they'd bothered.

Another month, another shopping trip. In July Weber popped

over to California and acquired a company called En-Linea. They created Internet sites for FIFA, and regional soccer. Next he was flying in to Athens to announce a television rights deal with the International Basketball Federation who controlled the sport outside America.

Then, something funny happened. Funny peculiar.

Weber's boys had of course been out selling. In July 1998 they sold a slice of the World Cup rights to Globo, the Brazilian television network, who made a downpayment of US$60 million. Nothing funny about that. But a US$22 million chunk of that money was supposed to go straight to FIFA. It didn't. Weber sat on it.

FIFA people started wondering, where's our US$22 million?

In September 1998 Michel Zen-Ruffinen wrote to Jean-Marie Weber, congratulating him on striking these, 'exceptionally lucrative' deals, but asking, Where's our money? And another thing: what's this contract you've signed with Globo? It left out the crucial clause that should be there to protect FIFA. Funds must be lodged in a special account to safeguard FIFA's money should ISL go bust. Zen-Ruffinen wanted Weber to restore the safety clause and hand over the money.

Weber didn't correct the contract and he didn't pay FIFA the money.

Instead, in November 1998 he plotted his, 'New Millennium Strategy Plan' a 'strictly confidential' 26-page vision of the ISL group's exciting growth over the next four years.

The parent company, called ISMM, which included ISL, En Linea, a sponsorship research company, and other interests, was now 'the leading global sports media and marketing corporation', said the vision document.

'We have an entrepreneurial spirit that constantly questions, creates and innovates' it said, and only after 'careful negotiation' would they 'ensure the right properties are acquired at the right price'.

The group boasted 'high ethical standards' and took a swipe at newspapers that questioned 'commercialisation' and ran stories alleging 'immorality involving money, tickets, drug-taking, match-fixing and racism'. This company would 'Strictly adhere to a high standard of business ethics.'

There was the tiniest hint of danger. 'Over past years, the financial performance of the group has not been satisfactory, partly because of high investments. The Group is now at a turning point.'

Turning point or not, Weber still hadn't paid FIFA their US$22 million and they wrote again just before Christmas asking him, please, to hand it over. But he didn't.

Was that embarrassing for Sepp? He and Jean-Marie met for early-morning coffee and croissants now and then at Blatter's office on Sunny Hill.

Monte Carlo, 23 April 1999. 'Champagne for everybody!' cried the jubilant salesmen as the applause died down in the gilt salon of the Monte Carlo Country Club. People clinked glasses and took in the view of the palm trees and the blue Mediterranean. Outside in the spring sunshine on the red clay courts of the most beautiful club in the world, tennis's top-ranked players smashed and volleyed for the 1999 Republic National trophy and the winner's handsome cheque. Today it seemed they played with particular enthusiasm. Those nice men from ISL had just given them a billion dollars more.

All the top tour directors from the ATP, the Association of Tennis Professionals, were there to celebrate the sport's biggest ever marketing and television contract: Charlie Pasarell from

Indian Wells, Butch and Cliff Buchholz from Key Biscayne, Gunther from Hamburg, Sergio and Adriano from Rome, Paul and Elaine from Cincinnati, and some other nice people from Stuttgart and Paris.

'This is an historic day and it's a very good feeling for us this morning,' said ATP chief executive Mark Miles. He compared the negotiations for tennis's most stupendous marketing deal to Winston Churchill's description of D-Day, the most difficult and complicated operation ever to take place.

'We needed partners with the right experience on a global basis, and the willingness and ability to make the right commitment of capital,' he said. 'In ISL we are absolutely convinced that we found just the right partners.'

New ISL managing director Daniel Beauvois beamed back and told them that ISL was going to make tennis bigger than ever. Jean-Marie Weber, sitting next to him, nodded. 'We want to go for the widest possible exposure ... the first success story of sports marketing in the 21st century.'

ISL had secured a decade's rights for a stunning US\$1.2 billion.

But to make money ISL would need to invest millions. The problem was they hadn't got any. Behind the fixed grins and firm handshakes in Monte Carlo, Jean-Marie Weber knew ISL were in trouble and only football could save him.

Jean-Marie went shopping again. And this time he wanted to buy Pelé.

In December 1999 Weber signed a 15-year deal to pay an astonishing US\$80 million to Flamengo, Brazil's biggest and best-supported team. Five times national league champions, they'd won the South American championship too.

It was a curious deal. Weber was buying the rights to market the club. He set up a new company, Latin America Soccer Investments, to handle the money, in the secretive British Virgin

Islands. The club would use ISL's cash to pay off their debts, build a training centre and buy new players. ISL would even provide 'a first-class stadium in the Rio de Janeiro area' with seats for at least 50,000 fans.

Pelé's name drifted in and out. Pelé Sports & Marketing were paid US$2 million for helping set up the Flamengo deal. In January 2000 Weber wrote to Pelé Sports chief executive Helio Viana. 'Following a year of excellent co-operation involving Pelé, yourself and Celso Grellet [Pelé's personal manager], as well as many members of Pelé Sports & Marketing, we write to you to review for a moment what we have achieved and to propose a way forward for our two companies with the objective of continuing and expanding our relationship.'

Weber wanted to draw Pelé into his group and hoped 'we could count on your continuous help and support, including a fair amount of time of Pelé personally.' Weber offered Pelé and Viana a five per cent slice of his group's business in Brazil. If the business were sold, either to private investors or on the stock market, that slice could be worth 'a considerable five-digit million dollar value'.

In the final paragraph of the three-page letter Weber spelled out his dream. 'Last but not least there remains our firm commitment to propose a worldwide marketing and licensing concept to Pelé for his name and brand.' Weber wanted to own the world's most famous, most loved footballer. Marketing bliss.

But the dream ended badly. By April 2001, when Weber's companies were in serious trouble, Weber and Flamengo agreed to tear up their contract, but not before the ISL group had kissed US$62.6 million goodbye. The Flamengo affair ended in litigation, heavy debts and cries of 'Where's all the money gone?' Another Brazilian deal, with the Gremio club, on which Weber had spent US$20 million, also bit the dust.

But that's jumping ahead. We're still in 2000 and FIFA getting nervous about the Globo money. In May Urs Linsi, who had replaced Erwin Schmid in the Finance Director's office ten months earlier, was notified of FIFA's earlier letter to Weber, the one from Zen-Ruffinen, dated 7 September 1998 that demanded the US$22 million and complained about the flaws in the contract. It was emphasised that nothing had changed in the previous two years. ISL's behaviour was highly criticised and it was urged that action should be taken.

In financial affairs, as in so many other things, a stitch in time saves nine. Some people at FIFA felt that Blatter should have been more assertive, taken control of the problems with the ISL group and acted swiftly, decisively, aggressively to protect FIFA's interests. Was he going to get tough now? It looked like Weber's company was in serious trouble and might drag FIFA down with it. People looked to their President to take action.

WEBER'S SHIP IS SINKING

Will Sepp come to the rescue?

EVERYTHING was going swimmingly for Jean-Marie Weber. At least that's what he wanted the world to believe when in July 2000 he came up with another 'Strategic Plan' full of hopes and opportunities. The company would be at the forefront of the internet revolution for sport, partners and fans and was a good bet for investors. 'Managing financial risk, understanding and controlling our exposure is an ongoing, integrated part of our existence,' he claimed. And the group would follow 'a high standard of business ethics and be transparent'.

'We are obviously very good at what we do,' he said. 'Our business was founded on the back of special personal relation-ships.' He added, 'Over the years we have built a network of close professional relationships with most of the major sports governing bodies which is second to none in the industry . . . we understand and respect the complex political and emotional inter-relationships within the sports industry.'

But they couldn't seem to make money out of tennis. ISL sold the ATP events to European satellite channels and within a few months the sport was barely visible. Less than a year after the champagne party at the Monte Carlo Country Club the complaints had started in the tennis world. Where was the big television exposure ISL had promised? Without ratings you couldn't sell branded product, players became restless, the sponsors didn't return calls.

So football mattered more than ever. 'The FIFA World Cup of 2002 will transform the Group – and sports marketing itself,' Weber claimed. They were forecasting an annual group profit by 2006 of getting on for half a billion francs. Buried in the back of the brochure was the throwaway line that this year, 2000, it would only be 1.5 million francs.

Their banks were refusing more credit and making noises about cancelling loans. Weber's group was close to catastrophe. He had to borrow a pile of money as fast as possible. If he couldn't, Horst Dassler's great creation would turn to dust under the demands of angry creditors. The whole shebang would be open to inspection by the liquidator's cold-eyed independent accountants.

INSIDE FIFA alarm bells were ringing. By late 2000 Sepp Blatter had problems of his own. His gift of US$250,000 a year to each of the 200 plus national associations, before the new money arrived from the sale of television and marketing rights for 2002, had done wonders for his popularity, but must have been putting FIFA finances under pressure. There were fears that that within three months paycheques to the staff might bounce. Incredibly, the world's richest sport was running out of money.

If President Blatter couldn't lay his hands on a lot of cash fast, he'd have to stop the handouts, forcing countless associations to abort development plans. It could be a catastrophe for FIFA and for the president who'd let it all happen.

Finance director Urs Linsi urgently negotiated a whopping great loan of 300 million francs from the Credit Suisse bank. It wasn't hard to get and at a cheap rate. FIFA had excellent security in the dozen or more marketing agreements, worth around 350 million francs, that had been signed with sponsors such as Coca-Cola and McDonald's. The burger company was a typical example, committed to paying nearly US$60 million dollars in stages up to the World Cup of 2006.

Financial crisis had been averted. Salaries could be paid, grants handed out and there was plenty in the cashbox for the kind of generosity that might help Blatter win votes.

But Jean-Marie Weber wasn't getting the same warm reception from his banks. In deepening trouble, he turned to President Blatter – and Sepp agreed to help.

In complete secrecy Weber sat across the table from FIFA finance director Urs Linsi and his advisors. By 25 November 2000 FIFA and ISL had a draft deal.

The deal was codenamed 'Project Dawn'. The project was raising funds to rescue the ISL group, and here's how it would be done. FIFA agreed to rewrite the 1997 marketing contract and let the ISL group raise money against the value of the individual contracts with World Cup sponsors.

ISL would have to raise its funds by a private placing because a public one would reveal the ISL group's financial difficulties. Very few people within FIFA were let in on the Project Dawn secret, and among those who got a sniff of it, there was strong disapproval.

Suddenly, more bad news for Weber. Jean-Marie and his chief executive officer Heinz Schurtenberger parted company. FIFA began to go cool on the rescue deal. Jean-Marie was furious.

He wrote angrily to Sepp, 'Dawn is of the highest importance for our group, and we therefore ask you politely and at very short notice, to call a meeting between FIFA and your partner of many years at the highest level so we can discuss the theme Dawn as well as other still open, important issues.'

Blatter declined to meet. For a brief while Weber toyed with Project Phoenix. After that came Project Faisal and then Project Sunrise and all the time the sun was dropping below ISL's horizon.

Weber was due to send a 66 million franc bank guarantee to Blatter by mid-December. It didn't happen. FIFA issued a formal 30-day notice: stump up the money or all FIFA/ISL group business is over. The Japanese marketing and advertising giant Dentsu came to Weber's rescue and put up the money.

The agreement insisted the terms must be kept confidential. Maybe that was because the security given was a sponsorship contract signed between ISL and Toshiba for 2002 and 2006. That sponsorship contract was held by an ISL group company called Lofa, based in secretive Lichtenstein.

In public Blatter showed no sign of the worsening financial crisis and led a FIFA delegation to the Vatican. They had an audience with Pope John Paul who urged Blatter to use his 'immense power' to promote moral values and solidarity. Blatter solemnly nodded his head. On the way out he gave a Cardinal 50,000 francs. A Swedish member of parliament urged the Nobel Committee to give their Peace prize to soccer. Then it was Christmas.

NEW YEAR 2001 began badly. News leaked that Weber was trying to 'renegotiate' his gigantic contract with tennis. Word spread that the ISL group was in serious trouble. Then one of

Weber's lawyers let slip that ISL was as good as insolvent and spent the next three months denying he'd said it.

In mid-January 2001 Weber begged Blatter for more time to hand over money that the ISL group had already banked from another television network. Blatter agreed to give him more time. And then even more time. Still, Weber didn't pay. Instead, he came up with a new demand. FIFA must lend money to help keep the ISL group afloat. And Weber had the cheek to demand that if the ISL group should fail to repay the money, FIFA shouldn't come after him and the other directors.

It wasn't forthcoming. Article 158 of the Swiss Penal Code prevented any such assurance being given.

On 20 January Weber wrote to his staff. He wanted to reassure them that he was making 'substantial progress securing the future of our Group and that all companies are able to meet their financial obligations'. Sadly there weren't going to be any bonuses this year. A similar letter of reassurance went to FIFA's sponsors, disputing rumours the company was bust.

In private every one of FIFA's many firms of costly advisors was telling them that the ISL group was a hopeless case. Then the banks issued Weber with an ultimatum: pay back 277 million francs or we close you down.

ISL tried to reassure Blatter. They sent him a piece of paper claiming the ISL group was 115 million francs in the black.

Blatter replied, ' . . . please be assured that ISL's efforts have been very well recognised and appreciated.' Blatter was worried. He'd asked for independently audited information demonstrating that ISL was healthy. And he hadn't got it. Please could Weber send FIFA some comforting reports? Sepp wanted Jean-Marie to know that he understood 'ISL's exceptional situation and difficulties'.

In the middle of March 2001 Sepp put his name to an austere

letter to Jean-Marie and now it had to be 'Dear Mr Weber.' Blatter reminded Weber that the ISL group had yet again failed to make an agreed payment. This time it was nearly US$8 million and FIFA had worked out a final timetable. Do it or die, was their unwavering message. Jean-Marie had to pay up and he must produce an auditor's report saying ISL could pay its bills. Do it or else. It was crunch time. (Again).

Sometimes you have to admire Jean-Marie Weber's cheek. Here's a man who owes you money. He doesn't repay it. He demands that you pay him some more. Plus, this time, he says you've got to agree not to chase him if he fails to pay up again. Always ebullient, he just keeps bouncing back, like one of his company cheques.

Weber was about to outdo himself in cheek. He was going to do something so fantastically shameless that hucksters around the world might cheer, stamp their feet and break out in applause.

On 20 March, two of Weber's advisors sat down at a table with some of FIFA's men. Weber's men said the ISL group was considering filing for bankruptcy in Switzerland. That wouldn't be good for FIFA, because FIFA might have to renegotiate all their sponsors' contracts. It might prove very costly in time as well as money. They let that sink in.

Then they said it didn't have to be that way. There was an alternative.

Jean-Marie could grab a quick flight to New York, hire a bunch of American lawyers and put ISL into Chapter 11 bankruptcy. Because most of football's sponsors were American, it should be easy. That way they could go on trading, get rid of their worst debts and take time to find someone who'd buy them. Everything would be fine for FIFA, all they had to do was sign a letter to an American judge saying they backed the scheme.

How could Sepp stop his old friend Jean-Marie taking flight to

America? He chewed over the options. It would have to be war, maybe nuclear war. That sounded a bit hard. What would Jack Warner's favourite film star have done? John Wayne would have taken decisive action and terminated the bad guys. Maybe FIFA should rush south to the canton of Zug, where ISL were based, see a judge and put the company into bankruptcy? Then a fax spurted out of the machine. Jean-Marie wasn't going to America after all. He'd found someone who wanted to buy ISL.

A week later Jean-Marie revealed his new buddies to the media. 'We are in the process of allying with a strong equity partner,' he said. Everything was coming up roses. There'd be time to complete a restructuring programme. The prospective buyer was the French Vivendi group. Weber said they just needed a little time to look through the books. Vivendi looked, and jumped on the next train back to France.

IN MID-APRIL Blatter called a meeting of FIFA's emergency committee at Sunny Hill. The elderly Nicolas Leoz didn't feel up to the trip from Paraguay but Julio Grondona, Jack Warner, Lennart Johansson and the little-known Adrian Wickham from the Solomon Islands turned up to hear how the ISL crisis was playing out. There was little to worry about, explained finance director Urs Linsi when asked about payments for television rights. 'The pre-payments were secured in a joint account and had been taken out so FIFA was on the safe side,' he said.

As the ISL crisis lurched towards catastrophe, Blatter had another problem on his desk. That 300 million francs loan from Credit Suisse that finance director Urs Linsi had fixed, godsend at the time, was now an embarrassment. The next year in Seoul the FIFA family would meet at their Congress and Blatter would be up for re-election. It wouldn't do to have to own up to a mighty hole in the finances. It would make FIFA look bad, and Sepp wouldn't look very good either.

Urs Linsi hadn't worked in credit leasing for nothing. There was a brilliant, brilliant way to turn disaster into apparent success.

If FIFA were to *sell* some of its biggest assets, the World Cup marketing contracts, the proceeds could be booked as income, the bank loan erased and the balance sheet would look great. Blatter could be proclaimed by voters as an inspired leader who'd steered FIFA through stormy waters, balanced the books, paid out massive amounts to every outstretched hand – and had plenty stashed away to keep up the flow of money.

Linsi's plan was opposed furiously inside and outside FIFA. General Secretary Michel Zen-Ruffinen and his assistant, the tall young Norwegian Jon Doviken, drafted a paper crackling with objections to the asset sale.

Zen-Ruffinen and Doviken picked up the argument that this asset sale didn't need to happen. In January 2002 money would start coming in from the television sales and FIFA would have adequate cashflow. What was wrong with extending the bridging loan from Credit Suisse? A bank loan was cheaper than Linsi's scheme, known in the money business as a 'securitisation', selling future income for money in the hand.

Linsi hit back with his memo. The loan he had already nego-tiated 'enabled the president to communicate a success story to the Finance Committee in Rome in early December last year'. This was essential, 'after the President was made aware that he and other executives would become personally liable for losses after the recognition that FIFA is over-indebted'.

Linsi was in a hurry. He had to arrange the securitisation quickly. FIFA was soon to change their accounting methods to conform with new international standards that didn't permit future income to be used in this way. If he wasn't quick, the window of opportunity would close and the 2002 report would reveal the starkness of the debt.

The deal went through and immediately Linsi was able to pump up FIFA's flagging finances with an injection of 690 million francs (US$420 million). Spread across the books for 2000 and 2001, it was a sight to gladden the eyes of FIFA's rank and file around the world.

Commentators in the international bond market guessed that securitisation had cost FIFA a lot of money. They noted that the deal had been done privately and that interest payments would not be disclosed. 'That FIFA had to privately place the deal tells you something about their judgement of its probable reception in the markets,' said a German bond trader. 'It's not usual to get a better price privately than in the market place.'

GREENHORNS TO THE RESCUE

FIFA family therapy, McKinsey-style

Zurich, 18 May 2001. FIFA and ISL had an over-close business relationship that 'lacked certain objective safeguards', claimed the Zurich newspaper *Weltwoche*.

These allegations were vociferously denied by FIFA.

Then *Bilanz*, another Zurich paper, revealed that ISL maintained a secret foundation named 'Nunca' – the Spanish word for 'never' – in the tax haven of Liechtenstein. Nunca, it was reported, was the slush fund from which top international sports officials had received pay-offs.

The *Berliner Zeitung* and the Munich *Süddeutsche Zeitung* picked up these stories and did their own research into the funny goings-on between FIFA and the ISL Group. They acquired some internal documents and claimed to have confirmation from a senior source inside the group that Nunca existed and was alleged to be the channel for bribes to key people in sport. It was alleged that Nunca paid the money and sports officials put their signatures to marketing and television contracts.

Again FIFA responded to these allegations by warning that it had contacted its lawyers.

A bankruptcy judge in Zug buried ISL on 21 May. A few days later Blatter met the press in the dark, windowless auditorium on Sunny Hill. We crammed into the rows of black-padded seats and Blatter bustled in and told us that everything was under control, he had taken personal charge of the crisis from the beginning and the World Cup was safe.

'Have you ever taken a bribe from ISL?' I asked him. The room filled with tension. Blatter looked genuinely shocked. He took a deep breath. 'I can tell you that in the 26 years I have spent at FIFA, attempts have been made to bribe me or to influence me in some form,' he replied, 'but never ever have I bribed anyone and I cannot be bribed.' Other reporters chipped in with questions about his probity. 'Please look into my eyes,' he said, 'I have nothing to hide. I am not a fraud, no, not me.' Asked if he would publish his tax declarations Blatter replied, waspishly, that if he were taking bribes he wouldn't be so stupid as to put them through his bank account.

The revelations took a new turn. Blatter claimed he was shocked when he was told that the millions of dollars paid to ISL by the Brazilian television network Globo had gone missing. It should have been paid into a special account and most of it should have long ago reached FIFA. But he definitely, absolutely certainly, hadn't known about Jean-Marie's duplicity until a few weeks ago.

'I followed the development of the ISL situation carefully,' said Blatter. 'ISL delivered payments on time, we had the money in our pockets, there was never a delay.' Then he insisted, 'It was only on 21 April [2001] that we discovered one payment didn't reach the right place.'

But hang on a minute. Michel Zen-Ruffinen was writing to Weber demanding the money back as long ago as September 1998. Why was Blatter saying they'd only just found out?

The secret wrangle inside FIFA about whether Jean-Marie should be forced to pay the money had bubbled for the past two years and eight months. Now that the US$60 million was lost, the recriminations began. In a secret memo General Secretary Zen-Ruffinen blamed Finance Director Urs Linsi for not taking action.

Linsi fired back his confidential reply. 'The decision not to push ISL and not to insist on a rectification of the Globo TV Agreement has never been the Finance Division's decision. It was a higher level decision within FIFA not to put too much pressure on ISL.' One level up from Zen-Ruffinen and Linsi sat President Blatter.

Once the bankruptcy let the US$60 million cat out of the bag FIFA had to be seen to be taking action and they made a criminal complaint to the authorities in Zug, alleging fraud and embezzlement by senior executives at the ISL group.

Blatter flew off to Japan and urged reporters, 'Let's not talk about bad things and about money, we should talk about the good things and going back to the roots of the game.' That sweet little song 'Always Look on the Bright Side of Life' seemed to be trilling in the air.

Blatter went on, 'The idea of the World Cup every second year shall no longer be closed in a safe where I have lost the combination. I should have a look during the next year if we should open again the safe door.'

*　　*　　*

Zug, 4 July 2001. Hundreds of people travelled to Zug for the first ISL group creditors' meeting. I was there. It was a hot sunny day and the air was close in the meeting room. When we broke for coffee I followed the liquidator, Thomas Bauer, out into the lobby. A tall man with a boyish grin, he'd been delving through ISL's files for six weeks. I didn't seriously expect him to answer a reporter's question, but you never know. It was worth a try and that's why I'd flown early from London and taken the train via Zurich to Zug.

I caught up with him. 'Excuse me, Dr Bauer, have you found any evidence of black money payments to sports officials?'

He smiled, 'Yes, I have found football-related payments from ISL. Some are very large, in excess of one million Swiss francs. I have tried to make connections between the payments and specific contracts, but this has not been possible.'

Dr Bauer added, 'All the payments went abroad. There are none to Swiss nationals. I have written to the recipients asking them to return the money. We are now in negotiation – and, if necessary, litigation – to get the money returned.'

Gobsmacked at his candour, I asked Bauer, would he be reporting these payments to the police? 'No. My duty is to reclaim assets of the company. That's all,' he said.

THAT SAME DAY Sepp Blatter was high above the South Atlantic on his way to a FIFA congress in Buenos Aires. He'd been preparing for months. While Weber had stood at the helm of the sinking ISL group yelling reassurance, Blatter was already making plans to put the best gloss on whatever trouble was coming his way.

His performance at the congress would have to be good. More than ever it would need careful stage management.

Blatter wrote to the head of McKinsey's office in Zurich on 9 February 2001 asking for help with the design and the 'concepts' he would deploy at the congress. Blatter told Jens Abend he had a budget of 3.5 million Swiss francs (£1.5 million) and they could spend it on completing the new FIFA business plan in time to show it off at the congress.

Blatter needed something stunning to impress the congress and help him bat away any attacks. In June, just before the congress, his old adversary Lennart Johansson was rumbling, 'I, and other members have for some time not been adequately informed about strategic matters which have been acted upon without proper discussion.'

Johansson and his supporters, roughly half the executive committee, tried to get answers to 25 questions from Blatter at a Zurich meeting. Blatter was furious. 'I and the administration of FIFA have been tackled from behind, this is not good,' he said after the meeting. 'I am sad, the sadness is when you are kicked or tackled from behind from within your own family. It is not good to bring all this dirty washing in public.'

As football's 'family' headed for the congress in Buenos Aires the news agencies were predicting that Blatter faced the 'toughest fight' of his presidency. The crack troops from McKinsey were already quietly checking every detail for his fightback at the congress centre at the Hilton Hotel in the ritzy area of Puerto Madero. Their advance guard had been out in Argentina working on the ambiance inside the congress hall. They were concerned that technicians from the Megalux decoration agency should light Blatter in the most flattering way.

On the eve of the congress McKinsey team members sat with Blatter in his suite into the early hours, rewriting and rehearsing the speech. Half an hour before he was due to go on the platform he sat down in an anteroom and was beautified by a make-up artist flown out from Switzerland especially for the job.

Blatter took his expertly crafted speech to the podium in the Hilton and performed for an hour and ten minutes. He did a great show. FIFA might have had a few problems but all was well now. Most important of all, every national association would continue to get its US$250,000 a year grant.

The puppet show was great too. 'How relieved and calm I am Mr President after hearing you,' said the Romanian delegate. 'I congratulate you, President Blatter,' said the new man from Haiti, 'We see you following Havelange with more solidarity and transparency.' The President of India's soccer federation applauded Blatter and blamed 'jealous organisations' – presumably UEFA – for seeking to undermine him. The applause began, the president showed his first smile.

Blatter called on another speaker. 'My name is Captain Horace Burrell, president of the Jamaica football association and many people may not know Jamaica but Jamaica is a small island in the Caribbean and is also the smallest country ever to go to the World Cup. This means we have a voice in world football and therefore we are getting up to support Mr Blatter and have confidence in him.' Then the man who put his girlfriend into Haiti's empty seat in Zurich sat down to ringing applause.

Next up, Libya. 'Thanks for so much transparency, Mr President.' Said Libya's man: 'We are with your integrity and your transparency. FIFA will never collapse under your management.' Speakers seemed to be reading from a crib sheet that had 'transparency' marked in bold. Peru and Cuba, Sudan and Congo offered total support.

Then Ivan Slavkov struck. 'Bulgaria approves all that you have said and we trust in you. It's time we showed our approval, Mr President!' General Secretary Michel Zen-Ruffinen had a point to make. 'The rules required a resolution and then a vote,' he said.

He tried to make himself heard above the cheering and clapping. Blatter, chairing the meeting, didn't help him. Sepp had his own ideas.

'Why not do it by acclamation?' he beamed at the congress. 'Are you happy, yes or no?' It was like a pantomime. He opened his arms to the room. The applause grew louder. Zen-Ruffinen was squashed. People got to their feet and gave Blatter a standing ovation that went on and on.

Then former president Havelange proclaimed, 'We should applaud Blatter day and night,' and a beaming Blatter replied, 'I'm a happy president because I have a united family, the executive committee and the congress.' Blatter's critics on the podium had been outmanoeuvred, again. One Argentine writer called it 'a festival of pandering'.

During the Congress, FIFA launched their campaign against racism. Executive committee member Nicolás Leoz, President of the South American confederation, reminded delegates of his humble origins. His father was an immigrant from Spain. He said, 'I was born in the Paraguay jungle, in a modest house, without a floor and in a place where there was just thirty people and a hundred Indians.' And that's all you needed to know about FIFA's fight against racism.

People whispered that nephew Philippe Blatter's team had given a helping hand to uncle Sepp. FIFA spokesman Andreas Herren said, 'The McKinsey team did not directly support the preparation of the Congress in Buenos Aires, nor did it prepare the speech for the president. And Philippe Blatter was not present.'

Herren must have been unaware of the extent of McKinsey's support for the Buenos Aires congress. The team had been on location preparing for the congress and working with the local Megalux company who decorated the hall. They'd also worked on Blatter's speech and how he presented it. Afterwards the FIFA President had been able to boast, 'The FIFA family was once again reunited.'

21

OWN GOAL!

Sleeping dogs wake up and bark

Zurich, 16 November 2001. Shocked to learn that some Koreans eat dogs and seeing a chance to embarrass a most capable rival, Sepp Blatter embraced his new friend, sex kitten turned animal rights activist Brigitte Bardot. He put on his socially concerned face and made a public demand of next year's World Cup host in dog-eating Korea, Chung Mong-Joon. Chung must take 'immediate and decisive measures to put an immediate end to this cruelty'.

Blatter warned that serving poodles with noodles was harming Korea's image in the world and urged Chung to be 'sensitive to vociferous worldwide public opinion and reject cruelty'.

FIFA, an organisation that was happy to take tea with murderous dictators and give the World Cup to a bloody-handed Junta, drew the line at pooches poached.

Satisfied at having twice in one statement linked his adversary to 'cruelty' Blatter turned his attention back to whistling a happy tune about the finances.

During his McKinsey-choreographed song and dance routine five months earlier in Buenos Aires Blatter had promised that KPMG would audit FIFA's books to find out what the ISL group's collapse had cost. He promised that the audit report would be done by October. There was no doubt he used the word 'audit'. The KPMG team there in the hall heard it too. They went away to work on his private instruction not to audit FIFA's books but to produce the briefest summary.

Lennart Johansson was asking questions, again, in the run-up to the executive committee meeting just before Christmas. Lennart and his twelve supporters on the committee had compiled another of their irksome lists of questions. They were telling reporters they hadn't a clue what was happening to FIFA's finances. 'What securitisation deals have been concluded?' Johansson asked. 'Will there be any more? Are there any bridging loans? What has happened to the audit?'

Five days before the meeting the dissidents delivered another letter for Sepp. They simply did not believe his promises or claims that he was a good manager. They cited 'a continued lack of transparency', complained about the secret power and salaries of Blatter's entourage of advisors, slammed them for being 'a double administration within FIFA', and, this was the most important part, they demanded that he set up an Investigation Committee.

They also wanted to know about 'Television contracts that are partly controlled by Members of this Executive Committee.' They'd heard that since the early 1980s Havelange had secretly arranged for Jack Warner to be given the television rights to screening the World Cup in the Caribbean. The cost? While others paid millions, lucky Jack coughed up a nominal one dollar a time. He'd sold these rights on to regional television stations.

Jack wrote Sepp one of his letters of support. 'My dear President, I have taken note of your pain, your hurt, your disappointment and your disillusionment and I do empathise with you.' Sounding a little like the schoolteacher he once was, Jack added, 'I take consolation in the fact however, that you have at least realised that in spite of all the posturing and the histrionics of some members of the FIFA Executive Committee the solidarity and the fraternity to which you aspire are nothing but an elusive dream.' He signed off, 'CONCACAF wishes to take no part in the destabilisation of the FIFA and do pledge to fight to the utmost for its unity and survival.' At the meeting he supported Blatter in opposing any investigation. They won that round.

'COMING HOME from hospital at 5 o'clock in the morning . . .' Johansson wrote to Blatter two days before Christmas. He'd missed the meeting because of cancer treatment. He was, again, disappointed in Blatter. 'We get flooded with facts and figures,' he complained. 'They are all well prepared but we get them the night before the presentation or after all has been presented. But these presentations do not answer the questions to which we want to have all the answers.'

Johansson rehearsed all that had gone before, the concerns about Warner's television windfall, Blatter's shadow administration – his F-Crew. And why did FIFA need to get its hands on money that wouldn't be earned until the 2006 World Cup? He ended with the question, 'Why do you oppose the setting up of an internal investigation group?'

There was no answer from Blatter. In late January David Will tried, this time, writing to finance committee chairman Julio Grondona about the KPMG report that had come in. What had happened to the promise of an audit? 'Honestly, I expected a 200–300 page document and could scarcely believe the two-page "review" that we finally received,' complained the Scotsman.

Johansson and Will were furious at the stonewalling of Blatter and his cronies. At the end of January Johansson and his twelve dissenters signed an ultimatum for Blatter. They were tired of him being 'negative' and they 'insisted' he call an extraordinary meeting to discuss one issue; setting up the investigation.

Blatter could hardly refuse. So he did the next best thing. He said yes, but it had to be done his way. Investigation Blatter-style with respect for 'certain practical and rational considerations'. Writing to the national associations he came up with a new reason for FIFA's troubles. 'The global financial consequences of 11 September 2001.'

As they approached the extraordinary meeting, scheduled to begin on the evening of Thursday 7 March 2002, the finance committee read a draft of the audit report being prepared for the Congress, three months ahead. Warner had something important to say. 'I am extremely assured FIFA is in good hands.' He added that the call for a special investigation 'was designed to weaken Blatter prior to the presidential election'.

Blatter went to work, whipping the executive committee dissenters into line. He packed his suitcase with sticks and carrots, flew to Madrid and eyeballed Angel Maria Villar Llona, the Spanish FA President. Before long, Villar Llona announced, 'I would also like to give my wholehearted support to the manner in which he is managing FIFA and its financial policies, on which I congratulate him most warmly.'

But it was one step forward, one step backwards for Sepp. Jack Warner's 76-year-old lieutenant Isaac Sasso, the Blatter loyalist from Costa Rica, sent word that he wasn't fit to fly. Postal votes weren't permitted, so Blatter had to make do with this endorsement from Sasso: 'I believe in the finance committee and Julio Grondona, and I believe in Mr Blatter, the president. Mr Blatter is a very good man, he is clean and he is white. Blatter brought democracy to FIFA. Now the organisation is very transparent.'

Blatter's problem was he couldn't win on a straight vote. He was outnumbered. He looked again at the demand for an investigation committee. It wasn't necessarily fatal. But there was one really dangerous demand: Johansson's point number 6, the right to investigate 'the Presidential Office'. All sorts of skeletons might spring out of that cupboard. Blatter's undisclosed bonus, his payments to favourites, to the F-crew and, oh dear, the Golden Goose might come hissing out.

The 7 March came around and the extraordinary meeting ran all through the Thursday into Friday. Blatter was cornered. He talked about possible breaches of FIFA statutes, he ranted about personal attacks, he denied corruption. But he seemed to be drifting Johansson's way. During a break he told reporters, 'We have a decision in principle.' Johansson believed they had won.

Principle was one thing, aircraft departure times were another. Blatter filibustered through the Friday and on Saturday morning slapped on the table a radically new document. Missing was any investigation into his presidential world. The arguments began again but this time several of his critics were looking at their watches. One by one, they left for Zurich airport. By the afternoon they were down to 16 and then Blatter struck. He had a majority and his version won the day. They would have an internal audit but no investigation and the presidential budget was off-limits.

Late on the Saturday afternoon Blatter summoned the hacks. We'd been kicking our heels for a couple of days. Communications Director Keith Cooper opened the meeting in the Sonnenberg auditorium. 'There will be absolutely no chance of individual interviews with the President, he has to go to another appointment. There is no point in running after him because you will not catch him.'

Talking to us, Blatter was tired but exhilarated, even flaunting his success in watering down the threatened audit. 'They can have a look at the secretariat of FIFA. But, I repeat, not on the presidential level,' he trumpeted. I couldn't resist adding to the fun and asked him, 'Why haven't you set up an inquiry into corruption?'

'I am not going to give any platform to those who doubt the results and the correctness of my election in 1998,' he barked, eyes tight. 'If somebody wanted to put into question the election result they have had according to Swiss law 30 days to make the protest. So, stop it! Finish! And that's good.'

Then he dashed off to grab a look-good, love-the-game photo-op at the Zurich Grasshoppers match.

On the following Monday Blatter was in Milan delivering a lecture at a business school. The new internal audit committee had been his idea all along, he claimed. 'I took the initiative at the end of January when I sent a letter to all national organisations saying that to give total transparency and clarification I proposed to install an internal audit committee.'

The committee included a member from each continental confederation. South America sent Ricardo Teixeira. Hollow laughter boomed from Brazil and leading football commentator Juca Kfouri, wrote, 'Yet again the fox is being put in charge of the chickens. It's very sad and makes you wonder if you can trust anything that FIFA does.' Brazilian Senator Alvaro Dias had just chaired an investigation into Teixeira's Brazilian Football Confederation concluding that it was 'a den of crime, revealing disorganisation, anarchy, incompetence and dishonesty'.

Chairing the new committee was David Will and he wasn't a yes-man. He got busy digging out information, and some of it looked like it might damage Blatter. Lawyer Will was even asking his witnesses to swear affidavits in the presence of Zurich notaries.

Now he was heading towards the offices of finance director Urs Linsi and general secretary Michel Zen-Ruffinen. Something had to be done.

Audit committee member Chuck Blazer went to his keyboard and wrote to Will. 'At the opening session I made the statement that this Committee was the formation of a political process.' Blazer was 'considerably distressed' and one of the things distressing him was that Korea's Chung had been talking about securitisation in an interview for an Australian television news programme. Blazer had also spotted David Will talking to a witness after a session had closed.

Blazer told Blatter and Blatter was shocked. 'In order to guarantee and to protect the interests of FIFA and the FIFA Executive Committee, I have to suspend the work of the Internal Audit Committee,' he announced on 11 April, 'pending an investigation in the matter of breach of confidentiality and the way documents which have been given to members of the Committee have been handled.'

David Will fumed and told reporters, 'I met with the President and he was not able to present to me one single example of information which had been given exclusively to the audit committee having been leaked, nor was he able to provide me with an example of any document having been improperly handled. In my view he had no justification for suspending the committee.'

Johansson said, 'Something must be rotten when the President does his utmost to stop an investigation that was only internal and only for the executive committee. It can only mean one thing: There is something that is being hidden.'

It didn't help that in the beginning of April 2002, Leo Kirch's media empire that had been selling World Cup television rights crashed into insolvency. FIFA took over the World Cup television rights that belonged to Kirch. Fortunately, most of the business for 2002 and 2006 had been completed.

THE FIFA ping-pong season opened officially. *Ping!* The dissenters on the executive committee wrote a detailed complaint to Blatter. *Pong!* Blatter replied, his style sometimes flowery, sometimes folksy, sometimes overhead-smash-violent, always moving the agenda his way. He copied his letters to the entire FIFA family.

Ping! The dissenters: What did he have to say about murdering the audit investigation? *Pong!* 'A smear campaign of insinuations and defamation about my work and me has been simmering for several weeks – a campaign designed to tarnish my image and to sow the seeds of doubt, but which ultimately risks harming FIFA itself and football at large.'

'Should we therefore content ourselves with what we have achieved? Should we stop improving what could still be improved and stop adding finishing touches to our operations and regulations, our development programmes and our competitions? Definitely not.'

A week after the tumultuous meeting that set up the emasculated audit committee Issa Hayatou, president of African football, had announced in Cairo that he would run against Blatter for the presidency. Johansson was at his side as Hayatou said he wanted to 'restore integrity, credibility and transparency' at FIFA.

Blatter was smart enough not to attack Hayatou directly. Better to ignore him. Johansson should be the target.

'It has become personal, especially with Mr Johansson attacking me,' Blatter told the BBC. 'I have not seen Mr Hayatou attacking me and I have not said anything wrong or anything nasty about him. It's dirty but not between the two opponents.

There's a third man in the centre of midfield and he's trying to tackle me. He is from the outside and there should be a referee eliminating people who enter the field of play with unfair play.'

That was one barrel. Sepp discharged the other days later in a letter. 'It is in your hands, Lennart, to set the tone for the coming weeks. I can hardly believe that you take any pleasure from the current conflict.'

Chung had stepped aside for Hayatou but that didn't spare him the Zurich lash. He got a letter, distributed everywhere. 'Dear Colleague (then in handwriting) Dear MJ.' That was the end of the pleasantries. 'In recent weeks, your attempts to discredit me in the eyes of the football world have increased dramatically. You have done so not only in public, but also in private letters to people, hoping that your influence will persuade them to change their positive attitude towards me. Your defamatory attacks do not anger me and they will have very little effect on me as a person. But the damage you are doing to the game of football is much greater and graver.'

And still there was two months to the election in Seoul.

The European associations, whose support must be wrenched away from Johansson, came next. 'Those who have known me for the past thirty years will be fully aware that I am incapable of what I am accused: buying votes, destroying documents, fear of the truth, dictatorial management of FIFA,' he claimed.

'This current campaign of vilification is reaching new dimensions of lies and unprecedented levels of defamation.' Blatter blamed the British newspapers – 'a directed press' he called it – for a 'pernicious climate, fervently organised'. He hadn't yet experienced the half of it.

*   *   *

'I THINK it's necessary to say officially that there are some things in FIFA which are not working,' said a new and dangerous voice of opposition. 'I have said this in a letter to the President on four occasions and I got no reply at all. I then went to members of the executive committee and my third and last tactic was to go to the press.' Michel Zen-Ruffinen, the loyal apparatchik, had finally snapped.

Blatter was genuinely baffled when Zen-Ruffinen put his head above the parapet in Geneva's *Le Temps* newspaper. Speaking like the lawyer he is, Zen-Ruffinen said, 'For several months I had noted dysfunctions in the financial process at the heart of FIFA. It is clear that the rules were not followed, either by the President himself or by the director of finances.' If that wasn't bad enough, Zen-Ruffinen then drove Blatter wild with rage, floating his theory on why Blatter closed down the audit investigation. 'I think that these manoeuvres were aimed at stopping me giving evidence because I could reveal some delicate details.'

These colleagues of nearly two decades were now speaking to each other through megaphones. Through the tightest of bared teeth Blatter called on Zen-Ruffinen to put up or shut up. 'He should take these unclear accusations and allegations regarding me and prove them in written form. What has happened in the last few days at FIFA is intolerable. The entire dossier will be given priority at the meeting of the executive committee on 3 May.'

A dossier? We salivating hacks couldn't wait for the meeting in Zurich, due in ten days. Zen-Ruffinen wound us up even more with the mysterious allegation that 'Things were found during the work of the audit committee.' Blatter added to our glee, ordering a ban on his general secretary handling or reading any financial documents.

*   *   *

Zurich, 3 May 2002. Blatter appeared at the boardroom door and ushered in a new friend. 'Please meet Dr Hans Bollman. He has some important advice to give us. We must listen.' Some executive committee members immediately showed hostility and began to boo. Bollman, a Zurich lawyer, pressed on and told them that they shouldn't listen to general secretary Michel Zen-Ruffinen.

Then Zen-Ruffinen took the floor. 'I have decided to stand up for the good of the game. I have been too loyal to the president for too long. FIFA is flawed by general mismanagement, dysfunctions in the structures and financial irregularities,' said Zen-Ruffinen. He'd prepared a 22-page confidential dossier. At the root of FIFA's problems, he said, was Blatter's parallel administration and the F-Crew. Appointing Markus Siegler to be his personal spokesman and Jerome Champagne to 'blatantly interfere in the affairs of national associations', to win votes for the boss, was sapping morale.

Did the executive committee members know that the president was interfering in the proper running of the bureaucracy and had snatched personal control of marketing contracts?

And look at this – consultancies for Blatter cronies, cash payments to Havelange. And what on earth did Blatter think he was doing using the Goal money to win himself votes?

One juicy revelation was that Blatter had secretly, without any authorisation, paid US$100,000 to Russia's Viacheslav Koloskov, the equivalent of two-year's executive committee pay, when he was taking a two-year break. That was under the headline 'Corruption'. Handouts to 'The Warner Family' took up a full page and another half page dealt with Blatter's refusal to reveal what he was paid.

After Zen-Ruffinen's presentation, five of FIFA's vice-presidents took Blatter into an ante-room and advised him strongly to resign. Issa Hayatou, one of the five, said later, 'He looked stunned, quite shocked. But he refused to go and said he was answerable only to the congress.'

The executive committee meeting went on for ten hours. Johansson and the other dissenters took Zen-Ruffinen's report to the magistrate's office in Zurich. He said it would take many months to investigate. Blatter took the opportunity to attack Hayatou. 'In the beginning, I considered him to be a fair man,' he said. 'But now, by signing the petition regarding the proceedings against me and by using some terms in the press that are not right, he has left the area of fair play.' Then the FIFA president went campaigning in Hayatou's backyard. The 1998 election had been won in Africa. Could it be won there again?

22

THE FIFA HOUSE IS BURNING

Who struck the match?

Monrovia, 23 November 1999. The sun shone, the crowds in Liberia's national stadium cheered and President Blatter opened the first project funded from the US$100 million Goal programme. President Charles Taylor warmly shook Blatter's hand and awarded him Liberia's highest honour, the Humane Order of African Redemption.

'Joseph S Blatter has kept his word in supporting us,' said Taylor. Taylor's bulky son-in-law Edwin Snowe, President of Liberia's national association, would return the favour in 2002. As Blatter campaigned on Issa Hayatou's home turf, Snowe set up 'Friends of Blatter in Africa' and attacked his fellow African: 'Hayatou has done nothing for any country in Africa.'

When the election was over Snowe left Africa for the Johnson & Wales private university in Denver, Colorado, which teaches courses in business, hospitality, culinary arts and technology. FIFA gave him US$50,000 to study Sports Management and

Entertainment Events in the USA. One of Blatter's spokesmen, Andreas Herren commented, 'It is normal that under this programme study loans are given to national association executives who aspire to further their education.'

Snowe's US$50,000 was a whole fifth of FIFA's annual US$250,000 grant to Liberia, a country so poor that they had trouble buying kit for their national squad.

Edwin didn't want to give up the president's chair while he was studying in America. You don't have to, said Herren. Former World Player of the Year George Weah is a loyal Liberian. He earned a lot of money in his playing days at AC Milan and he did what he could to help football back home. He didn't think much of Edwin's sabbatical. 'It's unfair to the football programme of the country. If the FA President is away for a three to four-year period on academic studies, there should be early elections for someone else to take over,' he said.

Despite President Charles Taylor's support (he'd appointed himself Liberia's Chief Patron of Sports), the national team seemed permanently broke, coaches weren't paid and it was hard to see what FIFA's development money was doing, other than educating Edwin. Charles Taylor offered Weah the services of his personal bodyguards and Weah, who's no fool, swiftly emigrated.

When Edwin came back to Liberia he turned his back on sport, resigned the association's presidency and using his expensive new education in football management, became managing director of the Liberia Petroleum Refining Company. In January 2006 the United Nations upheld their travel ban on Snowe, alleging that he was involved in funding the exiled Charles Taylor.

Taylor, who's held responsible for the deaths of hundreds of thousands of civilians in wars he started in Liberia and Sierra Leone fled to Nigeria and is now indicted by a UN special court. He's accused of murder, mass rape, amputation and mutilation, taking slaves, forcing children to become soldiers and attacking humanitarian workers. The UN estimates he stole at least US$100 million from his country.

Taylor learned his military skills in training camps in Libya, home of another Blatter support operation in 2002. The wealthy president of Libya's national association, Al-Saadi Gadhafi, son of Colonel Gadhafi, invited officials from 20 African associations, including Uganda, Rwanda, Libya, Sudan, Zimbabwe and Mauritania, to Tripoli in late April. It was a week before Zen-Ruffinen produced his explosive dossier. The African officials spent a happy week celebrating Blatter and then young Gadhafi gave them US$4 million.

Meanwhile Blatter was in Abidjan in the Ivory Coast, dropping by a meeting of French-speaking sports ministers. Jerome Champagne was doing the diplomacy, explaining 'President Blatter has not come here to campaign. But this is a good place to renew contacts with old friends. He has friends everywhere. They know what he has been doing for world football.'

African reporters must have been at a different convention. One reported, 'Blatter used the opportunity to lobby for votes. He knows very well that sports ministers in Africa have great influence on their football federations and urged the ministers to back his second term bid.' On the way home Blatter called in on Senegal for a few hours.

Moshoeshoe Airport, Lesotho, 7 April 2002. President Blatter's Gulfstream arrived from Botswana midway through his ten-nation sweep of Southern Africa. There was six weeks to go to the election. But he wasn't campaigning. He was just serving FIFA and popping in on some of his 'friends everywhere'.

FIFA's press office was busy keeping the world posted on news of every African nation that had been peeled off from Hayatou. 'Rwanda Football Federation gives full support to re-election of Joseph S Blatter', hardly caught the imagination but that didn't matter when Markus Siegler could add, 'Declarations from the Rwanda Federation and the Sudan Federation follow similar statements already made by the national associations of Lesotho, Zambia and Mozambique.'

Blatter cut the ribbon at new Goal-funded facilities in all three countries. In Lusaka he told football officials about his travails in Zurich. 'Investigations have been conducted and all allegations proved wrong,' he assured them. 'Those who made the allegations will be questioned.'

But who was paying for the chartered Gulfstream jet that swept Blatter from one airport greeting to the next? One of his companions, Mohamed Bin Hammam, revealed in Lesotho, 'This jet has been provided by a friend of mine, Saleh Kamil. We co-financed the trip. He is a Saudi friend of mine.'

Sheikh Salih Abdullah Kamil, then aged 60, ranked among the top 200 wealthiest men in the world with a personal fortune estimated at US$2.2 billion and a US$9 billion business empire. His Dallah Albaraka banking group was doing well but his Arab Radio and Television network was said by financial analysts to be 'a chronic money loser'.

The satellite network, which screened the English Premier league and the German Bundesliga, desperately needed top-class sports rights because Hollywood sex and action movies were unacceptable in the Islamic world. Why wouldn't a billionaire who wanted to screen the World Cup give the FIFA president a lift in one of his jets?

The English FA's switching support from Blatter to Hayatou was small consolation for the African. Knowing that some of his continental associations would always be vulnerable to Blatter and Bin Hammam, Hayatou was campaigning in Asia promising more World Cup slots. They would be taken from South America where the ten countries in the regional confederation had five slots.

Hayatou despatched his envoys across the Caribbean attempting to break Warner's grip on his block of votes. They visited the Cayman Islands and lobbied local association President Jeff Webb. They'd hardly left the room before Jeff was telling Jack that he'd allowed them to speak for five minutes and they'd done a presentation. What was most important to Jeff? Would Hayatou more than double the current US$400,000 allowed for each Goal project up to US$1 million? They couldn't say.

Jeff said that certain allegations were made about the President of FIFA and the President of CONCACAF, but that he'd refused to listen. Warner was delighted.

Not everyone in the Caribbean and Central America was delighted with their football president. After a dozen years at the top his confederation Warner suddenly felt the solid ground beneath his feet tremble. He was being threatened at the ballot box. Edgardo Codesal was the Mexican referee who'd waved the first red card ever in a World Cup final in Rome in 1990, sending off Argentina's Pedro Monzon. He did it again 21 minutes later, dispatching Monzon's team-mate Gustavo Dezotti. Now he wanted to blow the whistle on Warner and replace him as CONCACAF president.

Codesal received expenses as director of refereeing for CONCACAF and this got him a red card from general secretary Chuck Blazer. 'Our statutes prohibit paid members of the confederation from holding an elected office within the organisation,' said Blazer, rejecting Codesal's nomination for the regional presidential election. Mexican Football Federation president Alberto de la Torre shot back, 'Mr Codesal is not paid. He receives expenses and expenses are not payments because if they were, Mr Warner would not be eligible either, as he gets expenses. We will complain to FIFA.'

Warner immediately yanked Codesal from FIFA's referee's committee. Then he went ballistic when he found that he couldn't and Blatter couldn't intervene. 'We would kindly like to draw your attention to the fact that a member of a FIFA standing committee may only be replaced by the body that appointed him, the Executive Committee,' wrote general secretary Zen-Ruffinen to Warner.

When was the last time anyone had said no to Warner? It was hard to remember. 'What a strange world we live in!' was the best he could manage in a choked email to Blatter, copied to everybody. It got stranger and more infuriating. Zen-Ruffinen asked FIFA's legal commission to adjudicate on Codesal's wish to stand against Warner. Blazer erupted, calling for Zen-Ruffinen to be sacked or suspended for 'interfering in CONCACAF matters. This current action by Zen-Ruffinen has stretched his credibility to the limit,' boomed Blazer from Trump Tower.

Zen-Ruffinen called his lawyers. 'These attacks are an attempt to destabilise the function of the General Secretary, simply because he has insisted on adherence to the Statutes,' he said as defamation writs were prepared. 'The fact that the attacks emanated from CONCACAF, whose top representatives are often the subject of controversy, is further evidence of a destabilisation campaign.' Then Zen-Ruffinen made an intriguing disclosure. He had discovered that boxes of correspondence between Warner and FIFA from the years 1989, 1990 and 1991 had vanished. So too had another bulky file of Havelange documents.

They should have sold ringside tickets for this event. It's customary for FIFA's president and general secretary to attend the continental confederation congresses and Jack's was due in

Miami in late April. With all his natural charm Jack wrote to Zen-Ruffinen, 'I wish to advise you that, based on the prevailing circumstances that now exist between you and the leadership and management of CONCACAF, it will not be prudent for you to attend this Confederation Congress.'

That didn't go down too well in Zurich and Jack had to explain himself. 'While I acknowledge that English is the first language of FIFA, I am aware it is not your official language and I therefore understand what seems to be your inability to understand the meaning of the word "prudent". By no stretch of the imagination can anyone infer from my letter anything threatening or intimidatory and I am always one who speaks frankly and unambiguously.'

Chuck and Jack banned me from their congress in Miami but I hung out in the lobbies at Loews hotel on South Beach. A few regional officials met me secretly and told me what happened inside. Candidate Blatter was allowed to pitch for votes but candidate Hayatou was denied the floor. Jack finally permitted Codesal to stand, after announcing that the election would be by a show of hands. Only two countries, Mexico and El Salvador, dared raise their hands for Codesal. Jack got another four years.

Hayatou threw a modest cocktail party – a chance to talk with regional officials about his hopes for a new FIFA. He spoke to an almost empty room. One Caribbean delegate told me, 'Most are too scared of Warner to even attend, to hear the man.' The rest thought it safer to go to the beach.

BLATTER took his campaign to Dubai and the Soccerex sports business convention and told a sympathetic audience that his critics were nothing more than 'embittered rivals out to get me . . . their allegations of corruption and financial mismanagement are doing the game a disservice.' He refused to talk to the British press but told local reporters that 'More transparency than we are giving in FIFA now, it's not possible.' Then he looked around and said, 'I'm soccer's last romantic.'

The cities and countries sped past. Blatter was in and out of Bahrain, at the invitation of the Crown Prince, Beijing and Pyongyang where he schmoozed reclusive dictator Kim Jong-Il. That was a wasted trip. The North Koreans didn't turn up to the Congress. In Nuku'alofa in Tonga he shared a platform with Hayatou at the Oceania soccer congress. Still irritated by Zen-Ruffinen's insubordination, Blatter told a Zurich paper, 'My opponents are just waiting for me to sack him so they can say I got rid of the last person at FIFA who knows the truth.'

He got the emergency committee to ban the general secretary from talking to the press and ordered Urs Linsi to stop reporting to Zen-Ruffinen and instead report to finance committee chairman Julio Grondona who told a Buenos Aires radio station, 'Zen-Ruffinen isn't fit to run a troop of boy scouts. No disrespect intended to boy scouts.'

They all trooped off to Stockholm in late April for UEFA's congress and it was the best day of the year for Blatter. Somebody had done months of schmoozing and divisive politicking and the result was that Michel Platini was elected to the FIFA executive committee along with the Bundesliga's Gerhard Mayer-Vorfelder. One of Johansson's key lieutenants, Norway's Per Omdal was voted off and suddenly Blatter was back in the Zurich game. Johansson's slight majority had gone.

Blatter instructed a team to answer Michel Zen-Ruffinen's allegations of 3 May. It took them 15 days to come up with a 30-page response and they called it 'Rectification' which sounds painful, but according to my dictionary, means, 'the act of setting right'.

'Ladies and Gentlemen, dear football friends,' it began. 'For many months a campaign has been waged against me, largely through the media. It has intensified as the presidential elections approached. This smear campaign is bizarre and incomprehensible [and] is doing great damage to football.'

He went on, 'This document will leave you in no doubt that I am blameless and that the allegations made against me are both false and groundless. They will come back to haunt my accusers, above all the general secretary. The FIFA house is burning. Once you have read these documents you will see who struck the match.'

He wanted world football to know one other thing. 'The very serious allegation of corruption is also one I deny totally.'

But how did Blatter answer Zen-Ruffinen's charges? For instance, on salary and perks, Zen-Ruffinen had accused, 'He has never disclosed this to the executive committee or the general secretary.' What had Blatter's rectification task force got to say about that?

'The question pertaining to the President's remuneration has already been answered, on more than one occasion, during meetings of the Executive Committee.'

Well, actually, it hadn't.

Zen-Ruffinen had asked about the role of McKinsey. The rectifiers insisted that the finance committee had taken the decision to employ McKinsey and their decision had been approved by the executive committee at their meeting in Buenos Aires in early July 2001.

But, hang on a minute, Philippe Blatter's team had been hard at it in the chicken house the year before Buenos Aires, and Uncle Sepp had promised three and a half million francs (£1.5 million) for, among other things, working to showcase the President at that crucial congress.

Uncle Sepp's rectifiers were full of praise for the greenhorns, their sense of 'mission, vision and strategy development, business plan definition, organisation and implementation of complex large-scale projects, value creation through operational improvements etc'. What stirring language! It might have come from one of the greenhorns' own flatulent mission statements.

Michel Zen-Ruffinen had claimed that Blatter could have stopped Jean-Marie Weber's ISL group hanging on to the US$60 million paid by the Brazilian Globo television company.

'Groundless,' insisted the rectifiers. And to prove their point, they had a revelation that completely cleared the President. 'It was the FIFA Finance Division that drew attention to the risks for FIFA in the arrangements in the TV contracts. On 1 June 2001, the chief financial officer (Urs Linsi) wrote a memo for the attention of the President and the General Secretary.'

Hang on a minute. This was the memo Linsi wrote after the bankruptcy, after the court complaint, when all the world had heard about the money that went astray. This was the stunning memo in which Linsi claimed, 'The decision not to push ISL and not to insist on a rectification of the Globo TV Agreement has never been the Finance Division's decision. It was a higher level decision within FIFA not to put too much pressure on ISL.'

Perhaps the rectifiers couldn't spot that Linsi's June 2001 memo came 22 months *after* FIFA's letter in September 1998 to Weber about the missing money and the flawed Globo contract. Perhaps they didn't see the further reminders that FIFA had sent to Weber in May 2000, 13 months *before* Linsi's stunning memo.

How would the rectifers get away with overlooking all this evidence? Easy-peasy. All these documents were secret, buried in the archives. They've seen light of day for the first time here, in this book.

Having judged himself innocent Blatter went back on the road, warning, 'Those, who have made allegations and cannot prove them, they will go to prison.'

It was nearly time to pack for the Seoul Congress, the presidential elections and the World Cup. Cheering Sepp on the way was Robert Contiguglia, President of US Soccer. 'When we put aside all the negative rhetoric, histrionics, and embarrassing behaviour, we can come to only one conclusion,' said Contiguglia. 'President Blatter should continue as FIFA President.' In case voters hadn't got the point he added, 'Blatter is an icon of humanitarianism.'

WHILE Blatter and Hayatou and most of FIFA were roaming the globe in search of votes, one senior Sunny Hill official with important World Cup responsibilities was reporting on other matters. 'I felt wonderfully well after the massage and I touched and kissed you all over your warm body – I think that you enjoyed it also very deeply,' he emailed in mid-May to his new girlfriend, a football official he'd met on the road. 'I did not penetrate you – you did not ask me to – also you did not touch my sex with your hands, this I respected totally, that's why I gave happiness to myself as my desire was very strong.'

It wasn't the first time Mr Massage had featured in the Sunny Hill sex sagas. Some years back a very beautiful woman on the staff, let's call her Miss Sublime, was having an affair with one of FIFA's most senior and internationally renowned officials. Mr Big was often away for weeks at a time, so she spent some of those long, lonely evenings getting Total Respect from Mr Massage.

Mr Massage and Miss Sublime enjoyed each other deeply until one night during a FIFA tour of central Europe when all the big shots shared a hotel. Some helpful fellow whispered to Mr Big that at that very moment Miss Sublime was playing jiggy-jiggy with Mr Massage. So Mr Big picked up his phone and called Mr Massage in his room at two o'clock in the morning and growled, 'Do you know the whereabouts of Ms Sublime?'

'It's for you,' said Mr Massage, handing Miss Sublime the phone.

Mr Massage pleaded with Mr Big – no doubt with total respect – and kept his job. Miss Sublime got the sack.

23

BLATTER FOR TRANSPARENCY

'Every question can be asked and answered!'

World Cup Press Centre, Seoul, 27 May 2002. None of the reporters had ever seen an international sports federation disintegrating before their eyes, month after bickering month. This morning we sat in yet another auditorium in yet another continent watching the five dissenting vice-presidents again attacking their president. They hoped the media was their last hope, it might swerve their desperate messages around Blatter and direct to the voters who'd decide the presidency this week.

Julio Grondona and Jack Warner, the two loyal veeps, were in a hotel suite, huddled with Blatter, preparing for the next day's showdown. In front of us, sitting at a plain table on a brightly lit stage, were big serious Lennart Johansson, averagely-built Antonio Matarrese, big Issa Hayatou, small David Will and our tall, lanky Korean host Dr Chung Mong-Joon.

Johansson told us, 'Blatter has sold FIFA's family jewellery. This cannot go on. FIFA's President has taken FIFA to the brink

212

of disaster with his overspending, misuse of funds and inter-ference in the day-to-day running of the organisation.' We'd heard this now month after month and Blatter still bounced around the world denying everything and piling up his votes. The wildly partisan fifa.com had just reported that another ten Asian associations had pledged their votes to Blatter. Again, there was no space for any news about the countries backing Hayatou.

This morning's performance was part confessional, part seminar. The dissident vice-presidents said they should have done better and found out how Blatter was squandering FIFA's treasure chest. He hid the truth from us, they claimed. Star of the podium was silver-haired David Will, the now ex-head of the internal audit committee and he had a fistful of dangerous documents.

Yesterday Blatter's latest release claimed, yet again, 'FIFA is in a comfortable position to meet current and future financial obligations.' David Will took a different view. 'I feel I have an obligation,' he said, 'to clarify the financial situation.' Marketing income from the faraway 2006 World Cup had been inserted into the current accounts. He explained that the claimed 'profit' for the most recent accounting period was in reality a staggering loss of around 536 million Swiss francs. The richest sports association in the world may be insolvent, said Will, and perhaps it should declare this truth to the Swiss courts.

But Blatter talks of cash continuing to drip from FIFA's tree. How can he be wrong? Easy, said Will. Blatter has lopped a billion francs from estimated operating costs for the next four-yearly budget and – *Hey Presto!* – we're awash with readies and Sepp's the man to vote for.

Will told us the curious story of Blatter and Roger Milla's 50th birthday party. The goal-scoring phenomena of Italia '90 had hoped to raise some pension money staging an all-star game back home in Cameroon. Milla approached Blatter for help. Three months later he got a letter telling him 'FIFA will not participate and will not sponsor the event.'

Later Milla got wind that Blatter's campaign was claiming his support. Milla wasn't happy about that. He phoned Zurich, demanding to speak to Blatter who apologised and reached for FIFA's chequebook. David Will distributed a copy of a page from FIFA's account at the UBS bank. It revealed a payment of 25,000 Swiss francs to Roger Milla.

WE WANDERED out into the late morning bright sunshine. Seoul, nearly obliterated in the Korean War fifty years ago, was now a victory of poured concrete over planning controls and the fifth biggest city in the world. Wide, traffic-jammed fumy highways swept on stilts between the tower blocks. Construction crews on high, high cranes were busy building more of the towers at breakneck speed. Outside the press centre hundreds of black-clad and helmeted riot police carried shields and batons and looked wistfully at the trades-unionists demonstrating politely across the street. They might require some clubbing once the reporters had moved on.

We got in our cabs, gave the names of our hotels and hoped for the best. There wasn't a Seoul cabbie alive who'd admit he didn't know where the Hilton was. Many a reporter had screamed, as we hurtled along a freeway leading out of town, 'I don't want to go to the airport! Take me back!'

Every street light was hung with World Cup sponsors' messages and extra pylons had been erected for yet more. The pavements flowed with local citizens, fans and delegates to the FIFA congress with their tell-tale plastic-coated tags around their necks, still puzzled about having had to change their plans and arrive a day early for the first of not one but two congresses.

Ten weeks earlier, when Blatter seemed to be losing the arguments about FIFA money, he announced that 54 national associations had written to him demanding an Extraordinary Congress, the day before the scheduled one. They represented a quarter of the membership from all six continental confederations, and they said they wanted a public debate about the allegations of losses, the loans, the spending and the balances.

This was refreshing news. The rank and file having their chance to be heard. Diversity! Democracy! Maybe FIFA wasn't in such bad shape after all. Then somebody slipped me copies of some old faxes from Jack Warner's Port of Spain office and I began to have doubts.

The key day had been Friday 5 March 2002. The finance committee was meeting at Sunny Hill and Blatter's solid bloc of Grondona, Warner, Bin Hammam and Adrian Wickham from the Solomon Islands were at odds with Senes Erzik from Turkey and Ismail Bhamjee from Botswana over the state of FIFA's finances.

When UEFA members quietly briefed the press of the disagreement, FIFA media officer Andreas Herren responded to us. 'Two members raised reservations but when the chairman asked formally if the committee was in agreement to submit the report unanimously, there was no formal record of dissent.'

Warner left the meeting and called home. Harold Taylor, secretary of the Caribbean Football Union fired a fax to every national association in the region. 'Please find attached correspondence requesting an Extra-Ordinary Congress FIFA for which I am seeking your support. Kindly, as a matter of urgency, fax to the CFU Secretariat your support for this initiative. I am hoping to get your responses by 3.00 pm today. Same to FIFA by 5.00 pm.'

Later that day Richard Groden, secretary of the Trinidad & Tobago Football Federation, faxed Zurich. 'Dear General Secretary, In accordance with the article 11 of the FIFA Statutes we, the undersigned, request that an Extraordinary Congress be convened in conformity with the clauses of the above-mentioned article.'

FIFA spokesman Herren admitted later: 'The Caribbean Football Union did contact its member associations on 5 March. They must have been aware of the situation and were asking them to express their support to FIFA.' Only one UEFA member, Romania, backed the call but all ten Latin American countries signed up. Fiji and the Solomon Islands from Oceania signed, together with Tunisia and Edwin Snowe's Liberia. Qatar, Nepal, Oman, Jordan, Lebanon, Bahrain, Turkmenistan, Iran and Uzbekistan gave their support.

A week later Warner, President of the Caribbean Football Union, told officials at a seminar at the Dr Joao Havelange Centre of Excellence, 'In 90 minutes I was able to get 54 countries to call for an extraordinary congress of FIFA. And of those 54 countries, 30 came from CONCACAF and 24 of those came from the Caribbean. I was proud that in my confederation there were 30 members who in 90 minutes answered the call.'

I called a couple of Warner's lieutenants, asking why they supported him. Jim Fleming, President of the Canadian association, told me he decided to back Warner without consulting his committee because 'We support Sepp Blatter.' I asked Tony James from Jamaica, a vice-president of CONCACAF, why the demand for the special congress had been rushed through without local debate. He explained, 'There was no need for further consultation. This is a re-affirmation of our acceptance in Buenos Aires of President Blatter's explanation of the state of the finances.' James added, 'These countries have total faith in the leadership of Jack Warner.'

Two weeks later it began to dawn on the hard-pressed staff in FIFA's finance department how much this extra congress was going to cost. Vincent Monnier wrote to Jerome Champagne, Blatter and Urs Linsi predicting that there wouldn't be any change out of 500,000 francs. Even more expensive would be altering the travel plans and accommodation for several thousand delegates and their staff.

Grand Seoul Hilton Hotel, 28 May 2002. Blatter's dressers chose a white shirt for him with a beautifully cut wide collar and a pale pastel blue tie. That's all his audience would see of him behind the high podium at the crucial moments when he needed to swing the room behind him – so he'd better look good.

The clothes looked perfect but the president didn't. Had he had a bad night? Too much kimchi and rice wine? Poodles with noodles didn't agree with him? The skin across his cheeks was tight, nearly as tight as his eyes under the gantry of spotlights above the stage and he spoke in slow phrases, his usual charisma gone.

The surroundings wouldn't flatter anyone. It was gloomy in the high-ceilinged conference hall that could double as an aircraft hanger. Blatter was framed by a back wall of midnight blue, beneath him and to one side were the platform stalls and pale coffee-coloured furniture. Blue fluorescent light reflected back up onto Blatter's weary face and all in all, Issa Hayatou must have been cheered to see his rival so apparently under the weather.

The president adjusted his spectacles and peered into the half-light. 'Good morning everybody. Welcome in Asia. Welcome in Korea. Welcome in Seoul for the extraordinary congress of FIFA today. Welcome also to the big event,' and he spoke as slowly as the parson at a funeral, 'the FIFA 2002 World Cup.'

To one side, lined up along the top tier at the back of the stage sat the 16 members of his executive committee, Teixeira, Bin

Hammam, Blazer, Leoz, Per Omdal, Abdullah Al Dabal from Saudi and the rest of them. On the level below, closer together, sat the seven veeps. Warner was nearest to Blatter's podium and he slouched deep in his chair, looking as if he'd like to hold his nose because next to him was Italy's Antonio Matarrese and they didn't get on. Warner many times made clear he didn't give a toss what Matarrese thought about anything and, hurrah, this was the Italian's last Congress, he would be out of the executive committee after tomorrow. Next there was Johansson and Grondona, another pair with little to say to each other, then the rest of the internal opposition, David Will, Issa and finally Chung, as far from Blatter as it's possible to be without leaving the stage.

They gazed down to the front row, occupied by some old men, the honorary members. In their midst, honorary President Joao Havelange, two weeks on from his 86th birthday, hard gaze fixed on the youngsters running his federation. Behind him, in the dark, were row after row of delegations, 197 of them, big countries or small they all got one little oblong table covered in green cloth, with three Adidas footballs, three bottles of mineral water and three small chairs.

The President slogged on through his script, uninspired and uninspiring. 'Some are not happy, I am not happy, we are tense, our emotions are troubled and we are still missing our feelings of joy. What has happened to our proud and successful organisation?'

He summarised the collapse of the ISL group and then delivered his campaign slogan. 'We have hundreds of millions of Swiss Francs in our bank account.' Another pause. 'I am happy that 54 national associations were calling for this extraordinary congress, 54 national associations making use of their right. This is good for FIFA.

'Ask questions and we will give you answers. We have nothing to hide. All financial data will be at your disposal.' Pause. 'I hope this congress will go in a fair way, according to the principles of our game.' His speech over, he stayed at his podium.

Zen-Ruffinen strode quickly across the platform to an identical podium on the opposite side of the stage. 'I would like to take this opportunity to make a personal statement,' he announced. Blatter scowled in his direction. 'Today I shall not actively take part in leading this congress,' said Zen-Ruffinen. 'The reason is I have been restricted and prevented from any access to the finances of FIFA by the chief financial officer and by the President. The report on the finances being presented to you does not paint the transparent picture it pretends to do and on the contrary, some figures look better than they are.' He strode back to his seat and sat down.

They took the roll call and discovered that seven associations, Afghanistan, Cape Verde, Djibouti, Niger, Turks & Caicos, Eritrea and North Korea had not turned up. Blatter took off his glasses and started his explanation of the finances and when he got to the securitisation, he explained why they needed it. 'This is how we can serve the national associations, the competitions, the development programmes, the humanitarian activities, the congresses, the symposiums, the dialogue with the authorities.'

Everybody in the hall, from Blatter at the podium, his committee beside him, Issa Hayatou, the delegates, the reporters prowling at the back, the translators, waiters and all the officials in their FIFA blazers knew that every word spoken today was carefully chosen to influence tomorrow's election.

'We don't just want to talk about transparency, I believe in transparency, we have started to build transparency brick by brick from 1999 onwards,' said Blatter. Then he produced a small brick from his pocket and waved it about. Who thought up that bright idea?

Blatter mentioned 'transparency' three more times in the next minute and moved into his wind-up. 'We can be proud of what we have achieved under the responsibility of the finance committee, the executive committee and finally, under the responsibility of your president.'

This was greeted with a sprinkling of applause round the hall. Blatter smiled for the first time. 'Thank you, thank you.' He replaced his glasses and there was more applause. Now it was Linsi's turn. He peered at his script and read, woodenly, pausing after each word, his voice surprisingly high-pitched. 'We are all excited by football and the upcoming World Cup. Believe me, in recent months these facts and figures have become very emotional. You have just heard the general secretary saying that KPMG's report – a firm of global renown – does not show a true and fair picture. However, I can assure you reality looks different.'

Linsi's glasses twinkled on his nose. The stand-alone tuft at the top of his forehead quivered as he became aroused by his message. 'I want to tell you 11 facts about FIFA financials.' And up on the big pale green screens flashed his Powerpoints. There were pies, bars and lots of numbers, big ones. There was 'value potential' and 'recapitalisation' and as he wove his tongue around his jargon, he smiled in tender love for these poems.

Linsi adored his 11 points so much that he paused, and then went through them again. Again. And a fourth time. Our brains were wrapped in cotton wool and beaten with dumbbells. It was a relief when he stopped and produced his punch line. 'Good news for the FIFA family. There will be more money for development.'

Even with brains mangled by recapitulated value and value potential, everyone knew what that meant. Yippee!

Every public speaker has one joke and Linsi wanted to share his hilarious discovery about the funny side of securitisation. 'We are saving money through our SCORE programme.' Pause for dramatic effect. 'Smart Cost Optimisation and Revenue Enhancement!' It didn't bring the house down.

Blatter summed up – his second major political speech of the morning while Hayatou sat gagged – and we went outside for coffee.

THE PRESIDENT had got his confidence back. Shoulders back, his head up, colour flooding through his face. What had he been taking in the break? With hard authority he laid down the law for the second half of the day's business. 'We have to obey rules of conduct. Standing orders say the President should take the chair – and give permission to speak.'

But not yet. Blatter introduced his backing band. Over there was Fredy Luthiger. Fredy lifted his head and smiled. The two officials from the finance department. They smiled. The members of the finance committee. They scowled. There was even a Swiss lawyer present, we were told, in case of need.

'We will have discipline in the room and we will have to halt at 2pm.' Blatter looked around the room, 'Raise your hands,' he said and without hesitation shouted, 'Jamaica!'. As the powerful figure of Captain Horace Burrell in his silk purple necktie and matching pocket handkerchief, swaggered up to the podium, memories of Burrell's contribution in Buenos Aires drifted back. Was the fix going in again?

What was Burrell's question? He'd signed Warner's round-robin demanding to stage this inquiry session, what bugged him? Horace told the hall he had three important points he wanted to raise. Here came the first.

'Lennart Johansson is reported to have said that small countries like Jamaica and Tonga do not care about FIFA finances provided they are in receipt of assistance,' said Burrell. 'Ladies and

Gentlemen, I consider these comments about poor and small countries to be rude, out of order and rather insulting.' Burrell ranted on, full of indignation, repeating 'small and poor' and then, for unfathomable reasons, he told us that his was 'The smallest country to have qualified for three World Cup Finals', and as we screwed up our faces in disbelief he added, 'at different age group levels.'

The Captain's Point Two was a heartfelt endorsement of auditors KPMG. 'They were appointed by the Congress! What gives any member of the executive committee the right to want to derail this process?' Horace was now off on a solo trip to somewhere far away. 'KPMG is a company that has demonstrated integrity and indeed they have a great reputation for being above board in every part of the world and indeed my federation employs them.' Great stuff Horace, but where's your question?

'Mr President, I am worried because of some of the utterances I have heard from senior members who should know better. I am wondering, is KPMG going to take action against FIFA?' He paused, dramatically, and some of us in the back row wondered if Horace had been out behind the hotel kitchens in the coffee break, taking that stuff that put a smile on Bob Marley's face. KPMG suing FIFA? Oh dear.

The brave Jamaican Captain turned to David Will's documents and demonstrated that he could miss the point as well as the next man. 'Assistance was given to Roger Milla – 25,000 francs for his benefit game – and that is now becoming a big issue? I would ask you not to drag the great Roger Milla into this political nonsense!'

Burrell's boggled braying seemed to be unhinging the captain and his thoughts were becoming harder to follow. 'In concluding my presentation here I would like to ask those persons who continue to do so to show respect for the small nations, to show respect for the achievements of great football ambassadors like Roger Milla.'

There was still time for a question but that wasn't why Horace was at the podium. 'Again, let me thank President Blatter for all he has done for the majority, if not all, of the poor countries around the world. Let us support President Blatter! Thank you!'

He marched back to his seat, having used up nine minutes of the scarce time available to question the finances. I looked to see if Vincy Jalal was applauding him from the nearby Haitian table. But she wasn't there. This time they'd made it to a FIFA congress.

An independent chairman might have pulled Horace up a minute into his filibuster and asked, what's your question? Blatter said, 'Let us go to Libya.'

And here was his Desert Prince. Narrow-faced, bearded, in a dark suit, dark turtleneck and dark skullcap, Al-Saadi Gadhafi positioned himself as the master tactician for Blatter in Africa. Like Horace he went in for abuse, wild statements and he hadn't got a question. He put the sandal into Hayatou's ribs with the cry that 'The Confederation of African Football has not helped us out. FIFA has helped us out, especially the small nations.' He spoke for four minutes and 13 seconds and I counted four separate outbursts of whistling, jeering and booing from Africans in the hall.

Blatter, who had allowed this second speaker to get away with asking no question at all, told the hall that maybe it was best if there were no presidential campaigning. He called the man from Iran who praised KPMG for several minutes adding, 'I thank Mr Blatter for all he has done.'

Franco Carraro, President of Italian football and a longstanding IOC member, couldn't find a bad word to say about Blatter.

Neither could the official from Colombia. Around the hall, people were getting restless. The jokes were running. We might be in Seoul but this felt more like a political rally north of the border, in Stalinist Pyongyang.

Blatter scanned the hall and we at the back wondered, where was the public debate? Would we hear a critical voice? Where were the questions 54 countries said they wanted to ask? What was the point of this huge expenditure of money and time?

'Cayman Islands,' called Blatter. Up stepped Captain Burrell's bakery business partner, Jeff Webb. Another big man. 'My tiny country is not known for football but is known for finances. The Cayman Islands have over US$600 billion on deposit. We are ranked as the fifth financial centre in the world.' Jeff didn't mention that much of this money had headed in his direction to avoid paying tax at home.

Jeff actually had a question and we all craned forward. 'Is it fair to say that FIFA has greatly reduced its risks?' Could Linsi handle a toughie like this? With ease Linsi gave Jeff some answers and Jeff kept the faith, bellowing as he left the podium, 'FIFA is family and family must stay together.' Warner applauded from the stage.

'Seychelles,' called Blatter and their man said he was a senior partner in KPMG and didn't agree with FIFA having an internal audit committee.

'India,' called the President and the delegate who had been so helpful in Buenos Aires, came to the podium. The boos and whistling began as delegates registered their disgust at the way they'd been rail-roaded into attending a congress where only Blatter's fan club were allowed to speak.

India's representative praised Havelange. Let's nominate him for the Nobel Peace Prize! Nobody paid much attention to the rest of his ramble because the fun was all at the back. Somalia's Farah

Addo was standing up and asking to be called. Immediately behind him in the press seats Blatter propagandist Emmanuel Maradas began barracking Addo. Another member of the Somalia delegation turned, eyeballed the noisy Maradas and said crisply, 'If you ever come to Mogadishu I will shoot you.'

More boos, whistles, slow handclapping, this wasn't going to look good to the sponsors or on the television news. Maybe one critical voice should be permitted. 'Norway,' said Blatter and up to the podium bustled serious-faced federation secretary Karen Espelund. 'I would like David Will to be allowed to give his view of the financial situation,' she said. 'I would like the floor to be given to the other four vice-presidents of FIFA, I would like to hear Michel Zen-Ruffinen. I would like this debate to be extended so, in the President's words, "every question can be asked and answered."'

A lone critical voice, and she got roars of support in the hall.

Blatter ignored her. 'Peru.' The boos rolled again. As Blatter closed the emergency congress Hayatou stabbed a furious finger at him and David Will shook with rage.

OUTSIDE in the hotel lobby camera crews mobbed Karen Espelund. Radio microphones were thrust through the melee, some of us climbed on chairs to read her lips. 'It's been proved today, there is no democracy at FIFA, there is no transparency,' she said. 'It was obvious what was going on. He totally ignored everyone who is critical of him.'

David Will said furiously, 'He said he would not give me the floor, as simple as that, and I was very angry.'

Outside Leo Mugabe, President of Zimbabwe's association buttonholed me. 'It is shocking,' he stuttered, 'This is a travesty of democracy.' Was Robert Mugabe's nephew just saying what he thought I wanted to hear? Or did he think Blatter had been too tolerant in allowing that one dissident voice?

Seoul Hilton, Wednesday 28 May 2002. The décor had similar colour themes, creamy caramel and intense, quivering blue. The whole show had to move overnight because neither the Grand Hilton nor the ordinary Hilton could host FIFA for two consecutive days at such short notice. The confusion amongst the cabbies over which Hilton was today's choice didn't help with international harmony or good timekeeping.

So this was it. Yesterday was the phoney congress, now was the vote. President Blatter gazed down at his football family, same pastel blue tie as yesterday, looking fraught again, maybe mornings aren't his best time. 'We must maintain solidarity,' said the president, 'in the sense that we have to put a limit on the intervention of the speakers in order that we can correctly carry out the duties of this congress.' Yesterday, booed and catcalled for limiting 'interventions', Blatter promised an extra day, if needed, so that everyone would be heard. That 'believe me' assurance had been mislaid overnight.

The opening speaker was Korea's Chung, wearing his host's hat. We expected the usual platitudes of welcome and then more hours of conflict until the election.

'FIFA is now in a serious organisational crisis,' the tall Chung began. Battle had erupted as early as humanly possible. 'FIFA's pride, our pride is damaged. FIFA is divided. We, the concerned members, have tried to clarify all these problems through our internal audit committee but that was unilaterally suspended in March.'

Blatter's eyes went tight again. Gripping his podium with podgy hands, he glared across the stage to his elegant opponent.

You could see the jealousy cloud over Blatter's head. It wasn't bloody fair. He'd fought his way up through the dirt, the corruption, the hypocrisy to the very top of football and he was tired and irritated by carping critics.

Opposite him was a tall, handsome, graceful scion of the Hyundai family, wealthy and privileged and at ease with himself. Blatter could be forgiven for thinking, what did *he* know about having to dance around Havelange, kow-tow to Dassler, scheme with the deep and dark André Guelfi?

Chung continued. 'I believe this congress will decide the long-term fate of FIFA and world football. The real problems of FIFA will not disappear with the election. The issue is, will FIFA be able to restore our prestige and respect? I hope you all enjoy your stay in Korea. Thank you.'

'Thank you, Dr Chung, for that very unique welcome address,' said Blatter, his eyes raging.

The roll call ate up another 40 minutes. Then David Will's turn came at last. Will made his case. 'Last September it became clear that the 2006 money was already being brought into the 2000–2001 accounts.' Blatter listened without emotion. Will went on. 'Then we became increasingly concerned at FIFA's financial position.'

What was the truth about the money? And why, why, why was this rich organisation in so much trouble that it had to juggle with the numbers and treat future earnings as if they were current?

He went on, 'We lost 470 million francs in the past four years. If the ISL collapse only cost us 36 million, we have contrived to lose 433 million all on our own! If we were a company, not an association, we would be legally bound to report ourselves to a Swiss court as insolvent.'

Who could Blatter rely on to come to the podium and demolish

David Will? Finance chairman Julio Grondona? No. His deputy Jack Warner? No. 'Chuck Blazer,' said the President and up came his bruiser.

'I'm surprised that David Will has walked into a crowded theatre and yelled Fire!' said Chuck.

'There is no fire! Many of us have come to a different conclusion. They are not losses. That's only an interpretation. They are the investment that we've agreed to make in you!'

Blazer was appealing to greed. In the body of the hall were 197 delegations that had each received their first US$1 million, lightly scrutinised FIFA handout. Of those, 117 had also received or been promised US$400,000 worth of Goal project facilities. A few had pocketed bundles of the cash. How many in the hall cared if FIFA was living on expensive credit?

The critics weren't fair. 'The fact is that your president runs an executive committee where everything is unanimous. It's been a campaign of, if we throw dirt some of it will stick.'

Now Blatter was smiling, confident he'd weathered the worst of the storm.

The English FA's Adam Crozier backed Will and his numbers and added, 'Yesterday we believe the credibility of FIFA was damaged before the entire world. Our trust in FIFA is fundamentally broken.'

Ireland's Des Casey followed and said, 'Securitisation is robbing Peter to pay Paul.' He looked towards Blatter and recalled, sadly, 'You said in Buenos Aires this would not happen.'

Blatter's face was rigid. Casey was retiring in a few weeks. He'd deal with the English later.

Now, at last, after the months of ducking and diving, insults, rages, and allegations, it was time for the vote.

Blatter broke into that old charismatic smile and beamed towards the rows of officials. 'You were wonderful people,' he said and asked Grondona, as senior veep, to take the chair during the ballot.

Issa Hayatou walked to the podium, dropped his head and read a dull speech. Did he want to lose? The man seemed exhausted.

The old dancing master followed him. Blatter was all impish smiles, he kept his head up, spoke freely, worked the room with his eyes, gesticulated. He ended with a rallying call, 'Let's make the game better.' The portable voting booths were set up on either side of the stage and the roll call started again.

GRONDONA got to him first and slobbered on the re-elected president's neck. Helen Petermann rushed from backstage with a bouquet and kissed Sepp on both cheeks. Daughter Corinne appeared on stage clutching her 15-month-old toddler Serena. Grandpa embraced the child who promptly cried.

Hayatou and Johansson were stony faced. They hadn't thought it would be as bad as 139 to 56, a bigger majority than Blatter won four years ago in Paris. This was devastating and it showed on every dissident's face. Delegates formed a disciplined queue tailing back off the stage. They congratulated Blatter and asked him to autograph their Adidas balls.

Blatter grabbed Zen-Ruffinen's hand and bellowed to the hall, 'Shake hands with everybody! Do it, do it please! For the unity of football!'

As the hall emptied, Blatter started his victory press conference. 'Today the victory goes to football. Football is the game of the people. The people cannot lie. The people have the truth. So today is also a victory for the truth. You cannot imagine what it means for me, having been for months been accused by a certain directed press saying what a bad man I am.'

He paused, then he said, 'The general secretary says he is in trouble. He *is* in trouble.' Later Blatter told a Zurich paper, 'Tomorrow we take care of Mr Clean.'

A WARM WELCOME FOR MR SEPP ...

Boos all round

Sangam Stadium, Seoul, 31 May 2002. The booing began in one corner of the main stand and spread around the curves of the stadium like an aural Mexican wave. Some fans heckled, others whistled, there were cat-calls and hoots. Sepp Blatter was looking foolish. He'd stood up to make his speech opening the 2002 World Cup and this barrage of abuse wasn't on his agenda.

He'd manipulated the congresses, won the vote, trashed his critics, he was surrounded in the VIP stand by his favourite people, royalty, presidents and prime ministers. Beneath him, football's rank and file, the common people, 65,000 of them, were giving him the yell, the jeer, the finger, shouting down his ramblings about 'a sports festival of the global village'.

The fans hadn't forgotten the months of corruption allegations. The message from the congresses was that he'd got away with it, the fans knew it and they knew that in the weeks to come they would be shaken down on the streets with sky-high cash prices for tickets.

And here was their chance to send the message from the stands that they might have been screwed but they hadn't been fooled. Blatter tried his usual peace and harmony stuff. The crowd pumped up the volume. Blatter, embarrassed and angry, paused and croaked, 'Fair play, please.'

He stumbled on. This was 'the most splendid and perfect event ever'. Around him, members of the executive committee took in the scene. Some seemed shocked. Others laughed out loud. Welcome to the World Cup.

Seoul, 2 June 2002. Fans flocked into Incheon international airport for the World Cup. They passed FIFA Vice-President Jack Warner and his entourage on their way out. Out of Korea, out of Asia, out of the hemisphere, they were heading home to Trinidad as fast as they could to deal with something far more important.

Warner's friend Steve Ferguson had been arrested by the Anti-Corruption Investigation Bureau. He'd been accused of defrauding the government of millions of dollars during the construction of the new airport at Piarco near Port of Spain. The bail demands were huge and without Jack's intervention poor old Steve was likely to stay locked up with the lower classes for some time to come.

Ferguson, formerly chief executive of a financial services company, had stood shoulder to shoulder with Warner financing the UNC party. He was a comrade. Also arrested and bailed was another Warner friend and business associate, former UNC government finance minister Brian Kuei Tung. Steve was banged up and the court wanted TT$800,000 (£67,000) to unlock his cell.

Warner barked into his cell phone to try and raise the money while national association president Ollie Camps waited with him through the summer evening outside the Port of Spain prison. But they couldn't get Ferguson sprung. The magistrate wouldn't accept their sureties. Ferguson's lawyers kept up the pressure and a little after one o'clock the following morning went to the jail to liberate him.

The jailer, talking through a small sliding window in the big gate, told the lawyers he wasn't allowed to open up to receive their court order. Ferguson's lawyer demanded the man identify himself. The jailer told him, 'Hold on, I have to get permission to release my regimental number and name.' He slid the window closed and they never saw him again. The day shift let Ferguson out at sunrise and Warner headed back to Korea.

'MY DEAR President and Friend, I thank you for your kind invitation to the 2002 FIFA World Cup,' wrote Warner earlier in the year. He started listing the swarm of family, friends and functionaries he was going to bring along and that FIFA would have to pay for. There was Mrs Maureen Warner, and, 'please ask your staff to arrange for two extra rooms for my two sons'. Then there was Hubert Johnson taking time off from his job as a redcap at Piarco airport to be Jack's personal assistant.

Herbert was filling Harold Taylor's shoes because Jack got Harold a seat on a committee. Harold also needed paying for. 'Furthermore my personal secretary Ms Patricia Modeste will be arriving and I do thank you in advance for your assistance in providing accommodation for her as well in Korea and Japan.'

Jack wasn't always so free-spending with FIFA's money. On an earlier trip east he told FIFA, 'In Japan, I shall also have a travelling companion for whom a separate room shall not be needed.' But when it came to the tournament, it looked like Jack would need a whole floor. Big Melvin Brennan, Blazer's muscle who barred my way at that congress in Miami, got a free trip to Seoul and had a seat in the congresses. As well as Pat Modeste there was Marina helping out. Not forgetting Cheryl, too.

Alan Rothenberg from Los Angeles was nominated from CONCACAF along with his old allies Hank Steinbrecher and Bob Stiles. Jack had 27 of his officials in tow including the double act of Captain Horace Burrell from Jamaica – on the tournament's disciplinary committee where he'd pass moral judgement on players – and Jeff Webb, his business partner at the Captain's Bakery and Grill in the Cayman islands and the local Western Union office manager. Jeff was on the Protocol Committee for the World Cup. Its duties, I'm told, include setting out those little name cards at banqueting tables and making sure the invited dignitaries are seated in the right order in the VIP stand.

When Jack ran out of ideas he dreamed up the 'Special Duties' category and that got Chet Greene from Antigua and Colin Klass from Guyana out to the Far East, all expenses paid. Colin and Chet, squeezing a little time away from their arduous duties, made their way to a huge second-hand car lot in Kawasaki, Japan, where they took tea with the proprietor and promised to import lots of his vehicles into the Caribbean. A happy snap of Chet and Colin with the proprietor's family was pasted into the company's internet site.

In Japan Chet was too busy with his second-hand car business to go and collect his tickets. So he sent in his place a Swede, calling himself Osten Carlsson, direct to FIFA's ticket office for the pickup. Big, blonde, tanned and dripping with gold bracelets, Carlsson became a familiar figure to British fans wanting tickets as the World Cup went on, although there is no evidence that he was selling Chet's tickets for him.

Before the tournament FIFA had solemnly promised that this time they would outwit the ticket racketeers. Every ticket ordered would have to carry the name of the person it was intended for.

It's a good job FIFA did eventually abandon their rule about checking names on tickets. Otherwise the guards on the stadium gates might have got confused. What's this? A big red-haired Brit carrying a ticket with Mohamed Bin Hammam stamped on it. Isn't he one of those FIFA VIPS? Then, next through the turn-stile, a blonde from Glasgow. The name on the ticket? Mohamed Bin Hammam, from Qatar.

There was a row of Bin Hammams at the game on 2 June against Sweden. One angry English fan told me, 'When I got into the Saitama Stadium I was chatting with fans in the same row and they all had tickets with the same name. It's a disgrace.'

Then he discovered from the fan sitting next to him that Bin Hammam's name was on a ticket he'd bought on the street for the game against Argentina in Sapporo in five days time. Everybody had paid the touts a huge mark-up of US$500 over the face value of the ticket. Some fans paid £700 for £100 tickets.

Ticket trading was often planned far in advance of the tourna-ment. Some fans said they'd obtained their Bin Hammam tickets from the Beverley Hills, agents Razor Gator. During the Cup Razor Gator worked out of a 15th floor office in the Imperial Tower in Tokyo's Ginza district. One visitor told me the office was 'awash with World Cup tickets'. A company spokesman ex-plained, 'The name that appears on a ticket could be a company name, a sponsor name, a federation's name or an individual's name. We've never had a problem with any of our customers being allowed to enter the stadiums with these tickets in the seven World Cups that we've handled.'

Razor Gator sold tickets that had been issued to the football associations of Argentina and Qatar. Did the executive committee member from Qatar know about this? 'Mr Bin Hammam is as much shocked and disappointed with it as we are,' said FIFA spokesman Andreas Herren. Bin Hammam couldn't speak for himself because he wasn't there. It was the first week of the World Cup but Bin Hammam had gone home. Herren said perhaps Bin Hammam had given his tickets to friends who had sold them without his knowledge. The explanation that Bin Hammam did not know tickets bearing his name had been sold on is certainly credible; a man of his considerable wealth didn't exactly need the money.

English fans desperate to see the Argentina game were picking up tickets issued to sponsors that had worked their way on to the black market. One that ended up in my files was from 'C Cola' with a face value of US$60 and a street price of US$400. Another fan emailed me from Japan about buying tickets originally issued to the Ecuador FA. He concluded his message, 'FIFA are so bent.'

THE BOOING at the Seoul opening ceremony subsided but the fans knew their protest had been broadcast on most of the television screens on the planet. It became the thing to do when Blatter turned up at matches. In December the following year, when he stood up at a charity match in Basel, more than 32,000 Swiss fans gave him the same raucous, reception.

If the Swiss could do it – so could the Brits. More than 74,000 of them crammed into Cardiff's Millennium Stadium in February 2004 for the League Cup Final. Blatter came out on the pitch to shake hands with the teams and was greeted by boos and whistles from the fans. One veteran reporter told me, 'Of course fans love to boo the ref or players but I've never seen the dignitaries picked on before.'

And if the Brits could do it, so could the Chinese. Blatter, flanked by Mohamed Bin Hammam, arrived at the Beijing's Workers' Stadium in July 2004 for the opening ceremony of the Asian Cup. 72,000 fans booed the FIFA president. It's becoming a global habit.

BRAZIL WON the World Cup (again). Blatter sped back from the final game in Yokohama to his office on Sunny Hill and purged FIFA of its most loyal servants. General Secretary Michel Zen-Ruffinen was 'taken care of' as was his assistant, the tall bespectacled Norwegian Jon Doviken. Out of the door with him, guilty by association, went Zen-Ruffinen's senior administrator, Doris Valasek, paid off after 18 years' service.

As Blatter dumped long-serving and well-regarded officials, he managed all at once to hobble FIFA's effectiveness, to alienate surviving staffers and to throw away the institutional memory. He was also drawing a line under his past because there were few left who could attach proper significance to the names of Horst Dassler, Jean-Marie Weber and André Guelfi or had any knowledge of how these men had shaped FIFA.

Blatter gave Urs Linsi the 'acting' general secretary title for six months. Then Blatter's executive committee rubberstamped him into the job permanently in December 2002. They let him hold on to the chief financial officer's job too, driving a coach and horses through the separation of powers that was supposed to keep FIFA's money safe. What would the general secretary do now if he felt the finance chief was hiding something? Talk to himself? Blatter's highly-paid French advisor Jerome Champagne, perhaps hoping for Zen-Ruffinen's job, had to settle for becoming Linsi's deputy.

There was a bitter blow for communications chief Keith Cooper. 'I was called in by the acting general secretary – not the

President, whom I have known for almost 30 years, but who was unable to tell me himself – and told I was being dismissed as from today,' he said. 'It was really quite brutal. I asked the reason and was told there was no reason. Apparently under Swiss law you do not have to give a reason.'

Keith Cooper had impressed the international media with his competency. His departure made way for ultra-loyal Markus Siegler, Blatter's personal spokesman, to become communications director.

Cooper left with his salary paid until the year's end. Not for him the golden parachute that Blatter insisted on when his protégé Flavio Battaini was sacked by Zen-Ruffinen. Blatter had stepped in and shovelled around £600,000 of FIFA's money into Flavio's hands.

Next Blatter let go Roger Feiner, who had supervised the television contracts. Five more senior staffers were dismissed and more walked out when they saw how FIFA was being reorganised.

Presidential adviser Guido Tognoni had had a rollercoaster career and it was about to turn downhill again. Back in 1994, after the botched coup against Havelange, Blatter needed scapegoats and he nominated Guido to walk the plank. Sepp lacked the guts to tell Guido directly, so Erwin Schmid did it. Then, in Spring 2001, as the ISL group slipped under the water, Blatter brought him back in to advise on marketing. Sepp must have needed him badly, because Guido's secret contract – I've seen it – promised a £150,000 annual salary, plus a £25,000 annual bonus and the whole deal would run until after the 2006 World Cup. One clause says the contract is 'based on the personal relationship of trust between President Blatter and Guido Tognoni'. That trust ran out in March 2003 and Blatter sacked him again, but this time he got Urs Linsi to do the deed.

With a fixed smile on his face Guido headed off to live in the

Gulf claiming, 'I left on good terms and have signed a confidentiality agreement so I don't talk publicly.'

Up on Sunny Hill they reckoned he had fallen out with Linsi, now beginning to flex his general secretary muscles. Linsi took a little time out now and then to fire one of Blatter's favourites. Each firing sent a message to Sepp as chilling as a head on a silver platter.

Sunny Hill, 5 March 2003. Blatter and his finance team met privately with the new seven-member Internal Audit Committee that replaced the one he had disbanded a whole year before. He reminded them that the Zurich prosecutor had declined to take action over allegations made by Johansson and his supporters on the executive committee on the eve of the 2002 World Cup. Urs Linsi vigorously nodded his head. So did his back-up crew, deputy finance chief Markus Kattner and beancounters Michael Meier and Christoph Bollhalder.

Blatter went on, 'This shows us the important responsibility and dignity of committees like this one.' Andreas Herren, a FIFA spokesmen, nodded as well. Blatter's nodding employees were mirrored from the other side of the room by the KPMG representatives, Patricia Bielmann and Markus Ackermann.

Another nodder was the new committee chairman, Franco Carraro, a longtime survivor of IOC politics and president of the Italian national association. Blatter stressed the audit committee's independence; he and Linsi would attend only by invitation. Then chairman Carraro said, 'Let's make Urs our secretary.'

So Urs Linsi, the general secretary, who is also the finance director, is now going to be secretary of the 'independent' audit committee? They're supposed to be scrutinising him! That's the point of them. That's why they're there.

'This committee,' continued Blatter, 'will significantly increase

financial transparency, for the football family and for the good of
the game.' Brazil's Dr José Carlos Salim, a member of the new,
improved audit committee, couldn't argue with that. He liked
Sepp and the Brazilian football officials were grateful for Sepp's
support.

In 2000 Brazil's Congress and Senate had jointly launched
an investigation into allegations that three leading figures in the
national football federation were corrupt. Blatter denounced the
investigation as interference in football. He threatened, 'Brazil
will be suspended from all international activities. Brazil will
not take part in the 2002 World Cup, the World Youth Cup, the
Under-17 World Cup, the Women's World Cup and the Futsal
indoor tournament in Guatemala.'

The investigators produced a report in 2001 calling the
federation 'a den of crime, anarchy, incompetence and dishonesty'. Down the page they mentioned corruption, graft, money
laundering, tax fraud, inadmissible expenses, embezzlement,
generous salaries. There were US$2,000-a-day New York limou-
sine rentals, more than US$12,500 in restaurant bills, falsification
of documents. Money had been slipped to politicians' campaigns,
a horseowners' association and a football tournament for police-
men. The federation bought power and influence, sending five
senior judges and their wives to the World Cup in France – via
London, Budapest, Prague, New York and Los Angeles. A senator
on the investigating committee commented on the report, 'This
was just the tip of the iceberg.'

The three officials most tainted by the allegations were the
federation's president, FIFA executive committee member
Ricardo Teixeira (Havelange's son-in law), his uncle Marco
Antonio Teixeira and Ricardo and Marco's best friend, Dr José
Carlos Salim who had been in charge of finances. Salim? And now
Blatter had put him on FIFA's audit committee.

Nodding along in harmony around the table was Justino José Fernandes, head of Angola's soccer federation, a former governor of the capital city Luanda, and close associate of Angolan President José Eduardo dos Santos – godfather to one of his children. Angola's president can be touchy about suggestions that large chunks of the country's oil revenues end up in politicians' private foreign banks, leaving three-quarters of Angola's citizens struggling to survive on less than £1 a day.

Gun-toting cops kicked in Rafael Marques's front door at dawn one autumn morning in 1999 and hauled the reporter away to Labortório, one of the most notorious jails in Southern Africa. For ten days he was denied visits from friends, family or lawyers. Rafael declined to sign a paper absolving his jailers of responsibility in the event of his death in custody.

Rafael had written an article in the Angolan weekly magazine *Agora* accusing the Angolan government of 'incompetence, embezzlement and corruption'. Who went to the public prosecutor's office in Luanda and signed the request for Rafael Marques to be charged with defaming President dos Santos? On page 43 of the indictment is the name: Senor Justino José Fernandes.

Marques's 'trial' was behind closed doors, he faced a maximum eight years in jail and to speed things up, the hand-picked judge barred his lawyer. When the hearing was over, they wouldn't tell him the verdict. He heard on the radio that he'd got six months jail suspended for five years and costs and damages of US$6,500, a huge penalty in his impoverished country. He was also banned from leaving the country, unlike Justino José Fernandes who remained free to travel with the Angolan national team and to FIFA meetings with Sepp Blatter on Sunny Hill and attend meetings of the improved audit committee.

Perhaps Senor Fernandes isn't so smart as his friend Mr Blatter thinks. Rafael happened to work for the Open Society Institute supported by billionaire philanthropist George Soros. The US government quickly demanded his release, followed by Britain and the European Union. Within days Rafael went from dirt-poor scribbler in a faraway land to international symbol of heroism in the struggle for free speech. He was moved to another jail and allowed visitors but he still spent another thirty days locked up.

Two months later a colleague of Senor Fernandes told the Angolan parliament, during a debate on freedom of speech, that if 28-year-old Marques carried on criticising the government he should be 'advised' that he'd never see 40.

Rafael Marques emailed me confirming, 'Fernandes is the one who filed a criminal suit against me, on behalf of the president, which led me to a "nice" vacation in jail. Thanks for letting the world know about Fernandes. I hope he remembers what he did to me.'

MORE NODDING, more Blatter loyalists. Next at the internal audit committee table was Jeff Webb from the Cayman Islands, loved by Jack Warner because, as Jack says, Jeff knows how to 'keep the faith'. Jeff had told the extraordinary congress in Seoul the previous year that he hailed from the world's fifth biggest financial centre. That's one way to look at it. Another is that with no taxes the Caymans drain money out of other economies and has long been attractive to money launderers.

Jeff has nothing to do with that kind of stuff, he's in the bakery business with Horace Burrell. They've both shown extraordinary loyalty to Warner and Blatter. General Farouk Bouzo, President of the Syrian national association, sat next to the one man in the room who might cause problems, the independent-minded Mathieu Sprengers, President of the Dutch association.

He seemed to be asking questions that mattered, such as can we put out a press release about standards of corporate governance? Carraro seemed shocked. This kind of decision should be left to President Blatter and his executive committee. Rounding off the group was Australia's Basil Scarsella who had much to thank Blatter for. Three months earlier the president had helped give the Oceania region their own slot in the World Cup finals. If Australia could win the slot, that would bring in the money needed to pay the association's chronic debts.

The new improved audit committee met three times in 2003. At FIFA's congress in Paris the following year Fernandes, Salim, Webb, Bouzo, Sprengers, Scarsella, Carraro and their committee secretary Urs Linsi reported that everything was absolutely tickety-boo. Delegates could take their word for it.

THE PURGE went on. Once Blatter had neutered the internal audit committee, he turned to recreating the wider FIFA in his own image. There were loyalists to promote, scores to be settled and rebels got rid of. There were more than 300 seats on 30-odd committees.

First up, a score to settle. England was home of the beautiful game and home of Adam Crozier, the FA chief executive who'd dared speak out against Blatter at the Seoul Congress. The English had six committee places. Not for long.

Blatter got out his little chopper, and chopped off seats at the committees handling marketing, the club world championship, disputes and technical matters. Unchopped was FA president Geoff Thompson, who kept his seat on the 2006 World Cup organising committee. And Sir Bobby Charlton had a seat at the football committee, a decorative body that provided Blatter with photo-ops alongside people who had made a real contribution to the game. England also got a place on the not very important medical research committee.

So who got the powerful positions? Blatter surveyed the most unlikely candidates. Tonga, admitted to FIFA in 1994 and 176th out of 203 nations in the world rankings. Perfect! Blatter put local soccer boss, Ahongalu Fusimalohi, a member for the first time of the powerful Executive Committee, onto the finance committee and the marketing committee and the media committee too.

Tahiti, they'd only joined FIFA in 1990 and only ranked 113th in soccer performance. Three committee seats for them. One was on the big spending Goal committee and another on the technical committee. American Samoa, population 69,000, which joined FIFA in 1998 and was ranked 201st, got a seat on the important national associations committee.

Sucking up to Blatter paid off for Germany with 13 committee places, Argentina with nine, and the USA, Italy and Switzerland with eight each.

BLATTER could deny the corruption allegations for all he was worth. One thing he had to admit: they had damaged him. Who could he call on to help cleanse his tainted image? Who was the magician who'd whitewashed the old rascal Juan Antonio Samaranch? Why, Henry Kissinger!

In 1999, as Samaranch was sinking under the weight of corruption at the IOC, Kissinger was drafted in to talk up a bundle of painless 'reforms' created by the international image builders Hill & Knowlton. Kissinger even turned up at a Congressional hearing in Washington in 2000 to support Samaranch. Henry helped Juan. Could he help Sepp?

In early 2003 a little-known American organisation calling itself the International Amateur Athletic Association gave Blatter its Global Award for Peace. Apparently he had single-handedly ended the decades of enmity between Korea and Japan. On 18 February Blatter arrived at Manhattan's Waldorf Astoria with his newly installed third wife Graziella.

Kissinger told the 250 guests that his friend Sepp had a vocation to establish solidarity between the rich and the poor. Sepp replied that he had 250 million registered players in the world, all 'ambassadors for peace'. Then fifa.com announced that 'peace and football once again walk hand in hand'.

Buenos Aires, 5 July 2003. Julio Grondona wasn't keen on doing this kind of thing too often but he had an election coming up at the Argentine association and he hadn't been interviewed on TV for a while. So he said yes and sat watching the technicians make their final adjustments in the TyC Sports Channel studio for the Saturday lunchtime recording.

He wore his thinning grey hair swept back and cut neatly on the neck. The loosening of his face, the swelling of his nose, the slackness of the turkey wobble at the neck hinted at seven decades of good living.

He was most senior of all the FIFA's vice-presidents, chief of the finance committee, deputy to the president at the emergency committee that rallied round Sepp when the empire was under threat, chief again of the marketing committee that monitored the billion dollar deals that made life so good. The second most powerful man in world football gave the camera his disarming lop-sided smile.

'Good evening and a special guest tonight . . . .' said the young interviewer and off they went chat, chat, chat, all the expected stuff, clubs, players, Maradona, Menotti, World Cup winning coach Carlos Bilardo in Mexico in '86, happy times in the countryside with nice trees, free air and good wine. The show was going as it should when you are friends with the channel's boss, Carlos Avila, who you sold the TV rights for Argentine soccer (a deal that stretched from 1986 until 2014 – yes, really, 28 years on one channel.)

That was enough, it was time to start winding up. One final question. 'Don Julio,' the interviewer Ramiro Sánchez Ordóñez said, 'what about the myths we have in soccer in this country? Like, why do we not have any Jewish referees in the premier league?'

Grondona knew the answer to that one. 'I don't believe a Jew can ever be a referee at that level because it's hard work and, you know, Jews don't like hard work.'

Then it was thank you and good night.

'Are you happy Don Julio?' asked one of the two bigshots who had stood in the studio shadows during the taping, 'Want to change anything?' It was a courtesy offer to edit out any mistakes, anything he hadn't intended to say. 'Muchachos, todo bien,' he assured them. 'Guys, it's all OK.'

TyC Sports goes out on cable and didn't get a large audience that Saturday night. On the following Monday the TVR programme ran some highlights from the interview including that slur on Jews. A radio journalist broadcast a commentary on Grondona's gaffe; human rights lawyer Ricardo Monners Sans heard it and was gobsmacked. Before dusk the local branch of the Jewish Defence League was wheeling out Argentina's tough anti-discrimination laws.

Grondona felt he couldn't refuse when the Buenos Aires Jewish station *Radio Jai* summoned him to their studio for an explanation. But maybe he should have done. 'Well, you know, Jews are special people,' he blundered and when the unsmiling interviewer asked, 'What do you mean, special people?' the second most important man in world football couldn't explain what was in his mind.

Later Grondona said, as racists sometimes do, that many of his best friends were Jews. They were a brilliantly gifted people. 'I've been misunderstood, they've labelled me a Nazi and I'm not, never,' he complained.

Three weeks later Rabbi Abraham Cooper, who flew in especially from Los Angeles, went to see Grondona. The Rabbi held his chin high. He's a big man and his glare said there was a deep rage burning inside him. Next to him, in a staged picture of reconciliation at the offices of the Argentine Football Association was Grondona sporting a 'Please can I go and hide in the cupboard' lopsided grin. The two long-faced Jewish officials flanking them looked like they hadn't heard a joke in months.

Rabbi Cooper and his team, a delegation from the Simon Wiesenthal Centre, wanted more than apologies. If they didn't leave the building happier than when they'd come in, they were going to register a criminal complaint that could get the senior vice-president of FIFA up to three years kicking a ball around a jailyard. At their dictation Grondona dashed off a letter to President Blatter 'rejecting attempts by Arab associations to expel Israel from FIFA'.

The sports programme *El Sello* went off air as did Ramiro Sánchez Ordóñez and neither returned for half a year. TyC cancelled a planned programme celebrating the 25th anniversary of the Argentina World Cup staged by the former military junta.

Three months later, in November 2003, the Argentine FA re-elected Grondona for a sixth four-year term. All 40 clubs agreed unanimously to keep him as president, and he was well-loved in Zurich.

Sepp Blatter's voice leapt out of Buenos Aires' *Radio Rivadavia* and told Argentina, 'Senor Grondona is a monument – and not only to Argentine football. He plays a great role in South America and we are friends forever. Together we will defend football and transparency in FIFA.'

What did the FIFA president think about his deputy's anti-Semitic comments? I emailed Sepp Blatter and asked him. Lawrence Cartier, retained by Blatter and FIFA, got back to me.

Mr Cartier wrote: 'You omit to mention (notwithstanding that you are no doubt aware) that subsequent to the remarks being made Mr Grondona made an apology for them and shortly thereafter at a meeting with the Simon Wiesenthal [sic] Centre in Buenos Aires Mr Grondona stated, "My position and that of the entire Argentine Football Association executive has always backed an anti-discriminatory policy. Football promotes an un-restrictive and full union among people without differences of race, skin colour, religion or flag."' Apparently Grondona read that off the cue card without drawing breath at half time.

Mr Cartier went on: 'The original remarks were made without reference to and without the knowledge of my clients. They were not made on behalf of my clients and they do not represent my clients' views. As you well know my clients do not in any way condone racial or ethnic discriminatory remarks.'

Yes Mr Cartier, but what did Sepp think of Grondona's anti-Semitic comments?

I'd specifically asked Mr Blatter to comment on his friend's gaffe in the light of the two terrorist bombings against Jews in Argentina in the 1990s; more than one hundred people had been murdered and 500 wounded. Mr Cartier said, 'My clients do not consider there was any need for you in your e-mail to try and exacerbate a situation (which has already been apologised for) by linking the remarks to the tragic events which have befallen the Jewish community in Argentina.'

25

THE EMPIRE STRIKES BACK

Revolution in the Caribbean

'I'M SHOCKED,' said Sepp Blatter when he heard allegations that some of his most trusted colleagues had bought armfuls of World Cup tickets direct from FIFA and sold them to touts. 'This is something that shocks us,' repeated the President. 'Our disciplinary commission has the power to intervene and even to sanction them.'

Blatter was talking in Paris in July 1998. Six months earlier the office of the FIFA General Secretary had been sent a fax from Chet Greene. 'Please find attached the final and complete order for tickets for World Cup France from the Antigua Football Association.' Attached were three sheets, the official FIFA order form. It seemed that a substantial proportion of the 70,000 people of the twin Caribbean islands of Antigua & Barbuda, average wage £93 a week, wanted to buy tickets and travel to France. Antigua's general secretary ordered a total of 2,964 tickets, including 147 for the final. The request was passed swiftly

FOUL!

to FIFA's ticket office. So swiftly that they acknowledged Chet's order by fax the same day.

At the end of February 1998 Chet got bad news. Demand for tickets was so heavy that his order had to be cut back. He could have only 613 tickets. He got an invoice for 57,526.70 francs (US$39,763.33).

Chet attempted to get hold of more World Cup tickets . . . from Lennart Johansson! The UEFA president waited two weeks before replying, 'Mr Johansson has asked us to inform you that he unfortunately is not in a position to assist you with regard to purchasing tickets for the World Cup Final in Paris.'

Chet was close to the Bird dynasty – who'd led the fight for independence in Antigua – and he arranged for Prime Minister Lester Bird and the sports minister and his wife to attend the tournament. While in France, he got his hands on some more tickets from FIFA, including another four for the final. He – or rather the Antigua association – still owed FIFA 57,526.70 francs for his 613 tickets. Who was going to pay this? As of May 2002, this bill had not been settled.

'DEAR MR CHET GREENE,' faxed the American business-man from the Pacific North West, an exporter of sports kit to national associations around the world. 'You told me about FIFA's Financial Assistance Programme and how you were excited about it. I took advantage myself of this programme and have benefited from it personally. I would like to work with you on the US$250,000 a year programme. I am sure you understand how much profit awaits the hungry businessman such as you and myself. Call me and I'll tell you about my experience with the Liberia Football Assn and how much money I made with them. You won't believe it.'

Wrong, Mr Hungry Businessman. Chet did believe it and was writing cheques against FIFA's US$1 million grant over four years. The money started arriving in 1998. He bought a new air conditioning unit for the office, changed his mind and installed it in his home. He was so busy spending the grant that he mislaid all the paperwork for the first year, so it's been impossible to audit the grant for that period. In the years to come he didn't keep much more.

The following year it was decided that Chet would be paid from the grant a salary of US$1,000 a week – one fifth of the FIFA grant and five times the local average wage – for the part-time job of running the island's amateur leagues. The salary was paid by banker's order direct from FIFA in Zurich to Chet's account at the Antigua & Barbuda Investment Bank where it jostled for space with the salary from his government job as Commissioner for Sport.

As well as his two salaries Chet ran his own business importing and distributing sports kit. Umbro thought they had bought exclusive rights to sell kit at international matches on the island. They complained to Chet in July 1997 when they discovered rival kit manufacturer Admiral's goods were on sale at Antigua's ground as well.

Admiral weren't too happy either. In March 1998 they said Chet the hungry businessman wasn't paying his bills and refused to supply any more product on credit.

ANOTHER YEAR, another high-profile international tournament, another opportunity for Chet to use his clout with FIFA. It was the finals of Euro 2000 and one of Chet's associates, an Antiguan and his wife with an office in Tilbury, Essex had assembled a list of fans looking for tickets. They wanted 480, including 40 for each for the quarter-finals, semis and the final, and they faxed the list to Chet. Writing on the headed notepaper of the Antigua association, Chet approached UEFA's office in Nyon, Switzerland with the order. UEFA offered only 40 tickets for early round games, demanding cash with the order.

By the Spring of 2000, under Chet's direction, the Antiguan association had not only spent all the money FIFA had given it since the autumn of 1998, it had overspent by US$108,000. Where all the money had gone to was a complete mystery.

There was only one answer: ask for more. FIFA agreed, but with a few conditions. Chet must set up a new bank account for FIFA's money. And he must submit it to the scrutiny of a firm of Antiguan accountants. The money must be spent only according to a budget submitted by Chet and approved by finance chief Urs Linsi.

'That's fine,' said Chet. FIFA appointed the auditing company, CAS Hewlett & Co, and agreed to meet their fees. FIFA also agreed to send the association grants of US$612,000 over the next two years.

Raymond Doorgen, a slim-built East Indian from Guyana, was in his mid-forties and an employee of Hewlett's. He was made sole signatory on the FIFA grant account, and he celebrated his new job by flexing his fingers, unsheathing his pen and writing some serious cheques. He knew the best place for FIFA's money and over the next couple of years he moved around £200,000 to his personal accounts. Some of the money was eventually returned but the association's accounts were such a mess that no-one can say how much. Doorgen's hand never tired and he signed more than 60 cheques for his own personal benefit. The Premier Beverage company, the Epicurean, Southern Fry and the Food Court were always pleased to see Raymond Doorgen drop by with his FIFA cheque book.

The budget submitted to FIFA was fast forgotten. Chet wrote to Doorgen asking him to set up a £10,000 loan to the association. Then Chet and Ralph Potter wanted bundles of money to take on a trip to Brazil. 'Here it is,' said Doorgen, and he went along too, all paid for by FIFA. Doorgen took his responsibilities so seriously that he insisted on a trip to Miami, using FIFA funds, to examine some grass that might be used for a football pitch.

Doorgen was brilliant with the money. He approved a US$15,000 cheque to Jack Warner's Simpaul travel company in Trinidad for air tickets. He approved £400 for a gift to an Antigua cricketer who'd been selected for . . . the West Indies cricket team. According to the budget agreed with FIFA he should have been paying the fees outstanding to local football coaches. Budget? What budget? He'd torn it up long ago.

The money poured in from Switzerland and poured out to Doorgen's private accounts. Before long the association was in the red again and loyal workers at the office whose salaries, a fraction of Chet's, were part of the FIFA-agreed budget, were laid off for three months. Chet paid himself £10,000 in 'allowances' that definitely weren't allowed by the FIFA budget.

Now that all the money was gone, Chet temporarily closed the national football programme. He told the men's and youth teams to hang up their boots and some coaches were sent home without pay. This was 'to alleviate current financial difficulties'. The coaches weren't surprised to learn that times were lean, but then again, most of them had no idea so much money had flowed in. 'We never knew there was a FIFA grant,' one coach told me. 'We were never told about it.' Then Chet was off to Korea and Japan for the World Cup.

Chet had applied to the Goal project for another big grant to create a pitch, changing rooms and offices, promising to name it the 'Jack Austin Warner Football Development Centre'. In the middle of 2002, the first instalment arrived, US$161,439 from FIFA. A year later I visited the site where the pitch was planned and saw horses grazing in rough scrub alongside a wrecked beer lorry. I went to Chet's offices in a government building in Cassada Gardens to ask him about all those FIFA grants. He offered to throw me down a concrete staircase.

The association failed to pay a hotel bill for the national team in England, and football was falling apart in Antigua. In November 2002 a determined local reporter, Ian 'Magic' Hughes, began digging into Chet's ticket orders and asking what had happened to FIFA's one million dollars.

Just before Christmas 2002, Chet went off to Nassau in the Bahamas to get married and returned in time for the meeting the association called once every four years for elections. He assumed Ralph Potter would be re-elected president and himself automatically re-appointed general secretary.

No such luck. Many of Chet's individual supporters could not produce proof they'd paid their subscriptions, their right to vote was challenged by his opponents and the meeting was adjourned.

Reporter Ian Hughes ran another well-researched story about the manipulation of the FIFA money. It was crisis time. Something must be done, quickly, to roll back the attackers. Ralph had a brilliant idea. He told a local radio station that the association's money and the FIFA million dollars were safe because they had been managed by accountant Raymond Doorgen in his capacity as a 'partner' of the reliable local firm of CAS Hewlett.

'That's news to us,' said the managing director of Hewlett & Co in a furious letter to Potter. 'We were never appointed, orally or in writing, to manage the fund provided by FIFA. Raymond Doorgen did this on his own account without informing his employer.' Surely the game was up.

Not quite. Five days later FIFA deputy general secretary Jerome

Champagne came to Chet's rescue with a letter assuring everyone there was nothing to worry about. He recalled how two years earlier Chet, Jack and FIFA had agreed measures to protect FIFA's funds and he soothed, 'We are happy that the procedures have helped meet our joint objective of stabilising the financial situation of the ABFA.' He confirmed that 'Mr Raymond L Doorgen, a partner at CAS Hewlett & Co, has submitted regularly quarterly statements.' He copied his letter to Hewlett's.

The phone and fax lines between Antigua and Zurich throbbed for the next 24 hours. Jerome learned the truth. Raymond Doorgen was not and never had been 'a partner at CAS Hewlett & Co'. The man was no more than a book-keeper.

So Linsi and FIFA had been lied to. What would Jerome do now? Jump on the next flight to Antigua, knock Chet's and Ralph's and Raymond's heads together, and salvage what was left of FIFA's money?

Jerome called up the letter he'd sent 24 hours earlier, the one in which he'd described Doorgen as a 'partner' at Hewlett's. He deleted the word 'partner', inserted 'senior employee', and sent it off to Chet, for the record. No complaint, not a whimper. Everything remained tickety-boo.

It wasn't tickety-boo in Antigua. Reporter Ian Hughes published more damaging investigations in the Antigua *Sun*, revealing among other things Chet's gigantic salary. Chet and Ralph were in deepening trouble. Who else might save them?

Jack Warner dictated a letter. 'Dear Mr Greene, Your Association has followed the FIFA guidelines and, in many ways, represents a model for the rest of the region.' Tickety-boo! 'On the question of your salary which was recommended and paid by the FIFA, it is clear that there are persons operating out of malice and envy, and as such, I have no intention of dignifying the nonsense I have been reading with a comment of any kind.

'Suffice it to say that more goodwill emerges from the many administrative decisions that your association has taken over the last four years than your detractors will ever imagine,' insisted the FIFA vice-president, referring in passing to 'my friend' prime minister Lester Bird.

'In conclusion,' said Warner, 'I wish to state that, in every case, President Ralph Potter and you have represented your association, country and region with pride and, further, that your performance and representation at the regional and international levels have been nothing short of exemplary. Be consoled by the fact that people only throw stones at trees which bear fruit.'

The association's general meeting restarted at the multi-purpose centre at Perry Bay on Sunday 18 February and broke up after five hours' wrangling and no votes. They met again on 6 March and, with still no consensus on who was eligible to vote could agree on only one thing; somebody had to keep the association ticking over. The meeting appointed a three-man Interim Committee, led by the respected trades unionist Clarence Crump.

This new team wrote to Chuck Blazer in New York and Urs Linsi in Zurich asking politely for money to keep football happening in the island. Blazer and Linsi didn't write back. The general secretary of CONCACAF and the finance chief of FIFA would deal only with Chet.

They were happy to deal with Raymond Doorgen too, but all that changed when Raymond got a letter in March 2003 from his boss. 'The recent revelations in the news media and other sources, has made it clear beyond doubt that you have engaged in unlawful activity by allowing yourself to be appointed as an Accountant and Funds Manager, by one of our clients, in direct competition with us, while still working for us as a Semi-Senior Accounts Clerk.'

Hewlett's were not happy. 'We are informed that you

represented yourself as a senior partner and as a result obtained an engagement which was intended for a qualified Chartered Accountant, which of course you are not. You are also aware that your engagement with the client is fraudulent, and that possible legal action is pending.' Raymond was on the road with a month's pay in lieu of notice.

Meanwhile the interim committee was getting desperate. 'We are obliged to make contact once again,' they wrote to Linsi, 'to humbly request information on the status of our request for funding under the Financial Assistance Programme.'

At last FIFA responded. Not with help, but with a devastating blow for honest Antiguan footballers, fans and officials.

Zurich, 20 May 2003. 'The FIFA Emergency Committee has decided to suspend the Antigua & Barbuda Football Association,' announced Markus Siegler. Blatter's mouthpiece claimed 'the current chaotic situation in the administration of football in this country was preventing the national association from assuming its duties correctly.' He didn't explain what this meant.

As word of the suspension spread around the island, young men wept in sorrow and disbelief. Antigua's Under-23 squad were due to compete in the regional qualifying tournament for the Athens Olympic games. Now their Olympic dreams were dashed. Football supporters on the island petitioned IOC president Jacques Rogge. Didn't the IOC claim to stand up for the right of athletes to perform their sports?

The petition said, 'The athletes of Antigua & Barbuda Under-23 squad who through no fault of their own have been removed arbitrarily from the Olympic qualifying matches are now in deep despair as most of them will be too old to ever again compete in future Olympics. The team manager Mr Thadeus Price puts it into the proper perspective when he says, "The squad is hurting and Antigua and Barbuda is hurting."'

Antigua is small but it produces world-beaters. The petition was signed by former West Indies Cricket captain Sir Viv Richards, one of the greatest batsmen the game has ever seen, and fellow Windies team members Curtly Ambrose, Kenny Benjamin and Andy Roberts. Former world middleweight boxing champ Maurice Hope signed up and so did Maritza Marten Garcia, the Cuban discus Gold medallist in Barcelona who coached in the island. Most of Antigua's religious leaders and members of all political parties added their signatures along with representatives of most of the soccer clubs.

IOC President Jacques Rogge sent Blatter the mildest of letters asking him to explain why these athletes were being excluded, and left it at that. Blatter, who is also an IOC member sworn to uphold athletes' rights, replied that FIFA was sending a delegation to Antigua 'to look at the situation'. He didn't say when. So a generation of Antigua's finest were denied their one chance to compete at the Olympics. Sepp was there in Athens, beaming as usual from the VIP box.

'SERIOUS LEVELS of mismanagement, conflict of interest, abuse of power, negligence, financial irregularities and possible criminal activity that must be reported to the relevant authority,' was the summary of an investigation by the three-man Interim Committee.

Chairman Clarence Crump and his two colleagues published their report in June 2003, and it didn't look good for Chet Greene. Crump & Co accused Chet of 'unacceptable and abusive conduct that passed for effective leadership'. They asked him to produce receipts for the purchases he'd made and records of payments to sponsors. Chet was struck by a flash of memory. His office had been burgled. His records stolen. Was this crime reported to the police? Why, no, Chet was far too traumatized for that. It was gone, all gone, the receipts, the sponsor records, everything.

In January 2001 Chet had asked to be reimbursed for £5,000 he'd spent on 'equipment'. He didn't produce a receipt. Why should he? Doorgen was always happy to pay up without one. Asked later what the 'equipment' was, Doorgen couldn't remember. Years later a receipt miraculously turned up. A receipt from a company owned by Chet.

Crump & Co discovered that Antigua football had no up-to-date constitution, just a ten-year-old pile of scribbled updates that hadn't been put to members. Indeed, Chet hadn't called an annual general meeting in the past four years.

They signed off with a subtle but unmistakable rebuke: 'We wonder,' they wrote, 'how this situation could have existed over such a long period of time given the oversight that FIFA is presumed to have on national associations.' That did it. Chet's friends in CONCACAF and Zurich were furious.

Clarence Crump and his interim committee, their task completed, wanted to step down. They announced that elections for new officials would be held the following week.

Next morning they got another letter from Deputy General Secretary Jerome Champagne: 'Dear Sirs, We have been informed that an elective General Assembly of your national association is scheduled on 29 June 2003. Due to the current situation of football in Antigua and Barbuda we wish to inform you that we will not recognise any elections before a FIFA/CONCACAF delegation visits your country and makes a global assessment of the litigation with the parties involved.'

'Consequently,' added Jerome, 'we urge the latter not to take any steps that might lead to an even more difficult situation. Thank you for your attention to the foregoing.'

And what became of Blatter's pledge to the IOC's Jacques Rogge that FIFA would send a delegation to Antigua? Antigua was suspended in May and it was September before the delegation turned up. Stepping off the plane first was Jerome Champagne. Next came Harold Taylor, general secretary of the Caribbean Football Union and Jack Warner's enforcer. Taylor had already tried to intimidate Crump & Co, telling them that if they wanted any money from FIFA they must stamp 'General Secretary Chet Greene' on their requests, even though he no longer held the office. Lastly came Turkish executive committee member Senes Erzik, a nice man and no trouble-maker.

After three days the delegation left and Jerome promised that within 48 hours FIFA would send a list of proposed members of a 'normalisation committee' to steer Antiguan football back into grace. Privately Jerome whispered to the Antiguans that Chet wouldn't be one of them.

Before Jerome could get back to his desk in Switzerland Warner's man Harold Taylor intervened and sent out invitations to join the committee. Top of the list, Chet and Ralph along with their buddies, enough of them to outvote the dissenters. Days passed, then weeks as Warner arm-wrestled Jerome.

In the meantime some football officials reported Chet to Antigua's Director of Public Prosecutions, alleging theft of FIFA funds, but no prosecution has followed.

The normalisation committee was announced. Clarence Crump was to be chairman. And the secretary? Bitter laughter broke out all over Antigua. The secretary was to be Chet Greene himself. The face-saver for Jerome was that Chet was denied a vote. Chet and Ralph went off on an all-expenses paid jaunt to Doha in Qatar 'representing Antigua' at FIFA's congress for 2003. The suspension was lifted but too late for the young men who'd hoped to play in the Olympic qualifying games.

After a year of trying to make things work, Clarence Crump had had enough. He was invited to speak at the association's annual prize-giving at the beginning of March 2004, just as Antiguan football readied itself for elections that were a full fifteen months overdue. Crump delivered a blistering attack on Chet Greene and his cronies.

'Hiding and delaying information, deliberately incorrectly writing minutes, unilaterally taking decisions, selective leaking of information, ongoing press attacks through surrogate journalists were some of the many attempts to undermine and destabilise the normalisation committee and the game of football,' he said, angrily.

'Before the committee was officially formed the viruses were trying hard to fester themselves by forming a bogus committee and this prevented the announcement of the real committee, which was to be formed by FIFA,' said Crump.

Chet Greene's response was to call the accusations against him 'baseless and desperate'.

Come election day Chet stood for president of the association and was defeated 23 votes to 14 by Merv Richards, a former national player and coach and brother of Viv Richards.

Everybody assumed Chet was out of football. So how come he was wearing a FIFA blazer and attended FIFA's centennial congress in Paris in May 2004 and FIFA's player of the year gala in Zurich in the December? Warner created a new post at the Caribbean Football Union that kept Chet in the game. Chet, the man who had been instrumental in his country's young footballers being robbed of their Olympic dream, now had 'responsibility for all youth football in the region', well-funded and well-placed to wait and see if he could trip up Merv Richards and his new clean team and, in time, take back control of the money.

FURTHER west across the Caribbean was Jamaica, the football kingdom of Captain Horace Burrell. He never missed a chance to announce his belief that football should demonstrate the highest ethical standards. So when Jamie Lawrence, a new member of Jamaica's national squad, disclosed in a press interview that a decade earlier he'd been to prison for robbery, Jamie was out on his ear.

'It is the policy of the Jamaica Football Federation that if anyone connected to the sport is convicted of a criminal offence, he or she can no longer represent Jamaica,' Burrell dictated when he heard the news in June 2000.

Jamie Lawrence, aged 30 and born in South London, had made a success of his football career and was playing for Bradford City in the First Division when he was selected for Jamaica's national team. He'd also made a name for himself counselling kids against getting involved in crime. 'The fact he has since lived an exemplary life has no say,' added Burrell.

Four weeks later Captain Burrell was in Zurich receiving FIFA's highest honour, the Order of Merit, from President Blatter in the same hall where four years earlier his girlfriend had cast the vote of the absent Haitian delegate, Jean-Marie Kyss.

Captain Burrell sacked one Jamaican national coach because 'there has been a deterioration in the standard of discipline amongst the team members'. Blatter was so impressed he appointed Burrell to the special disciplinary committee for the 2002 World Cup.

A year later Burrell noted that elections were due and Jamaican football seemed to be getting tired of him. 'Burrell doesn't respect us,' said one official. 'He doesn't listen to us.' Other officials found him distant and arrogant.

Burrell appealed for help.

Blatter dropped everything and flew to Kingston with Jack Warner to be photographed with Burrell celebrating the sixth anniversary of Jamaica's qualifying for the 1998 World Cup. Blatter handed out special awards and broke the ground for new facilities to be funded by the Goal project. 'What we are doing today is for the future of the country,' said Blatter. 'Football can use it as the school of life. The philosophy of football is to offer hope to the population of the world.' Burrell was described in the press as 'gleeful'.

Blatter and Warner might as well have stayed home, because eight days later Jamaica's football family disposed of Burrell's services. Veteran administrator Crenston Boxhill won 54–49 and promised a new world of transparency. Burrell, cast out after nine years, was defiant in defeat. 'I have other football appointments,' he sneered. 'I'm a member of the disciplinary committee of FIFA, I'm also the first vice-president of the Caribbean Football Union and also a member of the disciplinary committee of the CONCACAF. So I still have a lot to do and maybe even more.'

Then he quickly added, 'First of all, I love country over self and whatever I can do for my country, I will.'

IT TOOK three months to put in place the campaign to undermine the Crenston Boxhill clean team. Warner turned up in Kingston again in March 2004 to launch the Caribbean Football Union's new marketing division. 'Under the astute leadership of Captain Horace Burrell and his dedicated staff,' said Warner, 'we in the Caribbean now have to harness the commercial energies of the region for the benefit of football.'

Regional football officials suspected this was a device to lure sponsors away from the Jamaican federation that Burrell had left with debts of more than £300,000. Burrell's deputy was Horace Reid who had previously been his general secretary. The voters didn't want them but Warner had to be seen to back his chosen officials – and send the message that anybody who opposed him or his placemen would get whacked. While they waited to return from exile, Jack would stand by Burrell and Reid just as he had stood by Chet Greene and Ralph Potter in Antigua.

As Boxhill and his team worked to reduce their inherited debts Burrell and Reid were jaunting to New York and then Zurich on vital FIFA business. In Switzerland they caroused with the discredited Chet Greene at one of Sepp's parties.

Next came the bogus stories. In early 2005, echoing the complaint of Antigua's Clarence Crump the previous year about 'press attacks through surrogate journalists', claims were planted in the Jamaican media that Crenston Boxhill was about to be ousted by a 'no-confidence' resolution. No such resolution surfaced. It was tosh.

Then came a letter from FIFA in February 2005 that simultaneously found its way to the Jamaican media. FIFA sought to block Boxhill's plan to sell and lease-back the Jamaican federation's offices in Kingston, in an attempt to reduce the debts Burrell had left behind him. Burrell had spent half of FIFA's US$1 million grant on the building.

'If it is confirmed that your federation in fact sells this building as part of the response to its current financial situation, please be advised that FIFA will consider this action to be a misuse of FIFA funds, and FIFA will ... take this matter up with all necessary bodies to take most severe measures against the JFF, including expulsion.'

The next day, on the eve of the federation's general meeting,

Horace Reid and another Burrell ally announced dramatically that they had been threatened with death if they turned up. Heroically, Reid said, 'I would much rather die for my principles and those things that I strongly believe in but I am deeply disappointed with that kind of skullduggery tactics. We have lost, it seems, all sense of decency and decorum in the football arena.'

In March 2005 the Jamaican federation lost patience with Burrell's sniping from the sidelines and issued a press statement accusing him of 'constantly undermining the organisation'. It went on, 'Captain Horace Burrell continues his sustained effort to seek to cast doubt on the current leadership of the JFF,' and reminded the country that Burrell's legacy was 'a heavily debt-ridden organisation and negotiated deals that limit the immediate possibilities for building a financially viable federation'.

By late 2005 Burrell's Captain's Bakery was sponsoring almost half of the island's parish football associations. On Christmas Eve he announced, 'I have been approached by people all around football ... If I am called on by my colleagues in the football fraternity for my leadership, I would not hesitate to offer myself.'

In early January 2006, as the annual meeting approached, Burrell continued in the same vein. 'If I am asked to assume the leadership of the JFF I would truly be honoured and would have no reservation about taking up the offer. Based on my past experiences and my successes as well as my contacts on the world stage, I know I am ready to make a success of the job.' President Boxhill riposted, 'The small group of detractors are trying hard but they are in it for personal reasons. They don't care about the development of the game in the country.'

Two days before the meeting, in an echo of the intervention 12 months earlier, FIFA wrote again to the JFF. This time, in a letter described by the local press as 'scathing' and 'stinging', FIFA instructed the JFF to provide 'detailed, legally relevant and complete information within five working days or the FIFA-funded Jamaica Goal Project will be cancelled'.

Boxhill's administration wanted to move the Goal project location from the site where Burrell and Blatter had broken the ground three years previously. According to FIFA's letter, 'the FIFA president was misled – and through that FIFA as a body'. Boxhill commented, 'All along we have been meeting the deadlines according to plans and we have been told that we are on track, so when I get a letter like this from the top, I was surprised and disappointed.'

The morning of the meeting the *Jamaica Observer* headline asked, 'Is this a stench from FIFA?' and answered, 'We are beginning to smell a rat – one that stinks to the heavens . . . the administration ought not to be undermined by international guerrilla tactics, which appears to be the case.'

That afternoon, when the no-confidence motion was tabled, Boxhill's opponents failed by 53–51 to win two-thirds of the vote and the motion fell. He commented, 'The election was between Burrell and football, and football has won.'

But Boxhill had only just started cleaning up the mess he inherited. He was unhappy with Jamaica's share of Carribean Football television rights arranged by Jack Warner. Boxhill wanted out of the deal, reckoning Jamaica would do better on the open market. Other Caribbean associations took courage from Jamaica's lead and said they might follow.

The first cracks were appearing in Warner's total grip on his empire and the assumption that he and Blatter would never be challenged.

The Caribbean's honest football enthusiasts had had enough of Jack and his big backers in Zurich. The empire was beginning to fight back.

_____

SEPP BLATTER BREAKS
MANDELA'S HEART

Twice!

BACK IN 1998, Blatter had torn African votes away from
Lennart Johansson by promising them the World Cup in 2006.
That promise, among others larded with bribes and inducements
from people who wanted Blatter elected, had given him the
presidency.

In early 2000, with the vote only months away on who was to
host 2006, it was time for Sepp Blatter to make good the pledge –
or start planning his retirement. If he wanted to hang on to those
50-plus African votes in the next presidential election, due in
Seoul in 2002, he had to be seen to be doing his utmost to steer
the tournament to South Africa. He'd made clear that he favoured
Nelson Mandela's rainbow nation over the other big gorilla in the
contest, Germany. Playing barely-noticed walk-on and walk-off
parts in the drama were England, Morocco and Brazil.

But if Blatter steered the tournament as promised to South Africa, then Germany might seek a harsh revenge, organising enough votes in Europe to push him out of the presidency. The challenge was to persuade South Africa and Germany that he supported *both* of them.

Jerome Champagne had the strategy according to my sources at Sunny Hill. Let everyone *believe* you're backing South Africa. Then, whatever happens, you hold the African votes. Tell the Germans you believe they are more capable of staging a successful competition. Then, whatever happens, they'll vote for you. Remind Franz Beckenbauer – not an official but hugely influential – and German executive committee member Gerhard Mayer-Vorfelder that you have to appear to be lobbying for South Africa. That way, you win long-term, whatever the result. Just pray you don't have to use your casting vote.

Nelson Mandela was South Africa's finest advocate. His people had won democracy but still, times were hard – unemployment stood at nearly 40 per cent. If his country won, said Mandela, 'It will lead to the uplifting of not only our people but will also contribute to the growth of our economy.'

His number crunchers said that hosting the tournament would create 130,000 new jobs and bring the government a tax windfall worth half a billion dollars. Who could say no to the Nobel Peace laureate when he said, 'The World Cup should be hosted by South Africa in 2006 and if that happened it would fulfill not only my dreams, but those of an entire nation.'

AFRICA HAD THE arguments, but they had fewer votes than Germany. The big continent had only four members in FIFA's ruling committee. Europe had eight of the 13 needed for victory in a straight vote. David Will from Scotland would back England on the first round but when they'd gone out and the serious voting started, he would re-join his UEFA allies.

It couldn't be any other way. Blatter had divided Europe in the presidential vote in 1998 and after that debacle, they knew they must vote as a block to regain credibility as the most powerful group in the game. They had to show their 52 members they had the clout to deliver a World Cup and the jobs and perks that would flow towards European officials.

The scrabble for the few floating votes intensified in the months before the decision, scheduled for the first week in July. Media mogul Leo Kirch put his chequebook behind the German bid. He already had the German television rights for the World Cup 2006 tournament and those rights would be worth a lot more if the games were held on German soil.

One of his subsidiary companies came up with a great idea. Have Germany's leading soccer club, Bayern Munich, play friendly games with Thailand, Malta, a Tunisian club and Trinidad. Pay each national association up to US$300,000 for the television rights to these games, regardless of whether anyone could be bothered to watch.

That made four voters happy. Malta's executive committee member Joseph Mifsud, Tunisia's Slim Aloulou, Trinidad's Jack Warner and Thailand's Worawi Makudi. 'Everything was cleanly done,' said former German star Gunter Netzer, a Kirch manager. 'The money was paid to the guest soccer federations and not to members of FIFA's executive committee.'

Nine days before the vote Germany's national security board met in private. The Chancellor and four other ministers agreed to reverse their policy on export of weapons and voted to deliver 1,200 anti-tank missiles to Saudi. Good news for Saudi's Abdullah Al-Dabal, a committee member with a World Cup vote to cast.

Germany was now so close to victory. The four votes in Asia –

from Saudi Arabia, South Korea, Thailand and Qatar – were in the bag. It was almost certain that the Asians, miffed with Blatter because they thought they deserved more World Cup slots, would vote against whoever was his favourite. That gave them 12 votes. One more would bring outright victory.

But Mandela wasn't going to be a walkover. Brazil admitted that its lethargic campaign was pointless and withdrew. The three Latin-American votes of Grondona, Teixeira and Leoz were pledged to Mandela. That put him on seven votes and catching up.

South Africa went to work charming Jack Warner. 'We have arranged a trip to one of our top game lodges, the famous Mala Mala,' promised a fax from South African bid team member Dr Robin Petersen. More good news was that 'Mr Mandela has expressed his wish to meet with you.' So apparently had President Mbeki.

When South Africa made Jack feel important enough he announced he was 'advising' England to withdraw. He would put his vote, Blazer's and Sasso's behind South Africa. Mandela, with Blatter's ordinary vote, had caught up to 11.

Then South Africa heard that the Oceania region had mandated its representative, 78-year-old New Zealander Charlie Dempsey, to vote their way. They'd made it! If Blatter kept his promise, spurned the Germans and gave his additional casting vote to South Africa, Mandela would be presenting the Cup in 2006 to the winners.

Mandela worked his heart out for his country. The old man got on the phone and campaigned to the end.

Sunny Hill, 6 July 2000. Morocco was chucked out in the first round of voting, followed by England. Mandela, who'd stayed home surely began to smile as the news came through from Zurich. Here was the third round . . . here was the result . . . and they'd lost!

What was wrong with the numbers? There was one missing. Confusion. Why was there no 12–12 tie? Where was Charlie, the man with the mandate? How could South Africa lose 11 votes to 12?

Blatter's casting vote hadn't been needed. Had Charlie died?

Somewhere high in the sky, Charlie Dempsey was alive and smiling and en route for a round of golf in Singapore. He hadn't voted. When the reporters caught up with him he told them, 'I have no regrets about what I did – none whatsoever. I had very strong reasons, but I'm not going into them.'

He muttered that he'd been threatened by 'influential European interests' not to vote for South Africa. He complained about being called early one morning by Mandela, a call most people could only dream of. How could this kind of pressure worry or frighten tough, Glasgow-born Charlie?

Some time later Dempsey was reported as saying: 'I was getting pressured from both sides to vote for them, so I abstained . . . The crux was I spoke to my lawyers in Auckland . . . I have the letter here that was sent to me and they said don't vote because it doesn't matter who gets in, you will be accused of accepting favours and bribes.'

Blatter hadn't been forced to make a choice. Africa believed he had tried his best for them. Europe had what it wanted and would return the favour with votes for Sepp later. The result was a triumph for him.

Two years after Charlie's abstention, despite the international scorn that it had brought down on him, FIFA made him an honorary life member, guaranteeing first-class travel, tickets and hospitality at future World Cups.

Warner, who had tied his reputation to personally handing Mandela the competition, was less forgiving. He wrote to Dempsey a month after the vote, to 'formally distance myself from you'. Dempsey had earlier agreed to track down some books for his friend Jack. 'Don't bother,' said Jack. 'I wish to inform you that I do not wish your assistance neither now or in the future. However I do take this opportunity to wish you the best of everything in the winter of your football career.'

Perugia, August 2003. 'Blatter knows that it was only me and Bin Hammam who helped him secure his post as FIFA President,' boasted the lean, lightly bearded Arab midfielder. After a training session with his Serie A team at their home in the medieval city of Perugia, a 170 km dash in his Ferrari down the autostrada from Rome, Al-Saadi Gadhafi told the press, 'Blatter came to me and asked me to help him against Hayatou. It was me and Bin Hammam who should get all the credit for him winning the presidential elections.'

The 30-year-old billionaire, who declined his wages as the club teetered on the edge of relegation, was talking up his country's bid to host 2010, the first World Cup that had been promised exclusively to an African nation. After Germany won the tournament of 2006, Blatter and his committee had ruled that in future the World Cup would be rotated through the continents and for 2010, only African nations need apply.

But which one? Libya, Tunisia, Morocco and Egypt and South Africa all wanted it. And Blatter wanted all of them to think they were in with a chance.

Critics had laughed at Libya's plans: they didn't have a single world-class stadium. Gadhafi insisted, 'It is not about infrastructure, it is all about relations and our relations with the FIFA people is very strong. After all, they owe us a lot. I am sure that Libya will win.'

His father, Colonel Moammar Gadhafi, autocratic ruler of Libya since seizing power in 1970, had promised as much as US$14 billion to spend on new stadiums and anything else that would indulge his third son who was president of their country's football association. And, whatever the critics might think of Libya's chances, Blatter and his friends were always happy to talk to the boy.

'I strongly believe that the personal relations I personally enjoy with FIFA's leading predominant figures will be a boost,' said young Gadhafi. 'We have fabulous relationships with Mr Blatter, Julio Grondona and Franz Beckenbauer. This will be vital for our campaign.' President Blatter had even turned up in Tripoli as a guest in August 2003 when Juventus, in which Al-Saadi owned a five per cent stake, beat Parma 2–1 in the Italian Super Cup, a pre-season warm-up.

Coach Francesco Scoglio led the Libyan national team to a string of impressive victories. And then, 'They sacked me because I wouldn't let him [Al-Saadi] play,' Scoglio told *Corriere dello Sport*. 'And I would never have let him play, even for a minute. As a footballer he's worthless. With him in the squad, we were losing. When he left, we won.'

Al-Saadi wasn't exactly a star at Perugia, despite recruiting as his personal coach the disgraced Canadian sprinter, Ben Johnson. Young Gadhafi still hadn't made it off the bench when he tested positive for a steroid. He said it must be the medicine a German doctor gave him for his back problems. Or an Italian doctor. Or a Libyan doctor. Perugia's boss blamed 'political reasons'. Al-Saadi was suspended for three months.

When he finally got on the pitch, Italian radio listeners voted him the second worst player in the country. The best quote he was going to paste in his Perugia cuttings book was, 'On the field, as in life, he mostly hangs around, waiting to be served.'

There wasn't much point inviting reporters to check out Libya's facilities because there weren't any. Libya packed its World Cup internet site with pictures of Roman remains, camels and stunning desert views. Anyone for beach football?

Al-Saadi held some press conferences in Switzerland, accompanied by Libyan reporters who greeted his every utterance with loud, sustained applause. 'We do not have any diseases here, unlike in other African states, and security is of the highest level,' was one of his winning claims.

The Libyans had good reason to believe that at least one of the executive committee's 24 votes would come their way. In 1995 Ricardo Teixeira and his Brazilian soccer confederation accepted half a million dollars from the Libyans to take Brazil's World Cup winning team to play in Tripoli. Another half a million bucks, paid by an agent of Libya, landed in an offshore account in the Bahamas belonging to the then Brazilian coach Mário Jorge Zagallo. The match wasn't played and the kindly Libyans didn't ask for their million back. Probing reporters acquired the documents and asked Zagallo, what had he done to deserve all this moolah?

It was for 'a newspaper interview', said Zagallo. That makes Tripoli's *Daily Soccer News* the world's biggest-spending paper!

It didn't take long to work out that all the money Libya might promise to FIFA wouldn't be enough. So Libya joined forces with neighbours Tunisia, another World Cup low-hoper with a wretched civil rights record. (*Reporters Sans Frontiers* ranks countries by press freedoms. Bumping along the bottom are North Korea at 139, and Tunisia and Libya at 128 and 129.)

When the pair announced their bid, Blatter hesitated. He needed lots of runners and riders to put on a show the media would talk up for him. Co-hosting was the last thing he wanted; Korea-Japan nearly broke the bank. Sepp didn't want to hurt Al-Saadi's feelings or upset Tunisian President Ben Ali so he said, if the other three rival African bids collapsed, this could be a great idea.

Sepp Blatter hasn't much interest in the nature of regimes hoping to host the World Cup (democracy, autocracy, who cares?), but he prefers them to be stable. Ben Ali, who'd come to power in 1987, struck a blow for stability, persuading his parliament to extend his presidency all the way to the 2010 World Cup.

New York-based Human Rights Watch warned that repression was on the rise in Tunisia. The regime was firing outspoken judges and favouring judges who turned a blind eye to torture allegations. Was Blatter concerned? On a flying visit in late 2003 he asserted, 'Your sports infrastructure is impressive.'

So too was Tunisia's performance in the African Nations Cup the following year. The first goal in their 2–1 defeat of Morocco in the final was scored by Brazilian-born Francileudo dos Santos. He'd got his Tunisian passport just before the finals. The winning goal came from a cross by his similarly re-badged compatriot Clayton.

At the Nations Cup in January 2004 we reporters searched for Tunisia's spokesmen and couldn't find them. Later that month Blatter – with masses of free publicity under his bed for 2010 – announced the inevitable: joint bids could not be entertained.

In March 2004, Sepp Blatter dropped in on Egypt – another tail-ender in the rankings of human rights and press freedoms – with his friend Mohamed Bin Hammam from Qatar. They spent two days enjoying the pyramids, the Sphinx sound and light show, and the warm respect of crowds of genuine people eager to welcome the World Cup to Egypt.

No-one appreciates a generous welcome more than Jack Warner. He encouraged, then gladly took up an invitation to bring the Trinidad team to Egypt for a friendly. 'Your country is more than qualified to host the World Cup,' he told his hosts, which didn't quite tally with the view from FIFA's evaluation people, who said the Egyptian budget 'requires complete revision'.

'WE WILL HELP to eliminate AIDS in Africa, improve education and tackle terrorism,' announced Saad Kettani, leader of Morocco's bid. 'Our scheme is called "Football Without Frontiers" and is aimed at using sport in general, and football in particular, as a means to fight despair all over a continent wracked by poverty and disease.'

It was touching that Mr Kettani, a wealthy banker, showed Morocco's concern for its less well-off neighbours in Africa. If Morocco won the right to stage the tournament, he said, they'd pay for the whole event and transfer the FIFA contribution of hundreds of millions of dollars, into this special fund for Africa. 'Yes,' Kettani insisted, 'Morocco could use the finals as an instrument of peace.'

That raised a bitter laugh among the 150,000 people in the refugee camps in the Sahara desert, driven into exile by Moroccan troops since 1975. Morocco is the only country in Africa that doesn't belong to the African Union, jumping out before it could be pushed in 1985 because it refuses to grant independence to the last remaining colony in Africa.

On the southern border of Morocco and running down the Atlantic coast is the territory of Western Sahara, slightly larger than Britain, invaded by Morocco in 1975 when the colonial power Spain withdrew. The International Court of Justice backed the people's right to independence, but Morocco built a 2,700 km sand wall, laced with landmines, down the centre of the country and proceeded to loot Western Sahara's rich resources of fisheries, oil, and phosphate.

Mariem Hmada, Minister of Culture and Sport for the exiled Saharawi Arab Democratic Republic, wrote to FIFA claiming that 'Morocco continues occupying illegally territories of Western Sahara, subjecting the people to forced disappearance, killings and summary executions, arbitrary detentions, torture, ill treatment, and summary trials.' Amnesty International regularly express concern about torture and forced confessions.

In January 2004 the Moroccan bid team was flying in teams of sports reporters and explaining to them their country's plan to bring peace to the continent. At the same time in Bradford, an immigration appeals tribunal granted Saharawi activist Aicha Dahane political asylum in Britain, ruling that her fear of persecution in Morocco was 'well-founded'.

Reporters flew home and filed glowing reports on the Moroccan bid. Saad Kettani was 'charismatic'. The plan to house the FIFA committee in a hotel Winston Churchill was said to have loved was newsworthy.

Kettani was said to be trusted by young King Mohamed and that's hardly surprising since the banker had just sold a large chunk of his businesses to a private trust owned by the royal family. The Moroccan media, mindful that their country lies at a lowly 89th in the ranks of countries with free media, reported cautiously that the sale concentrated most of the banking industry in royal hands, along with crucial stakes in other major industries. A successful World Cup bid would make the royal family and the nation's elite even richer than they already were.

Hobbling Morocco's bid was their terrorism problem. In May 2003 five young men killed themselves and 45 others in suicide bombings aimed at Jewish and other targets in Casablanca.

Moroccan terrorists were being blamed for other international outrages.

There was one man who might turn things around for Morocco.

'They know I'm Jewish, and I think it speaks volumes about what a special place Morocco is. It's a beacon of light in the Muslim world,' insisted Alan Rothenberg, consultant to Kettani's team, playing down the terrorism fears. Rothenberg was a fantastic asset, a FIFA insider who'd led the team evaluating bids for World Cup 2006.

The late Tony Banks, former UK sports minister, called Rothenberg's assessment, 'an absolute stitch-up . . . if he believed our football facilities were inferior to the Germans and only equal to South Africa then he clearly believed that Elvis Presley was alive and living on the moon.'

WHO WAS Sheikh Saleh Kamil backing? The short, 62-year-old Saudi billionaire with two wives, one thin moustache and a simple lifestyle had holiday and oil investments in Morocco, tourist developments in Tunisia and banks in Egypt. If his Dallah Albaraka Group hadn't already got a branch in Libya, it probably soon would have. The Sheikh's businesses were the biggest employers in Saudi and he was in Forbes' list of the super-rich.

He launched the first private television channel in the Middle East and is said to own the television rights to most Arab films ever made. Through his satellite station the Arab Radio and Television network, Kamil sponsors the Arab Champions' League, owns regional rights to the English Premier League and the German Bundesliga and has learned much from Rupert Murdoch about converting free television into pay television. 'If we don't give the poor free bread,' he asks, 'why should we give them free premium matches?' Kamil badly needs sport to screen because regional cultural inhibitions stop him showing Hollywood blockbusters with hints of cleavage and more.

Sheikh Kamil is one of the more important off-pitch players in the World Cup. In the summer of 2003 this Saudi businessman used his Rotterdam subsidiary to buy a 20 per cent stake in the Zug, Switzerland, Infront company that had acquired the rights to screen soccer's greatest competition. They came from the collapsed Leo Kirch Munich-based media empire that had in turn picked up the remainder of the television rights in the wreckage of ISL in Zug.

The German news magazine *Spiegel* claimed that Blatter had personally introduced Sheikh Kamil to former German star Gunter Netzer and the other owners of Infront. That was the least Blatter could do after the Sheikh, a friend of Qatar's Mohamed Bin Hammam, had so kindly lent him a Gulfstream from his hangar full of private jets to campaign for the FIFA presidency in Africa in 2002.

According to *Spiegel*, Kamil said, 'We hope that we will not only get the World Cup rights for 2010 but for ever more.' With his business connections to the Moroccan royal family it's reasonable to assume that Kamil was backing King Mohamed and fellow banker Saad Kettani. A World Cup staged in the Arab world would surely make it possible for him to jack up his charges.

ONE CANDIDATE for 2010 had something Jack Warner wanted more than anything else. South Africa had Nelson Mandela. And if they wanted his vote, Jack had to have his pound of Mandela's flesh.

Ten of FIFA's committee attended the inauguration of President Thabo Mbeki's second term of office in late April. Jack and his party got better seats than some world leaders and they even wangled a tour of Mbeki's private residence. There's a happy snap of the occasion: Warner, gold bangles jangling, pumps Mbeki's hand, reluctant to let go. You can almost read the thought bubble above a grinning Mbeki's head. 'I can just about keep smiling if this guy brings us the World Cup.'

Jack spent a night in the Presidential Suite that had been Mandela's. Sleeping in Mandela's bed! What more did the South Africans have to do?

Much more. Warner demanded an hour of Mandela's time and promptly invited him and fellow Nobel Peace laureate Archbishop Desmond Tutu to visit Trinidad. 'Just as I was received here, he can expect a most hearty welcome by the people of Trinidad & Tobago,' Warner told a reporter. Did Jack now presume to be Mandela's equal?

Mandela was 85 years old and his doctors wanted him to cut back on his international travelling. Desmond Tutu, 72, was having treatment for cancer. If Mandela and Tutu really, really wanted South Africa to host the World Cup Jack's invitation was one they literally could not refuse . . .

'IT'S A PITY that Nelson Mandela has got caught up in something like this,' said Trinidad & Tobago prime minister Patrick Manning. 'This visit is being unnecessarily politicised.' Manning leads the PNM party that routed Jack Warner's friends in the UNC government. Now Jack had found a headline-grabbing way to take the sweetest of revenges.

Who would greet superstar Mandela and share the blaze of flash bulbs when his plane touched down in Trinidad? Jack

Warner. Who would decide Mandela's itinerary? Jack Warner. Who would draw up the lists of people whose hands Mandela must shake if he wanted the World Cup? Jack Warner.

That's what Jack wanted but Trinidad's government weren't having it; a former state president must be greeted at the airport by the prime minister. 'No,' said one of Warner's sidekicks. 'He is our guest. We are not budging on Mr Warner greeting Mr Mandela, after which, he can be introduced to whoever else is at the airport.'

Who would drive Mandela into Port of Spain? 'Manning can come to the airport, but we will take Mandela,' added Warner's man. Warner demanded that Mandela address both houses of parliament, discovering later that only heads of state had this privilege.

'The government represents the Republic of Trinidad & Tobago, I am not aware that the Republic of CONCACAF exists,' snorted Manning. Warner had to back down when the South African government tip-toed in saying that Mandela was making an official, not a private visit.

Mandela was helped out of his chair at his home in Johannesburg and handed his walking stick. He went out to do battle again for his beloved country. He arrived late at night at Piarco airport and Manning, looking overawed, was first to greet him. Then came Warner pumping Mandela's hand and beaming gleefully as the photographers snapped away. With the support of a carved, wooden stick Mandela made his way down the red carpet. Then he was swept off to his bed. Archbishop Tutu had arrived earlier to an ecstatic welcome from local ministers and congregations.

The next day Warner planned to take Mandela to lunch at the swanky Trinidad Country Club. Local activists who had campaigned on the streets against apartheid in past years protested that the club had historically been a white enclave that barred blacks and Jack had to back down.

SEPP BLATTER wanted his pound of Mandela flesh. He rushed to Trinidad and elbowed Jack out of the way to take centre spot the day after Mandela's arrival. Sepp pumped the old man's hand when he arrived at the Oval, the largest cricket ground in the West Indies, to be publicly exhibited. Blatter had announced a few months earlier that they had so much in common 'such as our work for the good of the world's young people, for example'. Another FIFA man putting himself on a pedastal with Mandela. Was there room for them all? In high spirits up on the stage with him were Warner and Chuck Blazer and their hangers-on.

Frail Nelson Mandela was helped by an aide up on to the stage. He told the huge crowd that he had defied his doctor's orders to end all international travel to come to Trinidad & Tobago. 'This is my last trip abroad – I am here to plead,' he said. After 15 minutes he had to leave to rest in his hotel room.

Jack snubbed the government's offer of a free state reception where ordinary Trinidadians might catch a glimpse of Mandela and instead took him off to the Joao Havelange Centre of Excellence and charged £100 a plate to one thousand people. Mandela made his speech sitting down and had to stop after seven minutes.

Warner had insisted that once his two elderly captives had been shown off in Trinidad, they must fly onwards to the island of Grenada. If they really, really wanted his vote and the two others he could deliver, they must plead their case yet again, and this time in front of Jack's CONCACAF congress. Two of the world's most loved figures, symbols of goodness and heroic struggle would have to shake hands with Horace Burrell, and Chet Greene and the rest of Warner's lieutenants.

Then came the sad news that Mandela's first wife, Evelyn, had died. Mandela had to go home for the funeral. Desmond Tutu travelled alone to Grenada for further exhibition in Warner's circus.

Bribes to FIFA officials was usually a taboo subject but in the week before the vote, the South Africans, probably acting on their own secret intelligence, spoke out. 'If we have to choose between corrupting people and losing, let's just lose,' said Essop Pahad, one of Mbeki's ministers. 'We're not going to give any money to anyone under the table.'

Zurich, 14 May 2004. President Mbeki arrived with former President and Nobel laureate F W de Klerk at the Dolder Grand Hotel soon after seven in the morning, the day before the decision. Mandela followed shortly after. They must have been tired, travelling all night but as they checked in Warner and Blazer were on their heels in the lobby.

Warner said he needed another round of pleading because, 'Unfortunately, CONCACAF is still undecided.' Adoring his place in the spotlight Warner added, 'It's an historic occasion for me. In some ways it will decide the future of one country.' He got another hour's face time with Mandela.

Alan Rothenberg couldn't resist striking one last blow for Morocco, and he didn't care who it hurt. 'Everyone on the executive committee knows who Mandela is and what he has said and done and achieved,' he told reporters. 'We all appreciate him and his place in history, but that is it – Mandela is not a man of the future. He is a man of history.'

So was Alan's client's bid. Morocco went down 10–14 to the

South Africans on the first round. South Africa had won the World Cup of 2010.

And Blatter had emerged from two consecutive battles to host the tournament stronger than ever.

The Tunisians, Egyptians and Moroccans congratulated South Africa and went back to wondering if they had spent their budgets wisely. People swapped stories about who among Blatter's associates had pocketed the biggest bribes, who'd taken the money, pledged their support and then voted another way, who'd crossed the street for a bigger bucket of swill. Then there was the one about the executive committee member who'd asked for US$10 million. Not for himself, you understand. Just US$1 million would do for him. The rest he'd trade for votes among his colleagues.

Egyptian reporters were tipped off that during a behind-closed doors session of a parliamentary investigation into why they failed to get a single vote, bid leader Ali El-Din Hillal claimed he'd been asked for bribes amounting to US$67 million. Someone else in the bid team said this was news to him.

Libya went out in the dying days because their bid wasn't credible. 'The poor countries, which form the majority of FIFA's 204 members, should now seriously think of forming their own FIFA which can meet their ambitions,' screamed Libya's *Al-Shams* newspaper.

The daily *Al-Zahf al-Akhdar* dismissed Blatter's committee as 'a real mafia, with all its corruption, conspiracies inside clubs, drug and steroids trafficking, money laundering and secret gambling. That is the disease of FIFA.' Al-Saadi Gadhafi had discovered that courting President Blatter, helping out in his election campaign and inviting him to Tripoli had won him nothing more than a few headlines, mostly bad ones.

Four months later President Mbeki announced that South Africa was officially recognising the Saharawi Arab Democratic

Republic as the rightful government of Western Sahara. 'For us not to recognise SADR is to become an accessory to the denial of the people their right to self-determination,' he said. 'This would constitute a grave and unacceptable betrayal of our own struggle, of the solidarity Morocco extended to us, and our commitment to respect the Charter of the United Nations and the African Union.'

THE MONTH after his arduous trip to Trinidad, Nelson Mandela invited some journalists to his home and told them: 'I am turning 86 in a few weeks' time and that's a longer life than most people are granted. I am confident that nobody present here today will accuse me of selfishness if I ask to spend time, while I am still in good health, with my family, my friends – and also with myself.' He wanted to be the one 'calling you to ask whether I would be welcome, rather than being called upon to do things and participate in events'.

Then he said, 'My appeal therefore is: Don't call me, I will call you.'

POISONING, DRUG-BUST
AND KIDNAP

Meet Blatter's new PR man

Madrid, 18 December 2002. The FIFA family was meeting at
the Ritz for another football-foots-the-bill shindig. This time
the excuse was the World Player of the Year Gala. There was
Jack Warner whispering to Chuck Blazer in one corner of the
lobby, Ricardo Teixeira muttering to Julio Grondona in another.
Former International Olympic Committee president Juan Antonio
Samaranch was sporting his favourite shade of blue shirt, but
no jackboots today. But who's this? A new face in the crowd,
and he was looking my way.

'Are you Andrew Jennings?'

In his casual sports coat, with gleaming skull, straggly strands
of neck hair spraying out over his collar, middle-aged jowls
and tired walrus moustache, he might have been a racetrack tout,
hoping to sell me a tip for the next gallop, not a patron of the
glitzy Ritz.

'Who are you?'

'I'm Peter Hargitay,' said the gravelly mittel-European accent, 'special advisor to President Blatter. Can we have lunch some time? Here's my card.'

Mr Peter J Hargitay, 'Special Advisor in the Presidential Office', it said. His business was the European Consultancy Network Ltd with offices in Noel Street, in London's Soho; and his company, also, 'Advisors to the FIFA President.' It looked impressive.

We met in London at the *El Pirata* tapas bar and Blatter's new special adviser told me his life story. His family had fled Hungary in 1956 and he'd been brought up in Switzerland. He'd worked as a hard-nosed reporter for international publications that he never got around to naming, and he said the word 'fuck' a lot, as some hard-nosed reporters do. At some point he'd become a 'corporate affairs adviser', he'd worked at the very highest level and now he was working for Sepp.

Peter is the kind of PR man who knows how to flatter a journalist. He was most impressed by my work, kept referring to me respectfully as a 'senior writer', and he was so excited to be with me that, without warning, he flipped open his mobile phone and took a photograph – *click!* – inches from my face. I didn't like that. He gave me his word he would delete the picture.

When I expressed an opinion, he agreed with it. I mentioned a particular lazy reporter who liked to be spoon-fed. Absolutely. Lazy, spoonfed. Peter thought so too. About Jack Warner, what a problem for FIFA's image! Indeed, yes. Peter agreed. He even told me that he thought some of Jean-Marie Weber's ISL group executives would likely be indicted for allegedly stealing the Globo money.

Peter gossiped about his new colleagues. He hadn't much time for the young PR man Markus Siegler. As for Blatter's marketing advisor, Guido Tognoni, 'don't expect him to be around a lot longer', and Peter was right. Thirteen weeks later Guido was out of a job. So Hargitay knew his stuff. He even knew (and hardly anyone knew this) that Blatter was about to marry his girlfriend, a dolphin trainer, and she was going to move into his home with her floppy-eared hound called Queenie.

Peter planned to assemble for FIFA an 'international media advisory group' and invited me to be the first to sign up. I told Peter about times past when agents of IOC President Samaranch, infuriated by my disclosures about his members' corruption and his own fascist past, resorted to dirty tricks against me and my sources. Peter seemed shocked. Then we left together, sharing a cab. Kindly, he picked up the fare. I looked forward to our promised meetings in the New Year.

WE'D ONLY just met, yet Peter Hargitay gave every impression of caring for me, for my health, for my loved ones. In warm emails he encouraged me to 'rest a bit, surrounded by your family'. When Christmas was over he was back in touch, wishing me a happy New Year but 'above all, good health and much satisfaction in your professional endeavours'. It was a welcome change from the usually chilly Zurich press office.

My new friend hadn't rested over the Christmas holiday. 'I have given some more thought to the topics we discussed and I feel rather comfortable with the idea of the Media Advisory Board.' Peter assured me that his priority was 'to guarantee your complete editorial independence at all times'.

He seemed to feel personally responsible for FIFA's good name. 'In my opinion, there cannot (and must not) be any "hostile media,"' he said. It led to 'misunderstandings and possibly the wrong interpretation of "facts" obtained from alternative sources'. Unofficial sources, whistleblowers and leakers just got in the way of the truth. Peter was going to heal wounds, bring us together – and get me great stories.

Reporting FIFA would become much easier for me. 'You would not have to "chase" the information any longer, nor have to rely on secondary sources in your reporting.' This was going to save me so much time and effort. I could sit and wait for Peter to call me with terrific stories to put in the paper. 'We could re-activate the dialogue in early January,' he told me.

Maybe he could help me. There was something I'd been trying to get hold of. So I asked Peter for it: the Zurich magistrate's report of the investigation of Sepp Blatter. I waited. And waited. Sadly, Peter said FIFA couldn't part with their copy. He said, 'I feel very comfortable with the exchange of opinions we have had thus far and look forward to further intellectually challenging, thus rewarding exchanges.'

Peter told me FIFA was pleased I was writing this book, and could arrange to 'provide access for you in Zurich, including the President, without which – direct access that is – any book would be what the French call "hearsay", no?' At last! Blatter would take me into his confidence, tell me all the things he would never reveal to any other reporter. What a triumph for me. I'd win all the awards and make piles of money.

'A CHILD IS BORN. It is past midnight inside the dank labour room at the Sultania Janada Hospital, Bhopal. Three attendants wash the tiny infant and hold him up to give his mother her first glimpse.

'"Tumhara ladka paida hua hai (you have a son)," says one nurse as she pats the child to make him cry. There is no response. In the dim light, the skin of the child looks macerated and bluish. A senior doctor is called in. He looks down at the curled figure, asks for the mother's medical record and scrawls in the column for details of the birth: "Stillborn boy weighing four pounds, born to the mother."

'Outside there is silence as the father looks expectantly at the white-clothed figures washing hands in the waiting room. Then comes the sound of weeping from beyond the green curtains of the labour room.

'"Yeh bhi gas kand ka baccha paida hua hai (here is another child of the gas tragedy)," says the nurse as she shows the father the shrivelled face of his newborn.'

This was what reporter Ritu Sarin found when she visited Bhopal, capital city of Madhya Pradesh, for *Sunday* magazine in July 1985, seven months after the world's worst industrial accident.

Greenpeace estimates that 16,000 people have died and 500,000 more have been impaired in the twenty years since the discharge of tonnes of toxic gas from a plant operated by America's Union Carbide company. The disaster's victims continue to fight to establish Union Carbide's liability and obtain proper compensation.

When the polluters looked around to find someone to put a happy gloss on the tragedy, they called in Peter Hargitay. He's proud of his work. On his PR firm's website in 2002 he boasted, 'Some of our phrases have gained international recognition for their depth, unexpected message or plain content. "We accept moral responsibility," was the motto of a world-wide telecast when thousands perished in a terrifying accident. With that, we created a motto even the corporate lawyers could live with ... because it expressed the grief but rejected prima facie corporate and financial responsibility.'

* * *

WHEN the white supremacists in South Africa needed oil to fuel their apartheid regime a man called Marc Rich came to the rescue. The rogue commodities dealer, a fugitive from American justice and on the FBI's '10 Most Wanted' list, Rich was happy to bust international sanctions. From his hideaway in the Swiss canton of Zug, he bought oil from Nigeria and shipped it south.

In the 1980s he was convicted in New York, in his absence, of tax evasion and racketeering. Eventually he paid a bill of US$133 million but in 2001 New York State sought a further US$137 million. Mayor Rudolph Giuliani, said 'It was the biggest tax evasion case in United States history.'

Peter Hargitay made good money talking up Mr Rich. When I asked President Blatter's advisor about those days, he said Rich, 'was charged with tax evasion, which is a criminal offence in the USA but not in Switzerland'.

Hargitay moved from promoting the lovable aspects of sanction-busting Marc Rich to producing the musical *King*, based on the life of Martin Luther King, at London's Piccadilly Theatre. Hargitay told me, 'It closed after approximately three months with all bills paid.' Actually, the show opened on 23 April 1990 and closed on 26 May.

In 1995 the Zurich *Blick* alleged that Hargitay had been involved in a stock-selling racket in Hungary. Peter told me he was Hungary's Honorary Consul in Switzerland so he'd 'made a lot of enemies'. One of them was 'a Communist Army colonel caught running a pyramid scheme'. To save his neck he claimed that 'my Hungarian Consultancy – not I – had sold him shares that it subsequently never delivered. Later, the man went to jail. I did not.'

Peter told me the reporter behind the hostile article was biased because Peter had turned down his application for a job.

Peter got another run of bad luck in August 1995 when Jamaican detectives seized cocaine on a ship belonging to a

Hargitay company. The local press reported 16 kg. Peter says, 'Seven kilos of sugar and half a kilo of something mixed with a little bit of cocaine.' He was briefly locked up, tried and cleared.

Jamaican newspapers quoted Hargitay claiming to be a 'former diplomat and a member of the Swiss Army's intelligence arm'. They had Hargitay blaming his problems on the US government because he'd refused to help them kidnap Marc Rich.

In a letter to Jamaica's *Herald* J Michael Houlahan, Director of the US Information Service said, 'Mr Hargitay's self-serving, ludicrous accusations linking himself and the CIA in an alleged 1980s kidnapping plot involving an internationally known tax fraud felon are presented without a single bit of supporting evidence. It would appear instead that the organised campaign of vilification is being run by Mr Hargitay.'

A false imprisonment and malicious prosecution suit by Hargitay against the Jamaican government drags on, he tells me.

There burst upon the internet a previously unknown organisation, *The ADHOC Group for Human Rights*. 'We are,' it announced, 'a group of investigative writers, attorneys-at-law, priests and nuns, housewives and university professors, musicians and composers, managers and entertainers, students and teachers, adolescents and grey panthers, homosexuals and heterosexuals, believers and atheists.' Sadly, none of them felt able to disclose their names although the 'UK Liaison Office' was in Linden Gardens in London's upscale district of Notting Hill, coincidentally the home of Hargitay's son Steven.

At the heart of the website was an appeal for money, to be sent to an account in the village of Allschwil, near Basel. Potential donors were offered options. 'Don't just sit there and consume until you reach mental obesity ... Drop us a line if you want to exchange your La-Zee-Boy ride for a rough ride and a reality-check ... Or get fat and ugly and drop dead with heart disease.'

But they were toughies, no doubt about that. 'Once we have unearthed injustice in any given State that claims to be a democracy, we bring it to the open and are not choosy about our means, nor are we civil and nice. We collect information . . . We invade a system of injustice and operate from within the eye of the cyclone . . . We pull the rug under corrupt feet that dance to bribery . . . We investigate the persecutors and publish their foreign bank accounts.'

Hargitay didn't reveal how he got access to private bank account records.

As for the Bhopal tragedy, Marc Rich and the coke bust in Jamaica, that was 'dated material of no relevance to anybody, other than those who cherish gossip and strive on dirt'. All Peter sought was generating trust and understanding between the international media, FIFA and his client Mr Blatter.

CHARM AND DESTABILISE

Hargitay brings the press into line

IN MID-JANUARY 2003, Peter Hargitay sent an email inviting me to attend a 'media round table' with no less a person than Sepp Blatter. The venue, a swish hotel in London's Park Lane. Peter said, 'This first of a series of such talks aims at "de-mystifying" issues and to offer relevant information about anything you might find worthwhile, and which is of importance to FIFA and its President.' It was going to be an 'ongoing and meaningful dialogue . . . we are inviting but a few leading authors.'

And another thing, the Zurich public prosecutor's investigation had found that 'All allegations against FIFA's President were proven wrong in every respect.'

One evening the next week I turned up at the Metropolitan Hotel with the other 'leading authors', sports reporters from the *Daily Telegraph, Guardian, Financial Times, Reuters, Scotsman* and Irish *Sunday Independent*. Peter's son Steven shepherded us up to a tenth-floor meeting room with gigantic windows and wonderful views over Hyde Park at dusk.

The president bustled in followed by spokesman Markus Siegler carrying the mandatory bag of giveaway Adidas footballs.

There was so much nice chat I might have dozed off. Instead I asked Blatter what he was going to do about the vote-rigging at those FIFA Congresses in 1996 and 1998.

The friendly smile fell off Blatter's face, clanging noisily onto the floor. He spluttered, 'I was not involved in this matter but have been aware of the publicity about it. Perhaps mistakes have been made in the past and action needs to be taken. Perhaps we should have opened an investigation on these matters before, but it is not too late to do so now.' He said the allegations would now be referred to FIFA's Disciplinary Committee. At last.

I said, 'Presumably Mr Burrell will have to excuse himself from the disciplinary committee?' (It was Burrell's girlfriend who'd sat in for Haiti's Dr Jean-Marie Kyss in 1996.) Blatter said, 'He will definitely not be in this case, as a member of the committee.'

The meeting ended, the reporters trooped out and did Blatter kick Siegler's arse all the way back to Zurich? Perhaps, but not before Siegler had issued a press release, congratulating FIFA and its president on this Hargitay initiative. He had Blatter saying, 'When I spoke of transparency after my re-election in Seoul last year, it was not merely hollow rhetoric, but a promise that I shall keep.' He added, 'Neither FIFA nor its President have anything to hide, nor do they wish to.'

I wrote a story for the *Daily Mail* saying the disciplinary committee was at last going to investigate those vote-rigging scandals in Zurich and Paris. I quoted Blatter, saying that Burrell would be kept out of this investigation.

Next morning, in thundered an email from Siegler. 'President

Blatter never said that Captain Burrell would be kept away from that [investigation] at the Disciplinary Committee. He did not mention any names at all.' Siegler copied this message to Burrell in Jamaica.

I played back my tape:

Jennings: 'Presumably Mr Burrell will have to excuse himself from the disciplinary committee?'

Blatter: 'He will definitely not be in this case, as a member of the committee.'

The next week I offered Siegler my dossier of interview notes, documents and video tapes proving without any doubt both episodes of vote-stealing. Siegler didn't want them. I asked how the evidence would be assembled and who would do it? Who would take depositions, who would list the suspects, how could FIFA ensure an impartial probe when at least three members of the executive committee – Blatter, Warner and Blazer – might, potentially, be involved? Siegler wouldn't tell me.

Then Peter was back in touch, calling me 'dear man' and telling me his latest idea. He knew an investigative reporter in Jamaica. I should hand over all my research on Burrell. I declined.

WAR LOOMED. It was March 2003. American and British troops were poised to invade Iraq. Who could stop the carnage? Peter Hargitay had a peace-plan.

He booked a room in London and gathered together the potential peaceniks: Charles Clarke, then British Education Secretary, Sepp Blatter, Swiss Ambassador Dr Bruno Spinner and three cheerleaders, all from Swiss businesses. From English soccer came three chairmen, Geoff Thompson of the English FA, John Madejski from Reading and Daniel Levy from Spurs. A couple of commercial lawyers filled more seats together with an old friend of Peter's, BBC Arts Editor Claire Lewis, and she roped in BBC television journalist Mark Gregory.

Other doves-in-waiting were Richard Pulford of The Society of London Theatres, Leo Cavendish, an old friend of Peter's and a director of his PR firm, the European Consultancy Network, and Marc Berlin of the theatrical business London Management Ltd and again, a director of Hargitay's ECN Ltd.

Markus rushed out a quickie release headed 'FIFA President's round table assesses sport's role in defusing political tension.' Present were 'prominent figures from business, the arts, politics and sports business [who] sought to identify ways in which sport, and in particular football, could help to defuse social and political tension'.

Markus said that 'Charles Clarke praised FIFA for its efforts to harness the power of the game to increase understanding among people around the world. He also congratulated FIFA President Blatter on his initiative to hold such round table discussions.'

This was on 17 March 2003. Just 48 hours later, after Charles Clarke had voted in Cabinet for war, the Tomahawk missiles rained down on Baghdad.

Meanwhile Peter launched a new website. Out went his 'European Communications & Research Think Tank' that delivered 'sensitive investigative data to clients'.

In came his London-based 'European Consultancy Network' that boasted, 'A new attitude is the key. And so are the "unofficial means" by which relevant information can be obtained. Is being obtained, daily, hourly, by the minute.' He added, 'the most private affairs of a citizen, any citizen, can be invaded by simply typing a Social Security Number into a form'.

Sepp Blatter had promised us truth, transparency and openness. And here was his hand-picked PR man saying, 'The fully intended pre-selection and punctual withholding of relevant information by

a company or a high-profile individual of stature, must be the New
Objective of any thinking corporate leader today.'

Peter was offering 'Hand-tailored dissemination of information
. . . and hand-tailored can sometimes mean no information at all.'
If the client had big problems the answer was, 'powerful strategies
to "stay out of the media" and to prepare such briefs, news items
and alternative scoops that would divert, detract and destabilise
imminent media interest'.

And here was the Bhopal line again, about accepting moral
responsibility – but not the medical and other bills. Why had Sepp
Blatter warmed so quickly to Peter Hargitay?

I emailed Peter with some questions about the claims he used to
promote his company. Within hours his ECN site vanished from
the internet. Peter invited me to believe he was the victim of a
hacker. In a few days the ECN site came back and it had indeed
been hacked, from a vibrant 2,456 words to a minimalist 739.
Some of the most intriguing statements had got lost in cyberspace.

Hargitay told me he deplored invasion of privacy, of course he
was committed to openness. And, 'FIFA's communications policy
has never before been so open as it is today.'

Through his connection to Blatter, Hargitay landed the title
of Executive Producer on *Goal!,* a film part-financed by some of
FIFA's sponsors. His son Steven managed to obtain a marketing
job.

I was curious to know why three of Hargitay's associates
from the British theatre world (one with an MBE) were named
as directors on his ECN headed notepaper and his website but
weren't registered as such at Companies House. They told me
it was a cock-up by somebody who forgot to file the papers.
The ECN site has now followed previous Hargitay sites into deep
cyberspace.

Hargitay hadn't got much more to say about his old website

claim that he obtained other people's bank records, except to insist he never did anything illegal. He wrote to me saying I am 'deeply dishonest,' have 'selective ethics' and am 'disgusting and repelling *(sic)*'.

IN JUNE 2004 I was in Mayfair visiting friends when by chance I bumped into Hargitay in Davies Street. I said I would be sending him questions when this book was nearly completed. 'I don't give a shit what you write about me,' he said. Then he paused, and added, 'Give me a copy of your birth certificate.' He laughed and walked away.

His comment concerned me. Could he have been threatening to snoop on me? A birth certificate is well known to be the starting point for any professional investigation into a private individual. I'd been the victim of snooping in the past, twice – first when I was investigating corruption allegations against police officers, then again when I was taking a look at the fascist past of IOC president Samaranch. Both episodes came to light because the snoopers left a trail. The police officers had me secretly photographed and kept records that were later discovered by anti-corruption officers. President Samaranch himself made an embarrassing slip. He'd intended calling a senior police officer to ask him about my calls to a friend, a Barcelona journalist. By mistake he called the friend and blurted out his business.

So I knew a little about being illegally investigated and I didn't like it one bit. Perhaps Hargitay meant nothing by his birth certificate crack, but it bothered me. I called British Telecom and asked them to run some checks on my phone records.

'I think we'd better send a team straight away to sweep your house,' said the man from the British Telecommunications e-Crime & Computer Forensics Team. He said he was shocked at what he found. I have no idea or evidence that Hargitay was involved, but day after day, from mid-morning to mid-evening in 2003, callers posing as me had assailed call-centres, attempting to obtain details of my international calls. On one date, he told me, 'there was an awful lot of activity on your account – throughout the whole day. They were getting knocked back and knocked back. They kept trying and trying and trying.'

The sweep team began at my local exchange, swept the line all the way to my house and then set up monitoring equipment in every room, scanning for secret transmitters. Tapes of the assaults on my phone records have been stored for further analysis as more information comes to hand.

As for Hargitay, he'd told colleagues on Sunny Hill that Blatter had hired him 'to bring order to the British press' and he could boast some successes. The *FT* had been sublime. *The Guardian* and the *Sunday Times* published uncritical profiles and the *Daily Telegraph* were very friendly.

Then the old devil in Blatter surged to the surface. In early 2004, unable to control the dark undercurrents of suspender-belt voyeurism, he gabbled to a Swiss paper that he would prefer women players to wear tighter, more buttock-defining shorts. *The Guardian* picked it up on its front page, spiced the headline with the word 'hotpants' and world soccer erupted with hoots of derision.

SOME QUESTIONS FOR
MR BLATTER

. . . some answers from his lawyer

'UNDER THE GUISE of investigative journalism,' thundered Sepp Blatter in a furious letter at the end of March 2005, 'you have made a large number of allegations against me which have been completely and satisfactorily answered.'

That had me scratching my head. I'd tried every way I could think of to get him to answer the Big Question, the 300lb gorilla looming over his relationship with Jean-Marie Weber and the way that ISL got its television and marketing contracts.

Who had the one million franc kickback from ISL gone to, the embarrassing payment that arrived accidentally in FIFA's bank account after the last big contract was agreed in the late 1990s? Who got it?

I'd trekked to Blatter's press conference in Tunis in January 2004 to see if he would talk about it. I'd put the question about the alleged bribe and it was recorded by a German film crew. Ten months later their film portrait of Blatter, including my question, was screened. During the film the interviewer asked him: 'One million francs was paid to a FIFA account but was transferred?'

Blatter shrugged slightly, looked very serious and said, 'I don't know.'

The interviewer asked who the money went to.

Blatter grimaced, whispered something unintelligible, the interviewer said nothing.

There was a very long silence.

In March 2005 I tried again. I submitted written questions. What happened that morning when Erwin Schmid arrived at Blatter's office with the information from the USB bank? To whom was this payment forwarded? And who did Blatter report it to? Oh, and would he send me a copy of the bank document?

Blatter's reply, sent by Markus Siegler, was buried four pages into his stern, rebuking and sometimes threatening letter. After nearly 900 words, I got to it.

'The FIFA President has no knowledge of the matter you refer to.'

He didn't say it wasn't true. He wouldn't deny it happened. He didn't attack my sources, he offered no explanations. He didn't explain why he had dodged it in Tunis.

All he could say was, 'The FIFA President has no knowledge of the matter you refer to.'

DID BLATTER know anything about the 'inappropriate payments' that ISL had made to football officials, the ones that liquidator Dr Thomas Bauer had revealed to me over coffee in a break at the first creditors' meeting in Zug in July 2001? I asked the FIFA president whether FIFA had been asked to return any money – and did he know the names of anyone who had?

'At no point did the bankruptcy administrators ever ask Mr Joseph S Blatter for any repayment,' was the chilly reply. Blatter ought to know that Bauer had unearthed evidence that dirty money had been paid to football officials. So, surely he should have made it his business to find out who was trousering bribes. As President of FIFA, wasn't he eager to know who was on the take, so he could hound them out of the sport?

Whatever he knows, Blatter isn't talking. 'Any further enquiries in this connection should be addressed to the bankruptcy administrators,' was all he would say. And he concluded, 'I expect you to reflect in any forthcoming publication [that] I can claim to have played a fundamental part in ensuring that football is today a truly global sport and a universal language for hundreds of millions of people around the globe.'

Finished? He also put me on notice that if I continued my 'wholly unjustified and defamatory campaign', he would take action.

'FIFA TO SUE Andrew Jennings,' screamed out from the top of the front page of fifa.com one morning, two years earlier, in March 2003. I'd never seen the names of Pelé, Bobby Charlton, Franz Beckenbauer or Ronaldo getting that prominence on FIFA's daily newspages. What had I done to get Blatter out of bed so early?

The rest of it was short and not sweet. 'FIFA, world football's governing body, and its President Joseph S Blatter have today instructed their lawyers to file law suits against Andrew Jennings, a sports writer, and his employers at the *Daily Mail*, an English tabloid.' Apparently I'd written something libellous and Blatter had 'decided that a British court is the appropriate forum to establish the facts and expose the *Daily Mail's* fiction'.

Fiction? That morning I'd published an exclusive story that shed some daylight on what Blatter earned from FIFA. The little he'd ever given away in public hinted he was paid a salary. Nothing more. I had got hold of documentary evidence that he was paying himself a whacking great undisclosed bonus every year, a 'loyalty bonus' it was called, and that this had been authorised by former President Havelange just before he retired.

I had tried finance chief Urs Linsi who was always praising his own commitment to transparency. Would he run me through Blatter's pay package? The salary, bonus, perks and pension package that would be a matter of public knowledge if Blatter were the chief executive of even the smallest public company. Linsi ignored my questions. Press officer Markus Siegler had given me a similar brush-off. Just mentioning the subject of Blatter's earnings brought down an Ice Age on FIFA's communications department.

The speed of Blatter's before-dawn response told me that either my story was hopelessly wrong – or it was spot on and he was doing his best to deter other reporters from following up on my revelations.

A week later I followed the usual pre-press conference routine and emailed Blatter's pressman Markus Siegler to tell him I was coming to one on FIFA's finances. He replied, 'I just want to inform you that we will not grant you access to our premises.' What? Banned from a press conference! What was going on? Maybe they didn't want me showing my documents to a bunch of Swiss and foreign reporters. And asking more embarrassing questions about the boss's pay and perks.

WHAT'S THIS in the post? A letter from Lawrence Cartier, solicitor to Sepp Blatter, dated 25 March, 2003. 'Dear Sir . . . Our clients consider that the article contains seriously defamatory statements.' There was more: 'The waging of this campaign by you provides grounds for our clients to include, with their claims for defamation, claims for aggravated and/or exemplary damages.'

This kind of language has a way of making reporters feel queasy. I slipped my fingers inside the envelope. Where was the writ? I looked again at the letter. 'The continuing publication . . . of defamatory statements made against our clients constitutes conduct which our clients are not prepared to tolerate . . . our clients require you immediately to cease publishing articles of the nature complained of,' insisted Mr Cartier. So where was the writ? 'We are in the process of obtaining instructions on the details of our clients' claims as required by the pre-Action Court Protocol.' This was lawyer-speak for 'We'll soon be sending you a writ.'

A heavy envelope from Lawrence Cartier arrived. Is this the writ? No, it's a ten-page letter about my 'fiction'. Long before the end I lost count of 'unjustified', 'untrue', 'unfounded', and 'inaccurate'. Then there was 'misrepresented facts', and the recurrent 'defamatory'. Then Lawrence got down to the serious business.

'Our clients view this article as the very opposite of what is reasonably to be expected from a responsible journalist and are justifiably aggrieved . . . an apparent willingness to publish false allegations without regard to their truth.

'We require a full and unequivocal public withdrawal and apology in terms to be approved by us and to be published in a prominent position together with a written assurance and undertaking (a) not to repeat these or similar allegations and (b) to cease immediately this intentionally hostile and unjustifiable campaign against our clients.

'We also invite your proposals as to the substantial damages to which our clients are entitled for the injury and harm caused . . . including aggravated/exemplary damages.' On top of that would be FIFA's costs employing Lawrence to correct my 'fiction'.

But hang on a minute. I re-read a paragraph buried deep in the ten pages. It said, 'Mr Blatter never received a loyalty bonus.' Lawrence was adamant. My story was fiction.

Then Lawrence admitted, 'Mr Blatter did indeed receive a bonus (not a loyalty bonus) for his exceptional work as general secretary of FIFA and this was duly recorded by the FIFA Finance Committee and audited.' But Lawrence and Sepp were holding the line that it was a one-off payment and not backdated. I'd obtained a notarised document dated 2 May 2002, sworn by a former FIFA finance department official, which stated, 'I hereby confirm that Mr Joseph S Blatter, following his election as the President of FIFA, presented me with a document signed by his predecessor which awarded him an annual six-figure *prime de fidelité*, payable on 1 July, backdated in the first instance to 1 July 1997 . . .'

What was I to believe?

From his office in London's Lincoln's Inn Lawrence talked tough and he gave us a deadline. We had four days to grovel and retract. Or else. We didn't grovel. We didn't retract. No writ arrived. Once twelve months had gone by Sepp Blatter and Lawrence Cartier had missed their chance to go to court on the story they described as 'fiction'.

In the November of 2003 Sepp emailed me to say that from now on all my questions must be sent to Lawrence Cartier who would act as his press spokesman.

A month later Lawrence wrote me a letter, prefaced with the usual 'defamatory, hostile, unjustified' and then something rather surprising: 'You should also inform me of the organization which is proposing to publish your article and provide me on behalf of my clients with a copy of the article in sufficient time for my clients to respond before publication takes place.'

A copy of the article! In 35 years as a reporter neither I nor the newspapers, radio stations, television companies or book publishers I'd worked for had ever submitted a story for approval to anybody outside the company. Every cub reporter knows that you don't show your article, pre-publication, to anyone outside your newspaper. And you certainly don't submit it for approval to the subject. That just doesn't happen in countries with a free press and free speech. Perhaps Sepp was having delusions of grandeur and imagined himself the top man in a totalitarian state. Or maybe, after so many years of reading uncritical press reports, he genuinely didn't understand the difference between a press release (paid for, putting your point of view) and a press report (independent, free).

Later Lawrence went even further. 'Dear Mr Jennings ... responsible journalistic standards require that the manuscript of your book should be sent to us well in advance of any publication date.' This was so he and Blatter could correct any 'inaccuracies and misconceptions'. Indeed, 'a failure to respond to this request would lead our clients to believe that you and your publisher were not genuinely concerned about whether any criticisms in the book against them were valid'. But I am genuinely concerned. That's why I had been asking them questions.

I showed my manuscript to my publisher, my lawyer, my agent and my wife. I didn't show it to Sepp. And I didn't comply with their ludicrous demand that I should send my perfectly legitimate press queries to a London commercial lawyer, rather than to the well-funded and well-staffed press office in Zurich which exists, unsurprisingly, to answer questions from the press.

Lawrence wrote again. 'You appear to have missed the point of my firm's involvement. With respect it is not for you to decide to bypass my firm and contact my clients direct. Where a solicitor is instructed then it is the client's entitlement to expect communications to be sent to that solicitor and not to the client direct. I am instructed in this case because my clients consider you have acted in breach of your duties and legal issues of importance arise. My clients expect you to respect their entitlement for communications to be sent to my firm. Will you please observe this practice.'

It was all getting rather silly. Communicate through lawyers? Did Sepp think that he and I were getting a divorce? Had he forgotten that I was just a journalist and he was somebody I wrote about. Really, there was no need to involve lawyers at all. It was quite simple. He was a public figure. I was a reporter. It was my job to ask questions. He employed a team of press officers and it was their job to answer questions such as mine. Where was the problem? Why all the fuss? Did he, perhaps, have something to hide?

I carried on sending questions to Sepp. I asked him about his expenses, his salary, his tax bill, who paid for his election campaign? It has all been looked at by the Zurich prosecutor's office in 2002, he snapped back, and 'You know that the result of those investigations is that there is no substance or truth whatsoever in the allegations implied by the questions you have raised.'

Blatter quoted selectively from the prosecutor's findings. 'It cannot be maintained that Joseph Blatter engaged in unlawful conduct . . . this conduct does not merit prosecution.'

He added, 'I have been told by my Swiss lawyers, and give notice that it is a breach of Swiss law for you to raise again allegations which have been the subject of an investigation by the public prosecutor and dismissed by him entirely, as has occurred in this case.'

It was true that the Zurich prosecutor, Urs Hubmann, had closed his investigation into Sepp Blatter. Immediately afterwards Peter Hargitay and Lawrence Cartier trumpeted that the prosecutor found all the allegations 'entirely without foundation'. This claim was repeated in every newspaper and profile of Blatter.

Was it true?

I asked for an appointment to meet Urs Hubmann. He agreed to see me. I asked him, 'Did you really say that all the allegations against Sepp Blatter were entirely without foundation?'

He handed me a coffee. Hubmann was in his mid-forties, lean, muscular and wearing jeans to work in his modern office in Zurich's downtown. He chose his words carefully. He even pulled a big German–English dictionary off his shelf to check that he said what he intended to say. And what he said was: 'We cannot say that all the allegations were without foundation.'

Hubmann said there were 12 complaints against Blatter. 'Six of them were ridiculous.' The members of the executive committee who had brought the allegations to the prosecutor had forgotten that these six issues had been conclusively resolved at meetings they attended.

As for the other allegations, Blatter had produced documents that answered some of them. Hubmann paused. Two of the allegations, he said, 'had meat on the bone'. It was not true to say that he had found all the allegations without foundation. On the contrary, 'What I say, in two cases, was that I had insufficient evidence to proceed. Under these circumstances I could not see how I could bring a charge. I came to a similar view on a couple of other points in the complaint.'

Hubmann added, 'I have not concluded that Herr Blatter is innocent. He is innocent of certain things. That is not to say that nothing has happened. It simply means there isn't sufficient proof.'

I sent more questions to Blatter. And I asked him about something else that puzzled me. In 1998 people asked him whether FIFA was paying any part of his campaign expenses. 'Absolutely not,' he said. He was most vehement about that. So, I asked him, why, soon after winning the 1998 election, did he come back to his office and promptly fill in two expenses claims for 'Campagne présidentielle' of 12,527.70 francs and 56,032 francs?

Blatter declined to share the prosecutor's confidential summary of the case with me. He maintained he'd reimbursed FIFA in full, but whatever Blatter had repaid to FIFA, he'd often taken a long time about it. The prosecutor told me, 'The question remains open whether such a "credit" by the accused through FIFA is justified over such a long period of time in view of his salary. However, this is not a matter enough to accuse him.'

I asked again, would Blatter please reveal his salary, bonuses from various sources, allowances, car allowances, pension contributions, the terms of his contract and what his payoff would be if he were dismissed? No comment. I'd been told that FIFA gave him a monthly 8,000 francs housing allowance but he'd no comment on that.

Blatter had nothing to say about the stories the Swiss press had run about his tax affairs in three different cantons.

Blatter restricted his answer to 'I have always duly paid my taxes in my place of residence and the tax authorities are entirely satisfied with the procedure.' Yes, but what about your salary, Mr President? And isn't it true that FIFA pays your tax for you?

'All salaries and other payments are properly determined by the relevant FIFA bodies,' Blatter told me. But why did he absolutely refuse to disclose the details? Blatter said, 'It is in accordance with Swiss general law and recognised practice that individual details of salaries and payments are not published. The overall costs incurred for personnel (including the President and General Secretary) are published in the Annual FIFA Financial Report.'

The 2003 FIFA financial report listed 39 million francs

expenses for the whole FIFA staff. The projected figure for 2005 was 51 million. That's all.

I asked Blatter about some other things. About Havelange's and Jean-Marie Weber's grandiose plan for FIFA to endorse an US$8 billion dollar a year gambling business in the early 1990s. What did Sepp know and when did he know it? The answer came back. He knew nothing. I was curious to know what he knew about all that funny business with my phone records, the professional theft of private phone details that might be expected to reveal my contacts within FIFA. Did Blatter have anything to say about that? One word. 'No.'

DR JEAN-MARIE KYSS must be one of the bravest men in the world game. When not treating the poor women of the worst slums in the western world he resisted and defeated the government thugs who tried to take over Haiti's football association and steal the national stadium and the money it took at matches. He tried his best to play his part in FIFA's congress in Paris in 1998 that elected Sepp Blatter president but was turned back by the government gunmen at Port au Prince airport who wouldn't let him board his flight.

When I interviewed Kyss in the stadium back in 2002 he told me that he had called Jack Warner and asked him to draw the Congress's attention to Haiti's empty seat, to show the world that a government was interfering in the running of the game. 'That empty chair symbolised the interference of our government in our sport,' he told me. 'It was our gesture of defiance. That empty chair sent a powerful message to the world.'

Well, actually, it didn't, as we have seen. But Dr Kyss was never told that Warner's aide Trinidadian Neville Ferguson, not a delegate to the congress, had been fraudulently inserted into his seat.

If FIFA's disciplinary committee were fair and good it might
have investigated the voting scandal properly, invited Dr Kyss to
Zurich and honoured him with FIFA's Order of Merit. The entire
executive committee might have applauded him for standing up
to a corrupt government. The FIFA thieves complicit in stealing
Dr Kyss's seat at the congress, however high their rank, might
be named in banner headlines, and expelled from the game for
corrupting FIFA's parliament. It might also be recorded that
Blatter's election as president was tainted.

This isn't what happened.

Blatter considered it all done and dusted. At a press conference
in Zurich in March 2002 he was emphatic. 'If somebody wanted
to attack or put in question the election results in 1998 they had,
according to Swiss law, 30 days after 8 June 1998 to make their
protests or put in questions. Stop it. Finish. That's good.'

The following month Vice-Presidents Lennart Johansson and
Issa Hayatou demanded an inquiry into the hijacking of Dr Kyss's
vote. Johansson wrote to Blatter, 'I ask you to urgently investigate
this matter and to inform the executive committee accordingly.'
Later that month Blatter told Warner and his congress in Miami,
'The matter is now closed.'

The breakthrough came at the round table with reporters that
Peter Hargitay arranged for Blatter in London on 28 January
2003.

Blatter had gathered together a bunch of reporters he was
trying to impress with his openness, his transparency. I asked him,
when was he going to investigate the vote-rigging? What could
he say? This was his transparency round table. He had to say
something to impress. Blatter said he would refer the allegations
to the disciplinary committee and its chairman, Swiss lawyer
Marcel Mathier.

I wrote to Mathier asking – since so many FIFA officials were potentially involved, from the highest level down to the delegates who sat next to Ferguson and knew Kyss couldn't have mandated his vote – was he going to appoint an independent inquiry by people outside football? Would he follow the example of the International Olympic Committee who, embroiled in scandal over the corruption in Salt Lake City, had hired private investigators and posted the results of the investigation on the IOC internet site?

'I'm sure you will understand that when the inquiry is in progress, the FIFA Disciplinary Committee cannot make any kind of comment concerning the object of the inquiry,' said Mathier. 'Thank you very much for your understanding.'

I didn't understand but I offered Markus Siegler my dossier of video tapes, statements and documents and got no response.

Had Blatter really set up an investigation? It didn't seem like it. Lawyer Lawrence Cartier stepped in on Blatter's behalf on 19 May 2003 insisting, 'There was no such misconduct in respect of the election, let alone misconduct which resulted in his election or to which he was a party.' If Blatter said nothing wrong happened, surely he was prejudging and potentially influencing the inquiry – if there really was one.

In July 2003 Cartier changed his tune, confirming that there was an investigation in progress. Four months later, in November 2003, he revealed, 'The Disciplinary Committee has completed the first phase of its investigation. The Disciplinary Committee will report when its investigations are complete following which its findings will be published.'

Then we drifted into 2004. Month after month slipped by and still there was no news of the investigation that started in February 2003. In March 2005 I asked Blatter what on earth was going on. His reply was astonishing. The Disciplinary Committee had reached its verdict twenty months earlier, four months *before*

Cartier's November 2003 assertions that the investigations were still going on.

It looked like Cartier had been sold a dummy, passing on incorrect information given to him by his client Sepp Blatter or his minions.

So, there had been a disciplinary hearing. A secret one. And the result had been suppressed. Even to someone accustomed to the FIFA approach to truth and justice this was stunning. But what came next almost knocked me out.

Blatter wrote to me, 'The FIFA Disciplinary Committee decided on 27 June 2003 in Paris with respect to charges of rigging the FIFA presidential elections in 1998 as follows:

Messrs Jean-Marie Kyss and Neville Ferguson breached art. 12 of the FIFA Statutes.

As Jean-Marie Kyss is no longer subject to FIFA's jurisdiction, he cannot be sanctioned.

Neville Ferguson has been reprimanded.

1. *Neville Ferguson (Trinidad & Tobago FA) has been notified of this decision and CONCACAF has received a copy.*
2. *The costs of these proceedings will be shared between Neville Ferguson and FIFA (art. 122 FIFA Disciplinary Code).'*

Dr Kyss had been investigated, they said he'd breached FIFA laws and if he were still an official of the Haitian association he'd have been punished? I couldn't believe what I was reading. This was his reward for risking his life in violent Haiti to protect football's assets and independence?

And Neville Ferguson, who had deceived the congress, got a reprimand. What was it? It couldn't be much more than a polite letter from Blatter advising him not to get caught again because Ferguson carried on being an official of various Warner-controlled football organisations in the Caribbean and continued earning fees as an international match commissioner throughout the region. And why should FIFA share any of the costs of this inquiry with Neville? If he'd done something wrong, let him pay.

Missing from Blatter's terse message was the usual statement of facts that FIFA issues when it passes judgement on erring players, clubs and touchline officials. The normal practice – fifa.com has pages of them – is to state the complaint or alleged offence against FIFA rules, a summary of the evidence – reports from referees and match commissioners – and the defences offered by the accused. Finally, the wording of the punishment and the amount of money levied in fines and costs is provided.

This one had all been done in secret and unlike any other investigation by the disciplinary committee, not a word of it had been published anywhere and certainly not on their website. If I hadn't demanded answers, would Blatter and Mathier ever have disclosed the judgement of their kangaroo court and the savaging of the good Dr Kyss?

SOMETHING else was missing from Marcel Mathier's verdict. What had he done about the earlier case, the usurpation of Dr Kyss two years previously at the 1996 FIFA congress in Zurich by Vincy Jalal, girlfriend of Captain Horace Burrell? Her name is forever recorded in the official congress report as the accredited delegate from Haiti. Dr Kyss hadn't known about that either.

When Blatter had conceded at the London round table, 'Perhaps we should have opened an investigation on these matters before, but it is not too late to do so now', he had agreed that Burrell, a member of Marcel Mathier's disciplinary committee 'will definitely not be in this case'. Then spokesman Markus Siegler had denied the words were spoken.

Dr Kyss had clearly said that he had told CONCACAF's most senior officials that he couldn't make the trip to Zurich for the 1996 congress. My colleague videoed him telling me in the stadium in Port au Prince, 'I phoned CONCACAF and Zurich and told them I was unable to attend.'

Marcel Mathier had good reason to be additionally miffed with Horace Burrell. Before the minutes of that 1996 congress could be published they had to be scrutinised. Five national associations had been chosen for the job, including Jamaica. The Jamaican delegation, including Burrell, who had sat within reach of Vincy Jalal in the congress, had approved the minutes. Now Marcel Mathier had the opportunity to put things right. Nothing has happened.

How has Burrell fared since he helped rig the vote in world football? Not badly. In the year 2000 Blatter awarded him FIFA's Order of Merit, in 2002 Blatter appointed him a member of the disciplinary commission overseeing the World Cup matches in Korea and Japan and in 2004 Blatter appointed him as an instructor with their Com-Unity Programme. Burrell tours the world dispensing advice to football officials. For the good of the game.

FIFA FAIRY TALES

Clawing back the money

Autumn, 2002. And everyone lived happily ever after. President Blatter, re-elected, said he was carrying on 'for the good of the game'. Sports reporters watched the footie, retyped Blatter's press releases, merrily pressed SEND and repaired to the pub. A team of English and German professors put the finishing touches to their FIFA book, grateful for some generous help from Jerome Champagne, and happy to have made it clear once and for all that there was no corruption at FIFA nor any vote-rigging. How could there be? Hadn't all the allegations been withdrawn?

One man couldn't go along with the fairy tale ending. Swiss Magistrate Thomas Hildbrand was investigating what ISL executives had done with more than £50 million paid by the Brazilian network Globo to the ISL company for television rights to the World Cup in 2002 and 2006. The money should have been passed on to FIFA. It wasn't. Hildbrand obtained copies of the letters from FIFA to Jean-Marie Weber about the money, including the legal advice that FIFA ignored, urging them to make Weber stick to his contract and pay up.

When ISL went bust in the Spring of 2001 their siphoning off of the money couldn't be hidden any longer. FIFA had tried to talk down the disappearance but secrets that big don't stay secret for long. Eventually, FIFA reported the scandal to the economic crime department of the Magistrates' office in the canton of Zug where ISL had been based. They assigned Hildbrand to the investigation.

On 4 November 2002 Jean-Marie Weber and several other former ISL directors were arrested by Hildbrand and questioned for several days and their private offices searched. Weber was tight-lipped after his release. I caught up with him three weeks later in Mexico City on the fringe of an IOC meeting and asked what was going on. Weber said he'd been held in custody in Zug. 'But everything is fine,' he told me. 'Look, I have my passport, I am free to travel, we've just been helping with the inquiries.' He smiled, shrugged and walked away.

MEANWHILE, liquidator Thomas Bauer, trying to claw back money owing to creditors from the wreckage of ISL, found a curious thing in the company's accounts. For years ISL had, time after time, secured lucrative FIFA contracts. And for years they'd been making secret payments to football officials, including to FIFA.

I caught up with Bauer at the first ISL creditors' meeting. It was held in Zug in July 2001, seven weeks after the collapse, and Bauer was in good spirits and his eyes lit up when he told me, 'I have found football-related payments from ISL. Some are very large, in excess of one million Swiss francs. I have written to the recipients asking them to return the money. We are now in negotiation – and, if necessary, litigation – to get the money returned.'

For month after month Bauer doggedly negotiated with Weber, but after almost two years' wrangling he'd run out of patience. On 20 May 2003, Bauer went to the Zug court and filed a writ against ISL's directors. He wanted them to pay back the money they'd given to football officials. And he wanted them to hand over documents that would reveal the names of the directors, recipients and other parties involved in these curious transactions. According to custom and practice in Zug, Bauer's filing was kept secret.

A few months later I dropped in on Bauer in his small Basel office, crammed, floor to ceiling, with archive boxes full of documents that held the story of ISL's rise and fall. What I would have done for a peek! Bauer sat amid his treasure trove and laughed at my frustration. He wasn't telling the story, not yet he wasn't. It was November 2003 and he knew that he was close to clinching the deal that might get back all those millions paid to football officials, including the one million franc bribe that accidentally landed up in FIFA's bank account.

Early in the new year, on 18 February 2004, a special account was opened at a Zurich bank. It was named 'Escrow Number 1/Weber' and was the channel for football officials to repay the bribes from ISL. Opening the account, and negotiating the return of the money by an unspecified number of football officials, was Professor Peter Nobel, one of Switzerland's most respected lawyers who had previously represented Blatter and FIFA.

Nobel and Bauer negotiated amid the utmost secrecy. These were highly sensitive matters. Around the world, journalists carried on reflecting FIFA's happy face, and not a squeak of FIFA's troubles reached the public. Well, perhaps a squeak. At a press conference in Tunis in January 2004, I asked Sepp about the Bribe that went astray. He wasn't happy.

Professor Nobel secured a good deal for his secret clients. He got the demand reduced by a million francs to 2.5 million. And he got Bauer's agreement to close the case and not come back for more money later. The foreword to the agreement, dated 27 February 2004, says: 'Mr Weber wishes that the recipients of the money paid by ISL who are directly or indirectly involved in football business ('*Fussballgeschäft*') will not be asked to repay any further money.' It was also clear that Weber himself was not putting up the money. He was merely a vehicle for the bribe-takers to surreptitiously return some of their kickbacks.

A year later Switzerland's most senior judges looked at the document and concluded coldly that the money was 'paid by persons who had an interest that (Bauer's) lawsuit should never take place'.

ONE DAY IN APRIL 2004, Blatter and his Executive Committee checked into Claridge's hotel in Mayfair – it boasts 'one of London's widest champagne menus' – to begin celebrating FIFA's centenary in the country that invented the game.

I watched from an armchair in the lobby as Chuck Blazer and Peter Hargitay talked intently over coffee in a discreet corner. Blatter swept through, trailed by deferential English football officials. Then off they went to Buckingham Palace where Jack Warner told Queen Elizabeth and Prince Phillip that he was far from satisfied with the level of British business spending on football in Trinidad. Blatter called in on Tony Blair at Downing Street, then he and his entourage were off to the City of Love.

Why? Well, it was 2004 and FIFA had been founded in Paris in 1904, and everyone likes to party so FIFA invited all the world's football officials for a shindig.

President Chirac kicked off the merriment, congratulating Blatter on his 'brilliant career', praising his 'humanist vision of football' and making him a member of the Legion of Honour. FIFA splashed out on a chateau for an evening banquet and then Blatter handed out the Centennial Orders of Merit.

Gongs went to Adidas and Coca-Cola, to Havelange and Jack Warner. And there was one for Charlie Dempsey. Yes, Dempsey! The man who, on legal advice, didn't vote in the final round of the contest to stage the 2006 World Cup. More gongs went to billionaire Henry Fok, to Isaac Sasso, to Julio Grondona, Nicolas Leoz and Bin Hammam, to Denis Obua. Denis who? Denis Obua, President of the Ugandan federation, who within a year would be behind bars at Kampala's Luzira jail, accused of misappropriating funds of the national association.

Blatter gave an Order of Merit to his man in the Balkans, Ivan Slavkov, president of the Bulgarian association and an IOC member. Six weeks later the BBC's *Panorama* programme, taking a look at the bidding process for the 2012 Olympic Games, caught Ivan on camera naming his price for his vote. The IOC suspended him. Blatter swiftly came to his aid, proclaiming: 'For FIFA, he remains President of the Bulgarian FA and we are going to send a letter to him confirming that.' As FIFA President, Blatter is an automatic IOC member and in an IOC ballot on Slavkov's expulsion Blatter was among the few who voted against.

FIFA's troubles rumbled on. On 29 June 2004, FIFA did a curious thing. It wrote to Magistrate Hildbrand, quietly withdrawing FIFA's support for the criminal investigation into ISL's directors and the vanished Globo millions. No public announcement was made. If FIFA thought that would stop Hildbrand they were gravely mistaken. Hildbrand had other information and sources that he considered strong enough to merit continuing his investigation. Hildbrand kept on digging.

*   *   *

EIGHT weeks later, on 24 August, Hildbrand served a notice on Professor Nobel requiring him to hand over the names of the football officials who had repaid the 2.5 million francs to Bauer. Hildbrand also wanted the relevant bank records. He considered the information so important and so delicate that he instructed Professor Nobel and his employees that they were forbidden to reveal this to any third parties. Hildbrand seemed to be gathering evidence to bring a criminal prosecution for commercial bribery. This was very bad news for the bad guys.

Meanwhile Blatter was working hard on being a good guy. The *Financial Times* had given him a column and he used it skilfully a month after Hildbrand dropped his bombshell on Professor Nobel to proclaim how much he personally was absolutely opposed to a world of football where 'money rules and social conscience is of limited relevance'. Solemnly, he told *FT* readers, 'It was always my philosophy that those who have should give to those who have not.'

A few weeks later he led a discussion on Sunny Hill on 'the significance of football in society today'. The very next day he introduced FIFA's new Code of Ethics. Toothless, according to anyone in the know. Crucial, according to Markus Siegler, who averred, 'There is a lot of money in football, people might be tempted.'

Helpful Jack Warner weighed in, 'I am deputy chairman of the finance committee of FIFA. I oversee a budget of US$2 billion and I have never seen one iota of corruption.'

FIFA partied on for the centenary in Monaco in August and then Blatter led his team on a vote-gathering tour of central Asia, taking in Uzbekistan, Turkmenistan, Kazakhstan, Kyrgyzstan and Tajikistan, places where people live in fear of poverty, organised crime, arbitrary arrest and torture. Blatter's team saw none of that. Indeed they came home to report, 'every day is a celebration of tolerance through the harmonious coexistence of Islam and Orthodox Christianity, of Turko-Mongols and Slavs'.

Bauer held his second creditor's meeting, again in Zug. Weber's creditors were less than pleased to learn that out of the billions being claimed, less than 20 million francs had been recovered.

Blatter, continuing to clock up US$500 a day expenses, led a meet 'n' greet sweep through Latin America followed by another bout of ribbon cutting ceremonies at Goal sites in Africa. As Blatter travelled, Professor Nobel waited to hear from the Zug judges. He had appealed against Hildbrand's demand for names and documents. On 29 November 2004 the judges ruled that Nobel must comply with Hildbrand's demands and hand over the names. Nobel gave notice of appeal.

Back on Sunny Hill, FIFA poured money into the latest jolly. From all corners of the world football officials flocked to the Footballer of the Year awards in Zurich in December.

'Football meets Opera was held amid the opulent splendour of the fabled Zurich Opera House,' reported fifa.com. 'On a night of unmatched grandeur in Zurich, football itself was the real winner.' Brazil's Ricardo Teixeira, plagued by corruption allegations back home, was delighted to receive FIFA's Fair Play Award from Sir Bobby Charlton. Among the thousands of guests flown in at football's expense were Captain Horace Burrell and his pal Chet Greene. The marquee erected outside the Opera House reportedly cost 3.5 million francs for the night.

Lausanne, 17 January 2005. Professor Nobel lodged an application at Switzerland's highest judicial body, the Federal Court in Lausanne, to quash the ruling by the Zug court that the names, bank records and other information involved in the bribery repayments must be disclosed to Hildbrand's criminal investigation team. On 21 February the Federal court agreed to hear the appeal. All these legal manoeuvres were, as ever, kept secret. The same day fratricidal warfare broke out again up at Sunny Hill.

Urs Linsi had not found the transition from banking to sport easy. An executive in a Zurich leasing office until mid-1999 when Blatter hired him as head bean-counter, Linsi stumbled around the world of football.

Linsi's charismatic deputy Jerome Champagne deployed his long experience of the game, fluency in languages and easy rapport with officials to build a political base in the national associations. Did Jerome fancy his chances of following Sepp into the presidency when the old man quit? The future didn't look good for Linsi.

Zurich, 21 February 2005. Linsi sent a top-secret memo to Blatter complaining about Champagne's 'behaviour and attitude'. He wanted his deputy out of the building, out of his job. Blatter replied stiffly, 'I cannot approve this request at the moment.' Days later, Blatter approved something else: doubling the salary of executive committee members to US$100,000 a year, tax free.

I wrote to Blatter and Linsi in late March 2005, asking a clutch of questions for this book about their apparent lack of action since September 1998 when FIFA first discovered the Globo money had been diverted.

I told them I had seen the letters they'd sent to Weber and that I knew they had been told in May 2000 that Weber's handling of the contract and the money was wholly unacceptable. I wondered, did they feel any personal responsibility for the loss of the money? And had they told the executive committee this? I was curious about why Blatter had announced in April 2001 that he had only just learned of the problem. Hadn't he known since 1998?

I sent my questions via FIFA press officer, Markus Siegler. He sat on them for five weeks and then in early May he wrote back that I must 'address any questions for Urs Linsi to him personally'. I sent the questions again, this time direct to Linsi, but as this book goes to press many months have passed and still he hasn't got back to me.

Siegler did manage to pass my questions to Sepp Blatter. The president responded with the briefest of statements. 'The payment from Globo to which reference is made is the subject of a criminal complaint lodged by FIFA in Zug in connection with the bankruptcy of ISL.'

But this wasn't the full story. FIFA had withdrawn its support for the complaint, secretly, ten months earlier. But Hildbrand persevered.

ON Wednesday 11 May 2005 Hildbrand charged Weber and several of his associates with fraud, forgery and embezzlement of 118 million francs of Globo money and another 15 million francs belonging to the Japanese marketing company Dentsu. Hildbrand issued a statement revealing that his investigations had extended to five countries.

Hildbrand granted one television interview and looked composed, at ease with himself, a man with nothing to hide. His face tightened once – when he revealed FIFA had withdrawn support for the complaint the previous year. Hildbrand added, that 'the accusations made by FIFA', weren't the only allegations he had heard. He had taken into consideration, he said ominously, 'further facts and circumstances'.

Soon Blatter faced the cameras to respond. Had he tried to ban-jax Hildbrand's investigation? Certainly not, Blatter explained, they'd not *withdrawn* their complaint at all. They'd simply *refocused* it: 'We didn't show an interest any longer because we had found out in the meantime that . . . we stood a better chance of getting the money back in a civil case.'

TWO MONTHS LATER Urs Linsi struck again at his deputy Jerome Champagne with another memo to Blatter setting out a new list of 'incidents' which he said, 'leave me no other option than to submit a request for Jerome Champagne's dismissal as deputy general secretary as well as the notice of termination of his work contract'.

Why? Jerome was being so naughty. Senior officials of both the African and European confederations, claimed Urs, were furious at his interference in their affairs. One UEFA official called him a 'Spy'. Another had said they didn't want the Frenchman at their congress in Tallin.

Back at Sunny Hill, 'Champagne's behaviour and attitude towards individual members of the FIFA management has become a serious problem,' said the general secretary.

Six FIFA departmental heads wanted action taken against Champagne. 'Disregard of their wishes would lead to a split in the FIFA management.' Linsi shot a couple more arrows into Champagne's back then donned his undertaker's hat.

'The serious misconduct, lack of professionalism, disloyalty and inability of J Champagne just in recent months leave me no other choice than to take the appropriate – and obviously long overdue – action.

'Dear President, I recommend on the basis of the available facts to dispense with the services of Champagne and ask you for the good of FIFA to support my request. Best regards, Urs Linsi, General Secretary, FIFA.'

Lausanne, 11 July 2005. Federal Court President Féraud together with Justices Nay, Aeschlimann, Fonjallaz and Eusebio announced their verdict. It was 4,980 words long and considered the plea from Professor Peter Nobel that he should not have to hand over to Investigating Magistrate Thomas Hildbrand the names of the football officials who'd taken bribes.

For now, the names of the football officials who took bribes from ISL could remain secret. ISL liquidator Thomas Bauer said that there were no Swiss nationals involved. The Zug taxpayers paid the 3,000 francs tab for court costs.

Marrakech, 12 September 2005. The 55th FIFA congress backed Blatter's proposal to set up a special task force – 'For the Good of the Game' – to tackle match-fixing, doping, racism and other 'menaces' that he said threatened world soccer. The president lamented that 'some parts of today's football world are sadly not as wonderful as they should be'.

Mid-way through his speech, Blatter took a rest at the podium, stopped speaking and simply beamed at the crowd. Over the speakers came the sweet, mellow sound of Louis Armstrong singing, 'What a Wonderful World'. Listening in the gallery was gangling Jean-Marie Weber, a guest of FIFA, awaiting trial accused of stealing more than 100 million francs from FIFA, a man for whom skies of blue and red roses too might soon be a thing of the past.

Blatter got back to Sunny Hill and found Linsi still railing against Jerome Champagne. Blatter moved Champagne to his own presidential office, where Linsi couldn't reach him, gave him a new title of 'Presidential Delegate' and put him in charge of the 'For the Good of the Game' anti-corruption task force. So Linsi's attempt to undermine his capable rival Champagne bit the dust.

Near the end of the year Dr Thomas Bauer withdrew as ISL liquidator and was replaced by Karl Wüthrich, the formidable liquidator of Swissair, now renamed 'Swiss'. Then the almost unbelievable happened. At around 10.30 on the morning of 3 November 2005 Thomas Hildbrand arrived, unannounced at the front door of FIFA House with a squad of investigators and a warrant to search the offices of Blatter and Linsi. According to sources in Hildbrand's office in Zug, he had been given permission to launch a new inquiry, a 'spin-off' based on information obtained during the ISL investigation.

Blatter informed Johansson and other executive committee members but did not tell the public. News of the raid was broken by Swiss journalist Jean Francois Tanda three weeks later in the *Sonntags Zeitung*. Tanda reported that the reason given on the search warrant was *ungetreue Geschäftsbesorgung* – disloyalty to one's employer. FIFA spokesman Andreas Herren said, 'Nobody from FIFA or the organisation has been accused of anything. We think Hildbrand has over-reacted. Documents were taken and, to some extent, have since been returned.' Hildbrand declines to comment.

On 16 November 2005 the people of Trinidad & Tobago held their breath as their team took on Bahrain in the Manama Stadium in the Gulf for a place in the 2006 World Cup. Forty-nine minutes into the game Dwight Yorke took a sweet corner and giant Dennis Lawrence hammer-headed it into the net. Trinidad & Tobago turned wild with joy. For the first time in their country's history the Soca Warriors had qualified for the

World Cup. Life-long fans were prepared to raid their savings to go.

How would fans get tickets? Within weeks, the answer came in screaming local press ads.

'EXCLUSIVE: Tickets to T&T's First Round Games in Germany! Only Simpaul Travel Service can get you into the Soca Warriors First Round Games.' Ramming the point home the text announced, 'Ticket! or leave it.' Fans short of the readies could get 'low interest loans' from First Citizens Bank.

For T$30,000 (£2,730.53) fans got tickets for the three first round games and 12 nights accommodation in a shared room. Simpaul threw in a travel bag, a T-shirt, a national flag and a wristband.

What was this Simpaul Travel that seemed to have a monopoly on World Cup tickets? Lasana Liburd, a freelance writer working for the *Trinidad Express*, started digging. He asked Oliver Camps, President of the Trinidad & Tobago Football Federation. Camps replied that the federation had banned him from speaking about the tickets allocation.

'I do not know that is happening,' said Camps when asked if Warner was diverting the tickets to his own private company. 'Do you know who the owner of Simpaul is? Let us not go there.'

No wonder. Simpaul Travel was a company owned by Jack Warner, his wife Maureen and his sons Daryan and Daryll. Then Liburd contacted German hotels and calculated that Simpaul was making a profit of around £1,700 on every package.

The Trinidad *Express* carried Liburd's researches for three days over the Christmas period. He pointed out that Warner, a former linesman, although not an official of the T&TFF, appeared to control the Federation's every activity. The constitution had been changed in 1994 to disenfranchise the twin islands' football clubs. Only regional football associations and 'properly constituted bodies' like the Trinidad & Tobago Football Coaches Association and Football Referees' Association have the vote.

Next into the fray was the Trinidad *Guardian*, usually a supporter of Warner. 'There are also likely to be concerns that Mr Warner is using his position of supremacy in local and international football to benefit financially from T&T's qualification.'

The stories drew big mail bags, one writer wondering if Warner was breaching Article 2 of FIFA's Code of Ethics that states 'Under no circumstances may they [officials] abuse their positions to obtain personal benefits.'

On 1 January the Trinidad *Mirror* joined in. It reported that a London-based Trinidad businessman had asked the privately appointed committee handling the sponsorship for the team going to Germany what it would cost him to produce official team memorabilia.

The reply came from a Trinidad company registered as the Local Organising Committee 2006 World Cup Ltd (LOC 2006 Ltd) – set up by the Trinidad & Tobago Football Federation – and was signed by a man we've heard of before, Jack Warner's son Daryll, on behalf of Merchandising, Licensing and Marketing, LOC 2006 Ltd. As in 2001, when contracts for the Under-17 tournament in Trinidad and Tobago went to the Warner family, they seemed to be getting in on the act for 2006.

Daryll wrote, 'You and your firm would be entitled to pay T&TFF via LOC 2006 Ltd an immediate payment of US$80,000 via a certified cheque, bank draft or wire transfer in the amount of US$80,000 and T&TFF would be entitled to five per cent of your gross sales of your proposed merchandise.'

The tickets mystery deepened when Warner explained that his Simpaul tickets were not any part of the T&TFF allocation from FIFA but had been purchased through an un-named European tour operator long before Trinidad had even qualified for Germany. He didn't explain how this other company had obtained tickets.

On the morning of 3 January Warner, flanked by son Daryan, stood at the podium in the Crowne Plaza in Port of Spain. 'Warner in fighting mood,' reported the *Guardian*. 'I find myself here before you to defend my good name and that of my family against the mischief and character assassination,' he began.

'I believe that the three-part series which was published over the Christmas weekend is part of a well timed, carefully orchestrated character assassination.' Warner wanted people to know that the series was part of a government conspiracy against him and his party the UNC. It was a 'venomous, vitriolic personal attack with a clear political agenda'.

The articles by 'a creature called Liburd' – the name spat out and spelled in his release as 'Lie-burd' – were part of 'Operation Get Warner'. Warner called Liburd an 'unrepentant and inveterate liar' writing 'fabrications and inaccuracies' and 'gross misrepresentations'.

In view of this . . . 'No one should attempt to impute improper business practices and conflicts of interest to me.' Warner's 5,000 word tirade was posted on the T&TFF website.

Liburd, unruffled by the abuse, wrote calmly in the next day's paper that Warner had made an 'unusual response' and had in fact confirmed many of the facts he had dug out for his series of stories.

Warner's tickets scandal was picked up by the international wires and appeared in newspapers, radio and television worldwide. Worst of all, for FIFA's image, it played big in Germany. The *Berliner Zeitung* headlined their version 'Jackpot for Jack the Ripper', the Munich *Süddeutsche Zeitung* took a similar line and the domestic news service *DPP* fed it into virtually every newsroom in the country.

Trinidad's premier Patrick Manning said that his government would intervene to get fair play for fans and Warner snapped back, 'No Government in the world can intervene in FIFA's business, and that is the bottom line.' Trying to close the scandal down Warner added 'This thing is of no interest to me, no value to me. I want to move ahead.'

Liburd was soon back at his keyboard reporting that Simpaul's website was backtracking on its package offer, now announcing 'Match Tickets are not included and you must source these directly from T&TFF or via the FIFA Web site.'

He called Simpaul and a helpful salesperson assured him they still had tickets. Asked to explain the discrepancy, the Simpaul person suggested they had sold out their 'internet quota', whatever that was. The London *Independent* joined the fun and reported that when they called the T&TFF asking for tickets, the T&TFF directed them to Simpaul. The paper's reporter Nick Harris estimated that Warner could make a profit of more than £10 million on his country's ticket allocation.

FIFA kept its head down as the scandal grew but when Liburd asked Zurich to comment, spokesman John Schumacher had to admit, 'Packaging tickets with other services is not permitted. This is addressed in Article 3.7 of Exhibit B (FIFA Regulations relating to Tickets) of the Participating Member Association (PMA) Ticketing Allocation Agreement (TAA), which states: "Tickets may not be sold as a part of a package, or made available on the condition that other product(s) and/or service(s), including without limitation, catering, accommodation and/or transportation, are also purchased."'

So Vice-President Warner was scorning FIFA's rules, drawn up to protect fans and prevent profiteering on tickets.

Lasana Liburd had spent a decade reporting Trinidad football both at home and from the UK. Naturally, he planned to report the World Cup and duly wrote off to FIFA House for his press credentials. That was before his stories about Jack had appeared. After those stories ran, Liburd was astonished to learn that FIFA had decided he must be banned from reporting the World Cup.

Warner's press spokesman Shaun Fuentes announced, 'We've been advised by FIFA that he (Liburd) would not be accredited to FIFA tournaments. Apparently he's in their black book, I can't say for sure.'

News of the ban also appeared to be a surprise to FIFA. Spokesman Andreas Herren began the back-peddling and emailed Liburd, 'Please note that FIFA does not have a black book nor ever had one. One journalist (Andrew Jennings whom as I understand you know) was declared persona non grata for FIFA events a few years ago due to his various allegations levelled at FIFA and its President. Otherwise, all journalists and photographers are eligible to apply for accreditation in accordance with the procedures.' But FIFA didn't offer any hope that the banned Liburd might still make it to Germany.

And surely it was too late. Accreditation for reporters had ended eight days earlier. The lists were closed. Liburd must watch the World Cup on television, back home in Trinidad. Eventually Sunny Hill gave in and Andreas Herren asked Liburd to apply direct to them. He did and got the accreditation that should never have been taken away from him.

ON 27 SEPTEMBER 2005 Peter Nobel made an application to the court in Meilen in a suburb of Zurich. Nobel, you may recall, is the lawyer who opened the bank account through which sports officials could return to the ISL liquidator bribes that they had received.

This time Professor Nobel's clients were FIFA and its president Sepp Blatter. In secret, he asked the court for an immediate European ban on this book. Nobel asked for an order that I and my publisher hand over a copy of this book. If we didn't, we must suffer criminal and civil penalties under Swiss law.

Nobel claimed that publication would cause 'massive personal injury' to his clients. The application ran to a few dozen pages and demanded a permanent ban on disseminating and publishing allegations concerning FIFA and FIFA officials. The list went on and on.

Nobel said that I had been attacking FIFA and Blatter for years with 'dubious' reports and was considered 'a sharp and particularly unfair critic'. Sometimes, apparently, I am 'shrill'. There were echoes of Lawrence Cartier in the claim that my accusations were 'unjustified' with 'defaming judgements and false assertions'.

Professor Nobel did have some evidence to help sway the court. He produced a number of articles I had published and lectures I had given. This surprised me. One was the article about Blatter's secret bonus from March 2003 that Blatter and Cartier had threatened to sue over – but subsequently not done so. He hadn't even complained about the others – although they can be found easily on the Internet.

The Meilen court was also requested to rule that as soon as the book was 'published or sold in Switzerland or abroad'– including the UK – it should be confiscated 'by the competent authority'. And if we disregarded the court's banning order – we should be fined and jailed for up to three months.

Judge S Zurcher denied Nobel's plea – but ordered us to submit our arguments. My copy of the writ was delivered a couple of months later by a bailiff acting for my local court and at the expense of the British taxpayer.

On 3 March 2006, Judge Zurcher dismissed FIFA's and Blatter's application in its entirety. They where ordered to pay the costs of me and my publishers. They were also given leave to appeal.

Later that summer came the World Cup. Italy won it . . . and the story continues . . .

PSST, WANT A TICKET FOR
THE WORLD CUP?

Jack Warner's got thousands to sell

THE GOOD TIMES keep on rolling for the Warner family. Jack's son Daryan runs their Simpaul travel company, buys and sells thousands of World Cup tickets, manages several of his father's other businesses and at weekends races his Porsche Gembella. Daryan's also a director of the family-owned club Joe Public who play at the FIFA-funded Joao Havelange Centre of Excellence, between Port of Spain and the airport, where he is sometimes billed as Chief Executive.

Brother Daryll has been promoted. He's now a FIFA development officer, spending money throughout the region. That's handy for the family. He's approved a $600,000 FIFA grant for a world-class all-weather pitch at the Centre of Excellence Stadium where Joe Public play. The Sepp Blatter Hall, with room for up to 3,500 customers, stages trade shows, weddings and corporate events. The Sportel hotel and its special attraction – the Nelson Mandela Room – are advertised to business travellers.

Jack Warner seems to have long forgotten that FIFA paid for the Centre and still own it. Haranguing a local politician in 2006, Warner promised to give the fellow the keys to the Centre if he retains his parliamentary seat at the next election.

When the Trinidad & Tobago team reached the World Cup in Germany in 2006, chests swelled with pride. Shaka Hislop, Dwight Yorke and the team joined the roster of Trinidad's national heroes. Jack Warner marked the occasion by having his hagiographer, Tino Singh of the *Trinidad Guardian*, knock out a quickie rewrite of his biography with a new title, *Zero to Hero*. Hero? Really? If you asked Trinidadians to name their heroes you'd be three times round the islands before you found a single vote for Jack. Tino did squeeze in a mention of one true hero, CLR James. Shame he couldn't be bothered to accurately name James's classic cricket text. Tino, mate, it's *Beyond a Boundary*.

Poor Jack. All that jumping up and down and no-one gave him credit for the team's success. And then, finally, he gets some attention . . . but it's the wrong kind. Remember the ticket rackets disclosed in Chapter 30? Well, by February 2006 it was international news. Trinidad's Government decided to take a closer look at Jack. Keith Rowley, a senior cabinet minister in the People's National Movement government, revisited the extraordinary budget of the 2001 FIFA Under-17 championships. He ran his eye over the construction contracts. Hmmm . . . interesting . . . according to Rowley whopping cost increases had been attributed to items which clearly could and should have been anticipated in the initial costing.

Pushed and harried by international media reports, FIFA was reluctantly taking an interest in Warner's ticket scams. Now Rowley invited FIFA to examine what he called 'inflated stadia costs'.

When the PNM was last in power in the mid-1990s they'd approved a budget of US$26.4 million. Then, said Rowley, after

Warner's friends in the United National Congress took power, 'Contracts were awarded in a very strange manner,' and the bill more than doubled to US$58.4 million. The AP wire headlined their story 'Warner Faces New Corruption Accusation' and Sepp Blatter and his circle in Zurich stuck their fingers deeper into their ears.

MY LETTERBOX sometimes shows a happy smile on its brass face. The day the minutes of FIFA's secretive Ethics Committee slipped through, my letterbox grinned widely.

Relentless press interest in Jack's dodgy dealings had forced Jack and FIFA to do something. Jack came up with a bright idea: dodge all the flak by reporting himself to the Ethics Committee. They reached for the ethics code, dusted off the cobwebs and met to decide whether Jack had stuck to the rules. According to the code, members should not abuse their position to obtain personal benefits, should declare business interests and act with complete integrity.

FIFA's rules specifically say that tickets should not be resold at a profit and shouldn't be sold in packages.

Was Jack ethical? Had he broken any rules?

On 15 February 2006 the Ethics Committee met at FIFA House to discuss Jack's rackets – with Jack himself. In the chair was Turkey's Senes Erzik. Around the table, seven men from the regional confederations. President Blatter popped in for a few minutes but left general secretary Urs Linsi, spin doctor Markus Siegler and head lawyer Heinz Tannler on guard to make sure things didn't get out of control.

According to the minutes that slipped through my letterbox, Warner admitted that his Simpaul company had been doing FIFA ticket business for the last 19 years. He also admitted that that 'the company belonged to him, his wife and their two sons – and that one of his sons was responsible for running the business.'

What about those allegations that he'd grabbed a chunk of tickets and was knocking them out at a big mark-up? Completely untrue, ranted Jack, and part of a political assassination campaign against him in Trinidad.

Who was behind this conspiracy? Warner named . . . me!

Chairman Erzik swiftly rejected the political conspiracy nonsense, said he was surprised that Warner was still selling tickets and recommended they find him guilty of a conflict of interest. Mohamed Bin Hammam agreed that Warner's activities were unethical and that 'a FIFA vice-president should not be selling tickets for the World Cup.' Australia's Les Murray said it was 'a serious matter', a very simple and clear-cut case. He felt they had to take action. Juan Pedro Damiani from Uruguay agreed. Warner had been acting unethically for the past 19 years. France's Dominique Rocheteau chipped in that Warner had to obey the rules.

One member dissented. New York lawyer Burton K Haimes (nominated to the committee by one Jack Warner), explained that he wasn't there to support Warner – but he did. According to the minutes he said, 'It was clearly a local political conflict.' If Warner was guilty of a conflict of interest, there was nothing in FIFA's code about it. Indeed 'he had a problem seeing what he [Warner] was supposed to have done that was a breach of the Code of Ethics.' It had all been a misconception.

Thanks for that Mr Haimes, said the rest of them, and issued a press release stating that Warner had violated FIFA's Code and asked the Executive Committee, which would meet in mid-March, to decide his punishment. He faced suspension and possible expulsion from FIFA.

After Warner had been dispatched, general secretary Urs Linsi proposed that reporter Jens Weinreich from Berlin should be declared *persona non grata* – like me. Linsi didn't like Weinreich's continually probing into what happened that morning in November

2005 when Investigating Magistrate Thomas Hildbrand raided Sunny Hill and seized financial records. Surely the ethics committee, mindful that Weinreich is highly respected in Germany where the World Cup would begin in four months' time, would kick this barmy censorship into the long grass?

On the contrary. The minutes record: 'The Committee unanimously agreed the general secretary's motion and referred the matter to the Executive Committee for ratification.'

When their recommendation reached Blatter he saw the problems this would cause in Germany and refused to put it on the agenda for the next committee meeting. Linsi was snubbed and the matter died.

I read through the minutes again and again. This, I thought, was something football fans might like to see for themselves. And didn't FIFA have a commitment to transparency? I uploaded the minutes to my website.

A month later the executive committee met in Zurich – but Warner had an answer to everything. He said there's no story, I've sold my shares, I don't own the company anymore. They cleared him.

MEANWHILE Ernst & Young, at FIFA's behest, were doing an audit of ticket sales. Jack's high-volume business soon attracted their attention.

For nearly a year Warner and his son Daryan had secretly engaged in industrial-strength ticket touting, surreptitiously selling thousands more precious pieces of cardboard to tour operators to package with hotel rooms in Germany. The Warners also booked thousands of rooms, every new deal cranking up potentially vast profits for their Simpaul company, estimated at around £500,000.

They ordered 900 tickets for England's first round games. They sold 1,500 tickets to a Mexican company. Then they agreed to supply a stunning 3,000 tickets to Japan. All orders went through brothers Jaime and Enrique Byrom, whose Manchester-based company have the FIFA contract for distributing World Cup tickets.

The day-to day dealings with the Byroms in England were handled by Daryan. But how much money was Simpaul actually making?

As the first edition of this book was dispatched to the printers I joined the BBC's flagship current affairs programme *Panorama* to dig deeper and report on the corruption allegations at FIFA. We spent weeks filming in Switzerland and in May 2006, we'd come to the Caribbean to look at Jack Warner's football empire. He'd flatly refused to be interviewed.

We learned that Jack was due to speak at a political rally. Jack is deputy political leader of the UNC, a party in trouble. Three weeks earlier former UNC Prime Minister Baseo Panday had been found guilty of corruption and sentenced to two years' hard labour. The party needed a lift. A few hundred supporters of the UNC party gathered on this steamy tropical night around the floodlit platform in the market square in the small town of Rio Claro in south Trinidad.

Waiting for Warner out on the pavement was a *Panorama* crew: one man acting as lookout, two with cameras, and me. Warner's limousine drew up. He got out and walked towards the market place. I stepped out to greet him.

'Good evening, Mr Warner. Andrew Jennings, BBC *Panorama* programme. Would you give me an interview?'

Warner kept on walking.

I asked him again.

'How much profit do you expect to make from trading in World Cup tickets this year?' Warner paused, stared at me, then brushed past. 'Go f*** yourself,' he hissed. We left.

We drove off through the night. Inside the market square Jack took to the podium. Hundreds of browbeaten UNC supporters waited to hear some words of encouragement, perhaps an attack on the government. Instead, Jack's baffled listeners heard this tirade: 'No foreigner, particularly a white foreigner, will come to my country and harass me, intimidate me and push me around.'

Trinidadians pride themselves on being an ethnically mixed country. You can't spot a Trinidadian by his or her colour; the whole world is there. In Trinidad playing the race card is considered a cheap trick. Worse than that, it's an insult to the spirit of the nation. Warner's outburst went out on the local television news, causing deep embarrassment across Trinidad. For the rest of our stay strangers walked up to us and apologised for Jack's behaviour. We felt safe in Trinidad. The more Jack abused us, the more ordinary Trinidadians extended warmth and support. Some said they were used to rudeness and irrational outbursts from Jack, but this time he'd gone too far.

IT TURNED OUT THAT Jack had his own reasons for flying off the handle. I didn't know it at the time, but Jack did. The Ernst & Young investigators were closing in on him. (Since leaving Trinidad I've acquired Ernst & Young's confidential reports, so I can tell you a little more about what happened.)

Back in March 2006, Ernst & Young's Peter Coats and Christian Winter left their desks in Switzerland, and flew to Manchester to talk to the Byrom brothers. Daryan turned up. He pledged total transparency. Coats and Winter told him there were specific documents they needed to see. Of, course, he said, no problem. But they're in Trinidad; you'd have to make the trip.

A week later the investigators sat in the Trinidad Hilton, waiting for the promised files. Daryan turned up and handed them one document but refused to give them any more. Coats and Winter reminded him that Simpaul's contract with FIFA stipulated he must produce any information requested by the auditors. Daryan told them that FIFA would have to make a formal request and if they did, he would seek local legal advice on whether he need comply. And that wasn't all.

In their subsequent report to Urs Linsi, on 11 April 2006, the investigators quoted Daryan telling them: 'His decision to not meet further information (requests) was motivated by the fact that he had entered into similar transactions in the past.' In other words, what's all the fuss about? This is the way we've always dealt with FIFA. The investigators say Daryan claimed 'he would not have commenced these transactions without a confirmation that he would receive the tickets.' In other words, Daryan was confident that FIFA would supply the tickets because they always did.

So, well before *Panorama* and I landed in Trinidad, Jack was a worried man. And he wasn't just worried about the gigantic ticket orders going through Simpaul. I know, because I've since seen a little of his email correspondence, he was feeling anxious about the size of his own, personal orders for tickets. So anxious that he looked again at those orders, and tried to backpedal out of them.

In early May (by chance, only hours before he would walk into *Panorama* and me at the Rio Claro market square) Jack fired off an email to the Byrom brothers asking them to cancel his personal order.

Jaime replied: 'Are you sure?'

Jack wrote back: 'I do wish to formally advise that I have no interest in acquiring any World Cup tickets on any personal order of mine . . . please be advised that this decision of mine is FINAL even if I have already made a payment for same which payment I am also prepared to lose.' He copied the email to Urs Linsi,

Chuck Blazer and Jerome Champagne, as if to convince them he was cleaning up his act.

So, let's see this from Jack's point of view. There he is, under pressure, frantically locking stable doors long after horses have bolted. He pops out to address a political meeting and, oh dear, there's *Panorama* and me, asking difficult questions. Poor Jack. No wonder he responded with that ugly suggestion about what I should do with myself.

That night in Rio Claro I didn't know anything about Coats and Winter and the Byrom Brothers. I was on a different trail. Remember Jack said he didn't own Simpaul any more? I wondered, had he really parted company so hurriedly with the business he'd built up over nearly two decades? I went to the government offices and obtained Simpaul's registration documents. They recorded that on 6 March 2006 Warner and his wife Maureen had sold their shares to Ms Princess Rose Campbell, a veterinarian and to Ms Margaret Fletcher, a housewife. These ladies gave the same address at 177 Kitchener Avenue in the township of Barataria.

A vet and a housewife? What could they know about the travel business, about airlines, hotel chains, discounts and deals? And where did they find the money to buy this profitable company? I called them. A woman's voice answered. We established that she was Ms Fletcher but when I asked her about Simpaul, the line went dead. I called again, immediately, and this time a man answered. Ms Fletcher had 'gone out.' The line went dead again.

Ten minutes later, as the sun was setting, I walked up to the modest bungalow at 177 Kitchener Avenue. There was a middle-aged woman at the gate, talking to a neighbour.

I strolled over and said, 'Ms Fletcher?' She turned and raced back up her garden path, shot into her house and slammed the front door. I watched the sitting room curtains swish shut.

It's true these two ladies own one share each in the company. But the company secretary is still Pat Modeste, Jack Warner's personal assistant. In the company documents she gives her address as 113 Edward Street, Port of Spain. That's Warner's office. And Daryan remains managing director, doing Simpaul's ticket and room deals.

ALL OF TRINIDAD wanted to give their team a happy send-off. Trinidad & Tobago were playing Peru at the Haseley Crawford Stadium in a friendly just before going off to Germany. It was a rare chance for Trinidadians to see their boys in action.

When the Warriors had played their qualifying matches, fans had paid TT$100 for a ticket or TT$200 for the better seats. Now, Warner jacked up the prices. Fans had to stump up TT$300 and TT$500. People were furious and dismayed. Here was their last chance to see the Warriors, who were going to the World Cup for the first time in Trinidad's history and Jack had hiked the price so high that Trinidadians couldn't see their team play. The government protested.

With a day left in Trinidad we drove over to Piarco Airport to get some pictures of the T&T team who'd flown in to do a coach tour around the island, saying thanks and farewell to the fans before they left for Germany. We'd had no idea that Jack would be there, but there he was, waiting by the coaches, ready to join the party.

I strolled over and said, 'Mr Warner, hello again.'

He wasn't pleased to see me.

'Leave me alone, boy!' he shouted, and thumped me hard in the chest.

I'm not a boy. And I'm not a fighting man. I'm 62 years old. I write for a living. Jack had a strong punch. I staggered back. I managed to stay standing.

Warner's officials moved in. One of them blocked cameraman Steve Foote. Another shoved producer Roger Corke. They kept their cameras running.

Warner jumped on a team coach and hunkered down below the window. We could still see him though. I called through the glass, 'Hello Mr Warner, I know you're there . . . Hello . . . Mr Warner? He turned his head away. I bounced up and down. I tapped on the glass.

For all the trouble we seemed to be causing, we were making more friends in Trinidad. Players on the coach witnessed Warner's punch. They pulled out cell phones and called the BBC asking, Was I all right? Jack got in touch, too, but for a different reason.

His lawyer Om Lalla wrote to the BBC. He accused me of 'approaching our client in an aggressive manner and violently shoving a microphone into our client's face thereby causing injuries to our client's upper lip.'

That's odd. I thought *I* was the victim. And I hadn't been aggressive towards Jack. I'd used my best BBC manners. And what was this about shoving a microphone in his face? I wasn't using a hand-mike. The only microphone I had was a tiny little thing clipped to my shirt collar. And you don't have to take my word for it. It was clear to any of the millions of people around the world who watched *Panorama*, and to all the Trinidadians who saw their evening news. Why was Jack making allegations that were so demonstrably untrue? What was his problem? Was he cracking under the strain?

Maybe. He told the local media: 'When he pressed my lips with the mike it was not shown. It was not shown on television and it was not reported in the newspapers.' You had to admire Jack's pluck. Despite these terrible injuries to his upper lip he somehow managed to keep on talking.

And not content with whacking me in the chest, he instructed lawyer Om Lalla to hit me where it hurt. Lalla wrote to the distributors of this book warning them that Jack planned to sue them and me for 'serious libel' and 'false accusations'. He added, 'We have advised our client that he is entitled to substantial compensation.' We're still waiting for Jack's next move.

BERLIN, June 2006 . . . The 2006 World Cup. The Warriors were playing their hearts out. The Warners were working hard too. Daryan was flying around Germany doing ticket deals – some of which bore the name of the Football Association of Grenada. It was just a few months since he'd given the finger to Ernst & Young's Coats and Winter, and it didn't seem to have done him any harm.

On 14 June 2006 Daryan popped into the World Cup ticket office in Berlin and signed for 180 tickets on Jack's tab. They were quickly resold at four times their face value.

Within days, Jack was attempting another big ticket order. A very big ticket order and very late in the day. On 23 June he emailed the Byroms, cheekily heading his message with the Adidas slogan, 'Impossible is nothing.' He wanted 1,105 tickets for the later rounds in the tournament, including 95 for each of the semi-finals and 100 for the final. The next day he ordered another 30 for the final.

THE STORY I've told you here, about Ernst & Young's investigation and Daryan's shenanigans . . . all this was known to only a few people all through that World Cup summer. Then, in early September, someone tipped me off about a bitter row going on between Jack Warner and general secretary Urs Linsi who clearly didn't believe that Jack had detached himself from either Simpaul or its World Cup profits. Warner accused Linsi of a 'hostile tone and veiled threats.'

There was an executive committee meeting coming up. Surely by now they'd be acting on the Ernst & Young reports? I looked at the agenda. Nothing there. Does that mean the executive committee didn't know about all this? It was time to tell them.

I published a story in the London *Daily Mail* and posted the Ernst & Young reports on my website. Suddenly, with only three days' notice, the matter was added to the agenda for 15 September. The international press picked up the story. Now the world was watching.

The Executive Committee met. Jack's empire CONCACAF weighed in with a report commissioned by his friend Chuck Blazer from John Collins, a Chicago-based lawyer. Collins happens to sit on FIFA's legal committee. He found that Warner had done nothing wrong. Indeed Warner was the injured party, because someone at FIFA had leaked details of Ernst & Young's 'incomplete investigation' and this had caused 'significant harm' to Warner.

Attached to the dossier was a letter to Warner from another one of his lawyers, Mr Bruppacher of Zurich; he wondered about the possibility of suing Ernst & Young. And perhaps Urs Linsi as well for defamation 'under criminal and civil law.'

After the committee meeting Blatter sat on the stage in the auditorium at FIFA's new HQ and faced the press. Pale and sickly under the lights, tight-faced, he said the matter would go to the disciplinary committee but there was something more important to announce. Lord Seb Coe was to head FIFA's new Ethics Committee. Would Coe be looking into the Warner scandal, Blatter was asked. No, came the answer, only future issues. As for the disciplinary committee, we'd have to wait and see.

*   *   *

JACK WARNER is not a popular fellow in the Soca Warriors dressing room. In the past players have walked out of training sessions demanding payment of match fees and complaining about lack of basic facilities like medical supplies and water bottles.

They were looking forward to their earnings from the summer's campaign. Jack Warner had promised them 50 percent of the commercial profit revenues during their qualifying games and in Germany.

Trinidad accountant Kenny Rampersad worked out the numbers and produced them in early October 2006. Kenny assembles the accounts for most of Warner's various enterprises. Kenny hadn't found it easy to produce exact figures. He wrote, 'Please be advised that consistent with normal accounting principles we have made estimates in such instances where specific documentation was unavailable. In particular we have estimated the costs for hotel accommodation and players' fees and allowances.' No copies of hotel bills from just a few months earlier? Somebody had been careless.

And Kenny had another surprise for the team. He claimed that 'since many of the sponsors contributed to both the Germany campaign as well as South Africa 2010, the sponsorship income was treated in the following manner: two-thirds for the Germany campaign and one-third for the South Africa campaign.'

One-third of the sponsorship money being withheld? Almost £361,000 being taken out of the equation? To pay for a campaign to qualify for South Africa in four years' time? This was news to the squad. Then they turned to the bottom line. Millions had flowed in from sponsors, ticket sales and the sale of television rights. What would each man get?

£494.

These men are not by nature political. They love to play for their country. They didn't have an argument with Trinidad. Jack was the problem. They had to act.

The Soca Warriors said they'd go on strike. As Dwight Yorke told reporters gathered round him at the Haseley Crawford Stadium, 'The contracts that we enter into are not worth the paper they are written on.'

Showing all the tact that Jack's cronies are famous for, Trinidad Federation general secretary Richard Groden accused the team of 'delinquency' and 'less than honourable motives.' Warner told Canadian reporters they were 'greedy'. In the end, after media pressure and an angry response from the fans, Groden announced they would 'repatriate' to the players the money retained for the 2010 campaign. He said the Trinidad Federation was keen on 'maintaining our integrity in the world of football.' The team hired the firm Athletes 1 Legal who demanded a full account of the World Cup revenue.

Monday 4 December, Zurich Airport. Warner was in town for an executive committee meeting. It was a big one for him. There'd be a verdict from the disciplinary committee on his ticket operations. The BBC had asked him to give an interview about ticket deals and payments to the players – and again he had refused. So I was there with Steve 'Rocksteady' Foote again with the big camera.

Warner, clutching his Diplomatic Passport, had been ushered past immigration and customs by one of the airport authorities' Ms Meet 'n' Greet.

'Mr Warner, good morning, welcome to Zurich'.

He ignored me and speeded up.

I kept pace with him through the airport lobby.

'Mr Warner,' I said, 'can I ask you, yet again, how much profit did you make selling World Cup tickets this year?'

Warner looked around. 'If I could have spit on you I would've spat on you . . . I would not, of course, dignify my spit.'

Whatever was Warner thinking of? Perhaps he saw Tony Pasfield, our soundman with his boom mike, on the other side of Steve Foote, and guessed that was the only mike we had. What he said was picked up loud and clear by the mini-mike on my shirt.

'Why would you spit on me?' I asked.

'Because you're garbage,' said the FIFA vice-president.

I asked him again, 'How much did you make?'

'Ask your mother.'

'Ask my mother? My mother's dead actually, but it's nice of you to remind me of that.'

'Go find her, find her,' he said.

AFTER THE EXCO meeting Blatter came out to meet the press who were eager to find out what they'd decided about Jack.

'We have closed the file,' he said.

Marcel Mathier, the disciplinary committee chairman, chipped in, saying there was 'no concrete evidence' that Warner knew about the resale of World Cup tickets by Daryan.

That's all the press got from Blatter and Mathier. 'We have closed the file.'

As this paperback edition was going to the printers, I happened upon the minutes of that executive committee meeting of December 2006. Those minutes reveal that the matter was not in the least bit 'closed'.

They reveal that back in June, when Ernst & Young auditors estimated that Daryan might make a £500,000 profit from World Cup deals, the Exco had ordered Simpaul Travel to pay back to FIFA a whopping 754,375 Euros (US$992,652) which FIFA would in turn donate to its favourite charity, SOS Children's Villages.

Come December, the Warners had paid only US$250,000

351

'despite numerous reminders.' Blatter recommended to the Committee that FIFA should in future allocate no tickets to Simpaul. The committee agreed.

So why didn't Blatter tell the press about this? Because Simpaul's ticket deals were a private matter? Because Blatter feared Daryan might never pay up and then he'd look a fool? Because he didn't want to embarrass his friend Jack?

The official statement merely expressed 'disapproval' of Warner's conduct. The committee reminded him 'to exercise the requisite level of care in ticketing matters in the future.' Reporters rolled their eyes.

Blatter said: 'Jack Warner should ensure that his son Daryan does not abuse the position held by his father.'

'Oh, *bollocks*!' wrote Australian reporter Jesse Fink later that day on the Foxsports website. 'Warner's whole journey to the top of Caribbean football has been marked by a readiness to abuse his position. He should tell his son to stop? A father-to-son pep talk? Ha ha. This latest lettuce-leaf flogging of one its most ethically bankrupt executives has shown FIFA has no willingness to stamp out its own endemic corruption.'

CHASING THOSE BRIBES

Please, someone, speak to us!

WE'RE DRIVING THROUGH Switzerland in the world's fastest car. It's a rental car. All around us, snow-topped Alps, glittering lakes. The perfect setting for a romantic holiday. But beside me is James Oliver from BBC's *Panorama* programme. It's the spring of 2006 and we're heading for our next encounter with someone who probably isn't going to tell us what we desperately want to know.

Some things we already know. For twenty years ISL paid bribes to FIFA officials. What we don't know is exactly how they did it. We're searching for people who, we believe, know what really happened at ISL. We're scouring Switzerland, from Lausanne in the south, in the valleys around Lucerne and Zug and up to Zurich in the north. Here's the routine.

Ascend the steps of a prosperous villa. Ring bell. Wait. Clear throat. Smooth jacket. Wait a little longer. Admire view. Descend steps – nobody's in.

A quick look at the map, a sandwich, a cup of coffee, another Alp, another villa. Up the steps. No bell this time. Press the video-com button and smile into the lens.

The light flashes on.

'Hello, I'm Andrew Jenni . . .'

The light goes out.

On it goes, day after day. Villa after villa. No luck.

Then, another day, another villa, another door-bell.

'Hello, I'm Andrew Jennings.'

'Come in.'

A courteous welcome, not a warm one. Our host, let's call him 'Mr Brown', looks burdened. He sits us down. He's been expecting us. And, for reasons we still don't fully understand, Mr Brown, who worked at the heart of ISL for many years, wants to talk.

Horst Dassler, he tells us, had always made a point of mixing friendship with business. Of course he gave presents to his 'friends'. Of course he entertained them lavishly. He understood that people like presents, they like surprises. When a sparkling new Mercedes was unexpectedly delivered to a European football official on his birthday, it wasn't tied to a particular contract and it wasn't solicited. It was just an expression of 'friendship'.

But when Dassler went after the hugely valuable marketing contracts, like the football World Cup, things were altogether different. Key sports officials who could swing the business in his direction – or someone else's – demanded kickbacks.

Back in the mid-eighties, after Mr Brown had been at ISL a few years, he was told about the rackets. ISL paid bribes to sports officials and that's how they got their contracts, year after year after year. You had to keep paying or you didn't get the contracts. That was the game.

Even the sleepiest auditors tend to wake up when gigantic suitcases of illegal cash payments are bumped and dragged across the balance sheet. So Dassler had to come up with ingenious methods for getting the bribe money out of the company.

The plan he devised was that ISL would strike a deal with FIFA, the IOC, the IAAF or some other sports federation, making gigantic and very public payments in exchange for exclusive rights to market championships to sponsors and later to television networks. Under the contracts all payments from ISL to FIFA went to a named bank account in Switzerland.

All tickety-boo.

Behind the scenes, ISL made payments for 'Additional Rights'. Never mind that there *were* no additional rights. They were the cover under which bribes were paid.

'Additional Rights Payments' travelled to sports officials by various channels. Sometimes they went through law firms, sometimes through numbered Swiss bank accounts, to accounts held abroad, to offshore companies.

(Later, we got lucky on another front door in Switzerland and another man, we'll call him 'Mr Green', who'd worked in the bowels of ISL, recalled: 'Large payments were often sent to banks who had previously been given a list of names to forward the cash to. It was like paying salaries.')

The lake below us shrank from bright mirror to black pool. The lights in the glass-walled lounge came on, coffee was served and he continued talking in his dry, formal voice. Mr Brown seemed to loosen up – just a little. He gave a little cough, then he named to us the famous sports leader to whom ISL paid one million Swiss francs every six months – roughly one million pounds sterling a year – for more than a decade.

I didn't dare look at James. He didn't dare look at me. We both knew that if we showed our excitement we might scare Brown off.

Mr Brown named more beneficiaries. (Our lawyers won't let us repeat them.) Officials from several sports. One from Africa.

355

Mr Green said that an Italian, now dead, was the second biggest recipient. Another European was paid for more than a decade. Mr Brown named four from Latin America and in total, he believed, about twelve individuals were on permanent, contracted, kickbacks.

These were the salary men. Brown told us that ISL also made one-off payments to make certain things happen. When ISL badly wanted a particular football game to be played, he said, they came up with one million dollars that was shared between a top Italian club and its owner.

And the son of a leading UN official got a pay-off.

Then in the mid-1990s the whole business got more difficult. Just as new, more lucrative television contracts became available, ISL's contract with FIFA came up for renewal. FIFA officials knew the value of the contracts in their gift, and they wanted a slice of that money for themselves. Mr Brown told us that as the contracts got bigger the sports officials got greedier.

'The payments soared,' he said. (Later, I rummaged through my file. I looked again at the letter from IMG's Eric Drossart to FIFA in the spring of 1996: 'We do not believe that the World Cup representation question is being dealt with evenly . . . such obviously preferential treatment being given to other parties.')

ISL won the marketing and television rights in the mid-1990s to the World Cups of 2002 and 2006. Just as the bribes were getting bigger, there were more reasons to take more care over hiding them. Dassler family shareholders wanted to sell shares. A sale of shares would put the company accounts under greater scrutiny than ever before. ISL came up with new and more secret channels for the bribes.

As soon as the new FIFA contract was signed ISL set up the Nunca foundation in Liechtenstein. In 1999, our Mr Brown told us that ISL sent about 20 million francs – more than £9 million – to Nunca, to take care of future bribes. But the foundation didn't actually pay the bribes. Nunca moved the money again to Sunbow S.A., a wholly-owned shell company in the British Virgin Islands. Sunbow had the list of names who should be sent money.

That was it. We put our coats on, said thank you. James and I walked to the car without saying a word to each other, barely breathing. We got in, shut the doors. We breathed again. We'd got it.

WE WEREN'T the only ones who were excited about Sunbow's list of people who'd taken bribes from ISL.

Remember Thomas Hildbrand? He's the Zug Investigating magistrate who in May 2005 charged a bunch of ISL executives with embezzling the Globo television money that should have gone to FIFA. Hildbrand had the Sunbow list, but before he could use it he'd had to ask permission from a judge.

Under Hildbrand's interrogation, several ISL executives admitted paying kickbacks in return for contracts.

Hildbrand didn't stop there. In November 2005 he surprised everybody by raiding FIFA House and seizing files from the offices of Sepp Blatter and his general secretary Urs Linsi.

And he'd kept on investigating. Now he wanted to use the Sunbow list again, and again he had to ask permission. On Thursday 20 April 2006, Judge Martin Nigg in the Liechtenstein Royal Court in Vaduz said yes, he could.

A month later James and I got hold of a single page of the judge's decision from Swiss investigative reporter Jean-Francois Tanda, and what we found there blew our socks off.

It concerned the deal that ISL liquidator Thomas Bauer had struck with Jean-Marie Weber and lawyer Peter Nobel back in February 2004, a story I told in Chapter 30 of this book: 2.5 million

Swiss francs of bribe money was anonymously repaid to the liquidator. Well, I didn't have the whole story.

What Hildbrand told Judge Nigg was that the 2.5 million came, not from officials who'd paid the bribe, but from FIFA itself.

Yes, ISL had bribed FIFA officials. And when creditors demanded their money back, FIFA wrote the cheque.

Hildbrand wanted Nigg's permission to use the Sunbow list and other documents so that he could find out whether FIFA had acted illegally when it paid back the bribe money. Had FIFA officials broken Swiss criminal law? Had they defrauded FIFA?

And there was more.

It appeared from Nigg's judgment that ISL was still paying bribes as late as January 2001.

The company was at that time in mortal trouble, hadn't paid creditors for months and inside FIFA some people were urgently arguing that it was time to cut ISL off. Terminate the ISL contracts. If FIFA did that, it was all over for ISL. Still, the company kept on paying bribes. Whoever to?

I WANTED to ask Sepp Blatter why FIFA had repaid the bribe money.

It was early June, just before the Germany World Cup. Blatter was due to board a private Gulfstream jet in Zurich airport for the forty-five minute flight to Frankfurt. The *Panorama* team and I were waiting for him outside the door of the private charter terminal.

The Presidential Mercedes drew up. The driver opened the President's door and Sepp Blatter got out.

I walked over.

'Good morning, President Blatter. Why did FIFA pay back the ISL bribes?'

He reached inside the car for his briefcase and said nothing.

'Did you ever take bribes from ISL?'

He looked through me and said nothing.

'Can I ask you again, why did FIFA repay the ISL bribes?' He didn't speak.

He struck off towards the private charter building and said nothing.

I trotted after him.

'President Blatter, I must ask you, are you a fit and proper person to control world football?'

Sepp headed for the door. An airport official held it open for him. He slipped inside and the door closed silently behind him.

LIES, ADULTERY AND FABRICATION

How Sepp plays fair

SIXTEEN MONTHS AFTER the Boxing Day tsunami devastated coastal communities in southern Asia, Sepp Blatter blew in on a humanitarian tour. Dispensing cash and kind words, Sepp handed a football to some little orphans. 'The way they embraced the ball was special,' Sepp recalled. 'That moment, the unrivalled joy, will always remain with me.'

FIFA's slogan, 'My game is fair play', isn't just about football, it's about *everything*. It's about 'equality, peace, children's rights, health, education and the environment.' It's about racism and disability. It's about tsunamis.

FIFA's stated policy is to encourage 'fair play in society . . . leading by example.' Like Sepp says, 'As world football's supreme body, FIFA is responding openly to its social duty as an organisation of international status and renown.'

Does *FIFA* play fair?

Let me tell you a story. It's about global corporations and

sponsorship deals. It's a human story, and the human at the heart of it is Sepp Blatter.

Back in the summer of 2003, Blatter hand-picked a handsome Frenchman to shake up FIFA's sponsors. Jérôme Valcke's mission was to get more money, *much* more money, out of Adidas, Sony, Coca-Cola, Emirates Airlines, Hyundai and MasterCard.

The sponsors' most recent contracts would expire after World Cup Germany in 2006. This time around, FIFA would offer two World Cups in one big package and hike up the price.

Our story concerns just one of the sponsors, a company that has paid FIFA more than US$100 million over the past sixteen years to get *this* connection into our minds:

Football = Pelé = MasterCard.

The most fanatically followed sports event on the planet pushes MasterCard's message into homes in every country, on televisions in every bar. If you want to buy World Cup tickets by credit card, it's got to be a MasterCard – ideally one with Pelé's image on it. Each World Cup, millions of new customers apply for a MasterCard.

Football's value to MasterCard is so huge that it's protected by a clause in the contract: when the sponsorship comes up for renewal, MasterCard gets first shot. If, after 90 days, MasterCard *doesn't* want it, then *and only then* can FIFA offer it elsewhere. Lawyers call it 'first right of refusal' or 'first right to acquire'.

IN THE SPRING of 2004 Jérôme Valcke and his team couldn't stop thinking about VISA. Gigantic. A global turnover exceeding US$3 trillion. The world's number one payment system. Three times bigger than MasterCard. VISA had the Olympics all locked up. For years they'd wanted football too. What if . . .

Thanks to Court documents we know what Sepp's boys did next.

Jérôme sent his sales director Robert Lampman to chat up a

VISA executive at a conference in California. Lampman followed up the meeting with an email, to VISA's HQ in San Francisco, confirming FIFA's hopes for 'a relationship with VISA on an informal basis'.

By that summer, Valcke and his team were talking numbers with VISA's sponsorship chief Tom Shepard and his team at the Athens Olympics. We're offering two World Cups for US$225 million, said Valcke. Here's 'a genuine opportunity' to 'pursue a relationship'.

Shepard said, hang on a minute, doesn't MasterCard have 'incumbency rights?'

'FIFA is free to engage in any commercial relationship it desires post 2006,' Valcke replied.

It was the old story.

Are you married? I'm free. Completely free.

Valcke's team pitched up at VISA's head office in San Francisco in December 2004, and made a detailed presentation. Following this meeting, FIFA's Robert Lampman repeated there was 'nothing in our agreement with MasterCard that would prohibit us from doing a deal with VISA'.

Free as a bird.

Then Sepp Blatter took personal charge of the negotiations, inviting VISA's chief executive officer Christopher Rodrigues to Zurich in January 2005. They'd known each other for years: Sepp is on the International Olympic Committee and Chris is an Olympic sponsor.

Over an intimate two-hour dinner, Sepp told Chris, 'The potential of VISA being a partner would be welcomed.' Jérôme Valcke followed up with an email to VISA's Tom Shepard. 'We share the same wish, to be partners soon!'

Was this fair play? What about Sepp's obligation to MasterCard, his loyal partner of sixteen years?

John Stuart, MasterCard's vice-president of Global Sponsorship, was about to experience how it felt to be a cheated wife. In early

February Jérôme Valcke and his team dropped in on John Stuart at MasterCard's New York head office and played that old game: keeping your options open.

For the very first time, Jérôme told John the terms of the new sponsorship cycle – and he said he'd need an answer within 90 days.

But the US$225 million price tag was more than four times the amount MasterCard had paid before, and the terms – two World Cups instead of one – were radically different. They'd need time to crunch the numbers; they couldn't possibly sign a deal within 90 days.

Okay, said FIFA, but you'll need to be in 'good faith negotiations' – in other words, working through the small print – by then. Not one of Sepp's boys owned up that they'd already offered the sponsorship to VISA. By then VISA had been crunching the numbers for months.

Meanwhile Valcke was pushing VISA to sign a deal and bragging to FIFA colleagues, 'Soon we will receive a call asking for a signature!!' He told them to keep stringing MasterCard along: 'Yes, we have to play careful with MC.' They needed two signed contracts to put before Sepp Blatter and the board.

One hitch. Sepp's boys had been a little too greedy when they'd designed the sponsorship. To hike up the price they'd thrown in things like mortgages and current accounts – banking things. But VISA and MasterCard don't do banking, and they didn't want to pay for rights they couldn't use. Both companies turned FIFA down.

Valcke and his team stripped out the banking stuff nobody wanted and slashed the price from US$225 million to US$180 million. They called this new deal 'financial services light' and they offered it first to . . . VISA.

At VISA's San Francisco HQ in May 2005 Jérôme Valcke and Stefan Schuster said: if you agree to this, the FIFA board could approve a deal within four weeks.

Two days later FIFA offered 'financial services light' to MasterCard in New York.

Sepp's boys told VISA, blow-by-blow, how things were going in the rival camp, giving VISA a secret and continuing advantage over MasterCard who had no idea they were in a contest.

Here's how FIFA's Stefan Schuster saw it: 'If you tell your wife that you're cheating on her, it's a disruption to your marriage. If she doesn't know about it until the end, and you live until 90 and it was just one occasion, then maybe it's the better way. And we choose this one.'

But people talk.

In the autumn MasterCard's John Stuart confronted Jérôme Valcke. I've heard rumours about you and VISA, said John.

There's no truth in them, said Jérôme.

You're the only one.

So John Stuart carried on negotiating for another four weeks. Then, he said, let's get something in writing; we'll send you a 'letter of intent'.

'Entirely unnecessary,' said FIFA lawyer Tom Houseman: Our relationship is 'strong enough'.

Trust me.

Loyal John kept on talking.

On 24 October John Stuart told Valcke that, although US$170 million looked fairer, MasterCard was prepared to pay FIFA's US$180 million asking price.

Meanwhile, VISA offered just US$140 million in cash, plus a package of 'incentive fees' and 'value in kind' promotions that VISA reckoned was worth another US$15 million.

(That US$15 million 'value in kind' will matter in our story. In truth, FIFA prefers cash. In truth, Valcke believed 'value in kind' had 'no value'. But, as we'll see, truth is about to take a tumble.)

On 26 October in Zurich Valcke presented both offers to a

board chaired by Sepp Blatter. Strangely, some of the numbers had changed.

Now, Valcke said VISA was offering US$154 million cash, plus US$16 million in 'promotional value', a total bid, he claimed, of US$170 million. He said MasterCard had offered US$180 million in cash. The board unanimously declared the sponsorship 'sold' to MasterCard.

The next day Jérôme Valcke got on the phone to MasterCard's John Stuart. Did he tell John the good news?

No, he didn't.

He said VISA had offered US$170 million. However, the board had agreed to sign with MasterCard, so long as they paid the full US$180 million asking price.

Okay, said John Stuart, US$180 million it is.

That should have been that. But it wasn't.

Jérôme Valcke told his staff, who hadn't been at the board meeting, that they'd given him permission to close a deal with VISA *or* with MasterCard! And Valcke himself could decide!

Then he called VISA and came up with yet another story, telling Tom Shepard the board had approved concluding a transaction with VISA. Tom Shepard emailed back, saying VISA was, 'very excited about formalizing this agreement.'

Jérôme felt Tom was maybe a bit too excited. Actually, we've got 'two offers on . . . the table', he said. The board would make a decision, 'when and only when an agreement is signed.'

Then, Julio Grondona, chair of FIFA's finance committee, made a public announcement.

'Congratulations to MasterCard!'

What? At VISA's San Francisco office, Tom Shepard called Jérôme Valcke and asked, 'What *is* going on?'

'Julio's got hold of 'mixed information', said Jérôme. 'We have not finalized and are still in the process with both of you.'

He'd get Julio 'under control', make sure he 'shuts his mouth in the future'.

Then Jérôme rattled off a note to his immediate boss, Urs Linsi, FIFA's general secretary, saying: Tell Julio 'to stop!!' because 'we want to keep both VISA and MasterCard in the race to make sure we will get the best terms.'

HERE'S HOW FIFA'S sponsorship process is supposed to work:
- A deal is agreed.
- Then it goes to Zurich before a board, chaired by Sepp Blatter.
- It goes to the finance committee, on which Sepp Blatter sits.
- Finally it goes before the executive committee, chaired by Sepp Blatter.

Here's how FIFA handled MasterCard:
- A deal was agreed.
- As we've seen, the board, chaired by Blatter, declared the sponsorship 'sold' to MasterCard.
- Then Julio's finance committee said Yes to MasterCard.

Only one more step to go.
- The executive committee, chaired by Sepp Blatter, met in Zurich on 7 December. The board approved the MasterCard deal. (Later, when things go pear-shaped, FIFA will *lose* the minutes of this meeting and *find* an audio-tape that has a mysterious gap where the approval of MasterCard is supposed to be.)

After the meeting, Valcke told his staff that FIFA couldn't 'officially make a decision' in favour of MasterCard until Valcke and his team had got VISA to sign a deal.

And Sepp's boys carried on flying between Zurich, New York and San Francisco, chasing two deals.

By late January 2006 in New York MasterCard was ready to

sign the 'long form contract' that covers all the detailed business. Valcke said they'd 'execute the agreement' at the FIFA board meeting in March.

But, during February, Jérôme arranged to meet his VISA chums at the Winter Olympics in Turin

And he emailed VISA's Tom Shepard urging him to equal MasterCard's US$180 million cash offer and throw in that 'value in kind'. Do that by the end of the month and you'll get the sponsorship. 'There will be no discussion,' Valcke said, indicating that he could steer the board's decision VISA's way.

But Tom said VISA couldn't match MasterCard's price.

JÉRÔME VALCKE delivered the 'FINAL version' of the MasterCard sponsorship contract to John Stuart on 3 March. All Stuart had to do was get his top man's signature on it and send it back. Then, said Valcke, Sepp Blatter would countersign.

John Stuart was a very happy man.

He congratulated Sepp's boys on the 'great job' they'd done to 'bring a fair and balanced approach to the negotiation.' They all enjoyed a 'true spirit of partnership.'

Jérôme agreed: 'Our partnership will have such a good start.'

(John Stuart had the contracts signed. On 24 March he couriered them over to FIFA, as arranged, to be countersigned by Blatter.)

But on 3 March, the very day he'd sent the contract to John, Jérôme Valcke told VISA's Tom Shepard, I'm seeing Sepp next week. I want 'a clean version of our agreement with your final financial offer' so we can 'have on our table both agreements.'

Jérôme told Tom to get VISA's top man Christopher Rodrigues to give Blatter a call.

'VISA must come with an offer and signed agreement by Monday,' Jérôme said to Tom. It must be cash, US$180 million.

'I am giving you the wishes Blatter has expressed to finalize, now it is with you.'

And Valcke told his staff that FIFA preferred VISA.

MARKETING MAN Robert Lampman was troubled about how FIFA was treating MasterCard. 'There is no question, right or wrong, that MC believe they have a deal with us,' he told Valcke. 'If I had a vote, I think there is something to be said for the way we conduct business.'

But he didn't have a vote.

However, said Lampman, if we *must* go with VISA, we'll need to use the 'trademark issue'.

Ah, yes, the 'trademark issue'.

MasterCard, whose logo is two overlapping circles, had long ago challenged FIFA's efforts to register *its* two overlapping soccer balls in various categories including credit cards. The quarrel had rumbled on for years. During these latest contract talks they'd all agreed to set it aside, to 'park' it, for eight more years.

Lampman saw the 'trademark issue' as the 'only way out' with MasterCard.

Still, he didn't think much of his own idea, and nor did Stefan Schuster who told Valcke that the 'entire FIFA team' thought that digging up the trademark issue was a dud.

If we proceed with VISA, he warned, FIFA's 'market credibility will be lost.'

Jérôme Valcke wasn't listening to his staff. He was watching the clock.

FIFA's board, finance committee and executive committee were due to meet on 14, 15 and 16 March 2006. (Valcke had told John Stuart this was when MasterCard's deal would be formally 'executed'.)

But on 13 March, Valcke told VISA's Tom Shepard, hurry up: 'Send me your final offer by email. The Board is meeting at 8am!!'

With just three hours to go, Tom Shepard called Jérôme Valcke and said, Okay, we'll pay US$180 million cash. Plus the US$15 million 'marketing in kind'.

Just in time.

Jérôme Valcke rushed to the board meeting. He claimed VISA had upped their offer to a 'total consideration' of US$195 million!

That compared with MasterCard's $180 million! (Never mind that the difference between the two bids was the US$15 million of 'marketing in kind' that Valcke believed had 'no value'.)

Then, Valcke sang VISA's praises to the Board. They've got a 65 per cent share of the credit card industry! Compared to MasterCard with only 20 percent. They've got 'huge activation potential'! (Whatever that is.)

He didn't once remind the board about MasterCard's 'first right to acquire'.

Then, Sepp Blatter weighed in.

In real life he'd known for years about the trademark issue. But now, in the board meeting, you'd think he'd just become aware of it.

He was furious. MasterCard, was 'attacking the organisation.' He fumed, 'FIFA should not accept threats.'

General secretary Urs Linsi piped up: 'MasterCard has not always been an easy partner'.

MasterCard, the sixteen-year partner who, had 'done everything right in this process' had, as if by magic, become the enemy.

You had to hand it to Blatter and Valcke.

The board decided, 'A deal with VISA . . . will be signed.'

Nobody had the courtesy to tell John Stuart.

The next day FIFA's finance committee was due to bless the

FOUL!

MasterCard agreement that was all done and dusted. Copper-bottomed. Secure. US$180 million cash, guaranteed.

Instead FIFA and VISA spent much of the day trading calls, exchanging emails, desperately trying to firm up a commitment that was no more than a phone call from Tom to Jérôme.

Christopher Rodrigues personally phoned Sepp Blatter to assure him that VISA would come up with the cash.

But the two sides were still negotiating!

As for VISA's offer, it hadn't yet been approved by the VISA board!

FIFA's Tom Houseman broke off from talks with VISA's lawyers to tell his own team he didn't like the look of VISA's offer. Our 'ability to get promotional value out of the US$15 million marketing in kind is doubtful,' he said. As drafted, VISA's commitments were 'pretty meaningless.'

That's when Jérôme Valcke gave Tom Houseman a serious bollocking. Jérôme said Tom was totally missing the point. Obviously, VISA's 'marketing in kind' offer was 'of little or no value to FIFA', said Jérôme. But we *need* it to 'justify VISA over MasterCard'.

That same day – it was a long one – the finance committee met at last. And, sure enough, according to the minutes, they approved VISA, because, although both companies 'had offered US$180 million in cash', only one of them 'had also pledged an additional US$15 million in marketing-in-kind.'

The minutes also mention the 'unsuccessful' bidder's trademark dispute – those circles and balls.

Nobody had the decency to tell MasterCard's John Stuart that his deal was in the dustbin. As far as *he* knew, Sepp Blatter and MasterCard were still moving forward in a 'true spirit of partnership'.

*   *   *

370

BACK IN ZURICH, Sepp Blatter and Jérôme Valcke had got the decisions they wanted. Now, what to do about John?

Valcke and his team had an 'email conference' to cook up some 'excuses to give MasterCard as to why the deal wasn't done with them.'

Stefan Schuster came up with a ruse that would let FIFA 'still be seen as having at least some business ethics'.

They could tell John Stuart he hadn't provided a 'signed agreement in time for the board meetings.' (No matter that they hadn't asked him to; and VISA hadn't provided one either.)

Schuster said, let's tell them, 'VISA put – surprisingly – forth a higher offer at the very last minute.'

Then Schuster remembered circles and balls. Let's bring that up, he said. Let's call it a 'very big (decisive?) obstacle'.

So very big that MasterCard would have to pay an extra US$20 million to overcome it.

Valcke said, We can't do that. They might say, Yes.

It was all getting a bit hysterical.

Schuster said, Anything to 'make the whole f***-up look better for FIFA!'

Valcke asked Tom Houseman about circles and balls: 'What is the chance' that MasterCard would give up the trademark issue?

'Close to zero,' said Houseman. But, anyway, FIFA, 'had never presented' that as 'a deal-breaker.'

Robert Lampman chipped in, 'Guys . . . it seems like a dream . . . a nightmare that is!'

He said: 'It's clear somebody has it in for MC . . . this is going to be very ugly.'

And it was.

*   *   *

JÉRÔME VALCKE would 'string MasterCard along and keep them in play', until the VISA board had given the go-ahead. That should happen on 29 March.

How to string them along? Circles and balls. That might tangle John Stuart up just long enough.

On 17 March, Jérôme told John their deal had died – because of the trademark dispute.

John Stuart called Tom Houseman.

Tom! Circles and balls? *Are you serious?*

Er, yes, said Tom (who'd just told colleagues it *wasn't* a 'deal-breaker').

Neither Jérôme Valcke nor Tom Houseman said anything to John Stuart about VISA.

John Stuart urgently asked Valcke for a meeting with Sepp Blatter. Valcke set a date for 6 April, just in case the VISA board said, No.

On 29 March VISA's board said, Yes, and the next day Valcke phoned John Stuart. We've signed with VISA, he said. 'The dispute on the two globes vs MasterCard logo became a major issue. The main reason for FIFA's choice between MasterCard and VISA is on the mark.'

Then he thanked John Stuart for 'fair negotiation and agreement.'

MASTERCARD'S New York HQ shook with fury and rage. John Stuart rushed to tell his bosses about FIFA's betrayal.

MasterCard's top man, Robert Selander got on the phone.

Brring. Brring.

President Blatter's office. Hello.

Selander asked for Blatter.

I'm sorry. The President's just popped out.

Selander waited.

He called again the next day. Sepp had popped out again.

The weekend came and went. Selander faxed Blatter on 4 April, saying, honour our agreement or we'll sue.

On 5 April Blatter's office faxed back: Too late. We can't extend our agreement with you. We've struck a deal with VISA.

But he hadn't, not yet; Sepp Blatter and Christopher Rodrigues signed the *next* day at a private ceremony in Zurich.

MASTERCARD'S WRIT landed two weeks later at the United States District Court in Manhattan.

MasterCard accused FIFA of 'stunning bad faith' and 'shocking betrayal . . . blatant and deceitful violation of a right of first refusal.'

If the VISA deal went ahead, 'The harm that FIFA will inflict on MasterCard' would be 'irreparable'.

No amount of money would make up for it. 'Hundreds of millions of dollars' would not be enough.

MasterCard's lawyers immediately filed for 'discovery'. The Court ordered FIFA to produce, among other things, minutes of any meetings concerning MasterCard or VISA, emails, memos, handwritten notes, the lot.

In June, Sepp's favourite Zurich lawyer Peter Nobel told the New York Court: We can't possibly go looking for documents. We've got a World Cup on.

MasterCard's lawyers asked, on 'numerous occasions', for the minutes of that October 2005 board meeting, chaired by Sepp Blatter, in which Valcke presented both offers.

We can't find them, said FIFA. They don't exist.

Sepp Blatter claimed he didn't have any relevant documents 'in my office at FIFA Street in Zurich or anywhere else.'

MasterCard said, Are you *serious*?

Blatter burbled that what he *meant* was that he, personally, had 'no tangible documents' – meaning bits of paper – within the 'four corners of his office'. (His secretary files them for him.)

And 'anywhere else' meant Sepp's apartment in Zurich.

MasterCard lawyer Martin Hyman told the Court, 'The only thing we didn't hear was the dog ate my homework.'

ALL THIS TIME, FIFA'S lawyers had been filing motions to have the case brought home to Zurich, Swiss justice being the sort Sepp prefers. The United States, said Sepp's lawyers, was not 'an appropriate jurisdiction'.

On 10 August in a Manhattan courtroom Judge Loretta Preska said, Oh, yes it is.

Tall, thin, elegant, 57-year-old Judge Loretta Preska has great bone structure, perfectly coiffed silver hair, long fingers, flawlessly manicured. And a razor-sharp mind.

Oh, dear. Enter FIFA's star witness: Chuck Blazer.

Fat, shambling, 60-year-old Chuck has bushy hair, panda eyes, pudgy fingers and a mind that's . . . not exactly razor-sharp.

FIFA had to send *someone* from the executive committee. There weren't many volunteers. Sepp Blatter picked Chuck.

In an oak-panelled courtroom packed, wall-to-wall, with lawyers, Chuck spent many unhappy hours trying to explain how FIFA did business.

MasterCard's Martin Hyman asked him: 'It was OK in your view for Mr Valcke to string John Stuart along for a few weeks until VISA ratified the deal?'

Chuck babbled: 'I think it was OK for us to come back and make a determination at some point as one might have been needed again if the circumstances had turned out differently.'

Hyman: 'I have no idea what you just said, Mr Blazer.'

Chuck: 'What I'm saying to you is, without knowing the course of events over the ensuing days, it is impossible to determine how . . . '

And he blathered on until Judge Preska cut in: 'How does *that* answer the question?'

Hyman wanted to know: *Why* did FIFA choose VISA over MasterCard?

He took Chuck through some papers.

Here's Chuck saying, it was the trademark dispute.

Here's Blatter: 'The VISA offer we received was a higher one.'

Hyman asked Chuck: Who's lying, you or Mr Blatter?

Chuck said there was, 'a slight difference of opinion . . . I don't think it's significant.'

Hyman concluded: 'You're testifying here today because Mr Blatter was unwilling to come before this court to testify. Isn't that right?'

'Absolutely not,' Chuck said.

That was pretty much the high point for FIFA.

In his closing statement MasterCard's Adam Silverstein told the Court that any company should, 'have grave concerns about doing business with FIFA' where, 'lying and deception and bad faith are standard operating procedure.'

Hyman told the court, 'No lie was too brazen, and no excuse was too contrived for these people.'

Silverstein said FIFA hadn't played fair and 'deserves a red card for the way it treated MasterCard.'

That's exactly what Preska gave them.

She ruled that FIFA had breached its obligation to give MasterCard first right to acquire the new round of sponsorship.

She said: 'FIFA's negotiators lied repeatedly to MasterCard.'

They 'lied to VISA.'

And when they came to Court, 'The evidence of FIFA witnesses was generally not credible.'

About that 'mysterious gap in the audio recording' of the executive committee meeting back in 2005, the Judge said, 'FIFA has provided no explanation.' Nor had FIFA explained 'why the written minutes it produced do not comport with the audio.'

As for the 'trademark issue' . . . the Judge noted that Sepp Blatter had admitted knowing about it for years. And when he claimed, MasterCard was 'attacking the organisation,' he was just doing his bit to 'steer the FIFA Board's decision in favour of VISA.'

Sepp Blatter and Jérôme Valcke 'engineered the result' of that meeting, she said.

In court, Sepp's boys shrugged off their behaviour as 'white lies', 'commercial lies', 'bluffs', and even – ironically, as Judge Preska wryly observed – 'the game'. Judge Preska pointed to something more sinister, noting that FIFA ultimately confessed that, 'somebody has it in for MC.'

Then there was the matter of the dodgy documents.

MasterCard's Robert Selander had warned President Blatter on 4 April 2006 that he'd sue if FIFA signed with VISA.

Sepp and Chris went ahead anyway with VISA and signed on 6 April 2006.

But when FIFA eventually produced their version of the contract, it was dated 3 April. And Chris Rodrigues's signature looked funny. 'To the untrained eye,' said the Judge, it appears 'noticeably different from the signature of Mr Rodrigues on the VISA-produced version of the contract.'

In Judge Preska's view, 'No FIFA witness has provided an explanation for why the version of the VISA Agreement FIFA produced in this action is dated 3 April 2006'. Thus she concluded: 'it is reasonable to infer that someone at FIFA dated the document '3 April' to make it look as though the deal had been signed *before* Selander's threat of legal action landed.

As for Chuck Blazer, the Judge said, his 'testimony was generally without credibility based on his attitude and demeanour and on his evasive answers . . . '. Certain aspects of his testimony she even 'rejected as fabricated'.

JUDGE PRESKA delivered her red card on 7 December 2006, ordering FIFA to honour the MasterCard contract *and* – unusually in the USA – to pay MasterCard's costs and expenses.

FIFA said they'd appeal. FIFA 'fully expects to prevail' and 'remains convinced that at all times it acted in good faith,' said their official statement.

This time, not even FIFA believed FIFA.

Within days they changed their tune. 'The fact cannot be overlooked that FIFA's negotiations breached its business principles. FIFA cannot possibly accept such conduct among its own employees.'

And all four of FIFA's negotiators, Valcke, Houseman, Schuster and Lampman, had to walk.

What about Sepp? Judge Preska accepted that he'd *dined* with Chris Rodrigues, he'd '*steered*' the decision VISA's way, he'd '*engineered*' the result.

Shouldn't Sepp show himself the red card?

Oh, and Sepp, I've been wondering, why *did* FIFA go to all that trouble to engineer a deal with VISA when it had a deal, for the asking price, with MasterCard?

'The answer is blowing in the wind somewhere in Zurich,' was MasterCard's best guess.

Can you tell us, Sepp?

Sepp?

Sepp?

(Oh, dear. I don't think Sepp's listening.)

POSTSCRIPT

IT DOESN'T SEEM like Sepp is listening to anybody inside FIFA – or feels any need to. The MasterCard debacle has cost an estimated US$5 million in legal costs. He's lodged an appeal and if he loses that, the costs will be even greater. FIFA is losing nearly US$2 million a month in revenues without a credit card sponsor.

Sepp didn't listen to the howls of protest when he interfered in the UEFA presidential election in January 2007, backing his man Michel Platini against Lennart Johansson. Platini won. Another new face at the FIFA table is John McBeth from Scotland. He's replaced David Will in the seat reserved for the four British home nations.

But Sepp must be listening intently for the footsteps of Zug Magistrate Thomas Hildbrand. The trial of the ISL executives accused of embezzling around £50 million from FIFA is scheduled for late 2007. Hildbrand's second investigation, into who repaid the bribes, continues.

Tick. Tick. Tick.

APPENDIX

CHAPTER NOTES

Chapter 1

page 1. The story of the bribe that was wrongly addressed: Multiple sources inside and outside FIFA and ISL. Parts published in the *Daily Mail*, 27 May 2002 and again on 5 December 2005. Also published in various Swiss and German newspapers. More in Chapter 7.

page 4. Repression in Tunisia is widely recorded by varied organisations from the *New York Times* to the BBC and NGOs such as *Reporters Sans Frontiers* and Amnesty.

page 5. The decision of the Zurich prosecutor and his investigation of allegations against Sepp Blatter are dealt with fully in Chapter 29.

page 6. The author's question to Blatter was taped by a film crew from Denmark and subsequently broadcast in many European countries. The film's producer and interviewer was German journalist Jens Weinreich.

Chapter 2

I am grateful to Morley Myers and Keith Botsford who reported from the Frankfurt Congress and to Christian Jannette who shared his memories of working for Dassler.

I have published more on Dassler's team and its operations in three previous books *The Lords of the Rings* (1992), *The New*

Lords of the Rings (1996) and *The Great Olympic Swindle* (2000) and in numerous television films and articles.

Chapter 3

page 22. Chowdhry's involvement in international amateur boxing is chronicled in my previous Olympic books and most recently, *The Great Olympic Swindle*.

page 24. André Guelfi tells his story in his autobiography *L'Original* published by Robert Laffont, Paris 1999. There's more in contemporary French press reports of the Elf-Acquitaine scandal and subsequent trial.

page 26. Dirty tricks against Kaser: Kistner & Wienreich, *Das Milliarden Spiel: Fusball, Geld und Medien* (Fischer Taschenbuch Verlag, 1998).

page 28. André Guelfi's comments about Blatter's hiring by FIFA and Kaser's pay-off following his falling out with Dassler, were recorded by Barbara Smit for her story of the Adidas-Puma family story, published in the UK in May 2006 by Penguin as *Pitch Invasion* and in several translations.

Chapter 4

Thanks to Ezequiel Fernandez Moores for his guidance on all matters Argentine. His work on FIFA senior vice-president and Finance Committee chairman Julio Grondona has been a blessing for foreign reporters.

page 35. Blatter's attempt to succeed Havelange was reported in detail by Kistner and Weinreich in *Das Milliarden Spiel: Fusball, Geld und Medien*, and in contemporaneous reports.

The issue came up again in 1998 when Blatter ran for FIFA president. See 'Soccer-Johansson launches blistering attack on Blatter,' *Reuters*, 27 March 1998.

page 35. Pelé accusing Havelange's son-in-law Ricardo Teixeira of corruption: *International Herald Tribune*, 15 December 1993.

page 36. Investigation of Havelange in *Playboy* Brazil, 1994 by Roberto José Pereira.

page 36. Ellert Schramm, quoted in Kistner & Weinreich, *Das Milliarden Spiel: Fusball, Geld und Medien*.

page 37. Havelange and 32 teams in the WC Finals – quoted in Kistner & Weinreich, *Das Milliarden Spiel: Fusball, Geld und Medien*.

Chapter 5

Birth of the FIFA gambling plan: I am grateful to Rodrigo Mattos and Juca Kfouri in Brazil for their assistance with this investigation.

Much of the detail of the gambling plan is revealed in a memo from Richard Herson to Blatter, 28 May 2001.

page 45. The detail of the Machline helicopter crash is recorded at the National Transportation Safety Board http://www.ntsb.gov/ntsb/brief.asp?ev_id=20001206X01950&key=1

page 46. The 1,600-page report by Brazil's Congress on football corruption was published on 4 December 2001. It gives fascinating detail on the other financial relationships of the main players in the FIFA gambling plan.

Chapter 6

The shock of the ISL directors on losing the Olympic contract and the need to retain, at all costs, the FIFA contract is reflected in the ISL board minutes of 7 December 1995.

Chapter 7

page 60. The wrongly addressed payment. The anonymous quote from a former FIFA official was checked with him before publication.

Chapter 8

page 61. Havelange 'honoured' to be a guest of President Abacha, in 'Havelange apologizes to Nigeria', *Reuters*, 8 November 1995.

page 63. *Sunday Times* article 'Havelange defends Nigerian plans despite condemnation,' by Peter Wilson quoted by *Reuters*, 12 November 1995.

page 64. David Will rejects gifts, quoted in *Badfellas*, by John Sugden and Allan Tomlinson (Mainstream, 2003).

page 66. Dr Jean-Marie Kyss was interviewed by the author in his surgery and also in the national stadium in Port au Prince in April 2002.

page 67. Vincy Jalal named as the delegate from the Haiti national association on page 6 of the Minutes of FIFA's 50th Congress, Zurich, 3/4 July 1996.

page 70. Johansson; 'I will push for an independent accountant,' *AP*, 21 March 1998.

page 71. For more details of Chet Greene's ticket order – see Chapter 28.

page 72. The UEFA-sponsored resolution to force Blatter to declare his candidacy was dated 12 March 1998. The meeting was reported by *Reuters, AP* and *AFP* on 12 and 13 March.

Chapter 9

page 75. Platini: 'I'm a man of conviction,' *Reuters*, 18 May 1998.

page 75. Blatter will be transparent: 'Blatter Says He's Near FIFA Victory,' *AP*, 5 June 1998.

page 75. Johansson expects a dirty campaign: 'Blatter is Havelange's puppet, says Johansson,' *Reuters*, 29 March 1998.

page 77. Braun's comments were at UEFA's congress in April 1998, open to the media.

page 78. Johansson in Kuala Lumpur: 'Havelange is not neutral,' *Reuters*, 14 May 1998.

page 79. Blatter's brief visit to Nairobi was extensively reported at the time in the *Daily Nation* and *East African Standard*.

page 81. Blatter's US$135,000 election budget, reported by *Reuters* on 5 June 1998 and then US$300,000 by *AP* later the same day.

page 81. Platini objecting to 5-star hotels: 'FIFA presidential hopeful says he's near victory,' *AP*, 5 June 1998.

page 82. Farah Addo was interviewed in Bamako, Mali, in January 2002 by the author with Christoph Mueller of Swiss TV, SFDRS.

page 85. Emir's plane: Blatter interviewed in *Tages Anzeiger*, 23 December 1998.

Chapter 10

page 89. 'Bomba' Mthethwa in the *Swaziland Times*, 5 June 1998.

page 90. Neville Ferguson of Trinidad passing himself off as the delegate from Haiti is recorded on Page 9 of the minutes of the 1998 FIFA Congress. The episode was recorded on the official FIFA video.

page 92. Corinne Blatter on African support, *Reuters*, 8 June 1998.

page 92. Warner's 'pivotal role', *Trinidad Express*, 12 July 1998.

page 92. Rumours of US$50,000 bundles being handed out to African delegates were reported in the *Washington Post*, 9 June 1998 and elsewhere.

page 92. Blatter 'vehemently' denying: 'Blatter threatens to sue over rumours,' *Reuters,* 9 June 1998.

page 92. Graham Kelly and Alec McGivan: 'England relieved with Blatter victory', *Reuters,* 8 June 1998.

Chapter 11

page 96. Blatter charging his election expenses to FIFA (and subsequently repaying this sum) is evidenced in his claim form and other documents seen by the author.

page 99. The author has seen a notarised statement sworn by a former FIFA official stating the facts of Blatter's bonus. See also Cartier letter to author on page 306.

page 103. Markus Siegler revealing that FIFA Executive Committee members do not have to produce receipts when they submit expenses; email to *Daily Mail,* 2 September 2003.

Chapter 12

page 105. Urs Linsi's declaration that FIFA is transparent, posted in January 2003, appears to have been erased from fifa.com. It was at: http://www.fifa.com/Service/MR_A/51043_E.html

page 106. Chung letter to Warner regarding Blatter's salary, 18 January 2002.

page 107. Warner's reply to Chung letter, 21 January 2002.

page 108. Blatter's Appenzell tax affairs featured in *Blick* in September 1995. The story was picked up by most of the Swiss media in the following months.

Chapter 13

page 115. Johansson 'I have no proof of this and I refuse to speculate' in 'Blatter threatens to sue over rumours,' *Reuters,* 9 June 1998.

page 115. The membership of FIFA committees can be found at: http://www.fifa.com/en/organisation/committee.execom.html.

page 116. Warner's wealth: *Trinidad Guardian*,13 January 2000.

page 118. Koloskov's $100,000. See Michel Zen-Ruffinen report of 3 May 2002 and Blatter's subsequent 'Rectification' document.

Chapter 14

page 122. Thanks to several French reporters who helped me with background on Jerome Champagne.

Chapter 15

Sources include: a) Warner's authorised biography *Upwards Through the Night*, written by Tino Singh, sports editor of the *Trinidad Guardian* and published in 1998 by Lexicon of Trinidad Ltd; and b) 'The Story of Trinidad and Tobago Football 1983–2000' compiled by Valentino Singh (Chapter 12 – 'Austin Jack Walker' and Chapter 15 – 'Aftershocks') – T&TFF website: www.tnt.fifa.com.

page 131. Blatter praises his 'wonderful and loyal friend' Warner, 25 September 2001.

page 132. Diplomatic Passport – from Prime Minister Panday on Warner's 57th birthday, 26 January 2000.

page 132. Warner says his opponents are 'Taliban', *Trinidad Express* 26 November 2001.

page 132. Warner promises sports facility to La Brea constituency, *Trinidad Express* 26 November 2001.

page 133. Warner nominated as Speaker of Trinidad parliament; *Trinidad Guardian*, 10 April 2001.

page 134. Warner's three sets of books. *Upwards Through the Night*, page 136.

page 137. Warner printed thousands of extra tickets, Trinidad v USA World Cup Qualifier 1990, *Upwards Through the Night*, pages 25–47 and 'The Story of Trinidad and Tobago Football 1983–2000,' Chapter 15.

Chapter 16

page 141. Blazer on the CONCACAF election and most of his quotes, in *Upwards Through the Night*.

page 141. Warner's 'sordid' fax to Blatter, 28 April 1990.

page 142. Blazer's gambling business: 'FIFA boss who wants to take your bets on the World Cup', *Daily Mail*, 18 December 2001.

page 144. Blatter pledges a code of conduct: 'Blatter embarks on moral crusade with a Code of Conduct' *Reuters*, 19 December 2001.

page 145. Warner a 'beneficiary' of his community. 'Warner waits in the wings' – profile by Irving Ward, *Trinidad Express*, May 1998.

page 146. Grondona & Blatter $6 million loan letter to Warner, 14 December 1999.

page 147. Warner's seminar $77,000 . . . and request for financial assistance made to Blatter on 21 August 2001.

page 147. Warner's request for funding of a second seminar including Pelé, Charlton, Parreira and Houllier: 12 March 2002.

page 148. Warner's son becoming a registered football agent: *Upwards Through the Night*, page 226.

Chapter 17:

page 152. Trinidad & Tobago Contractors Association letter to Prime Minister Panday; 20 September 1999.

page 152. Keith Thomas report dated 12 March 2001.

page 152. Sandra Bachir 'things which we cannot change' from 'More $ for Warners,' *Trinidad Express*, 1 September 2001.

page 156. Warner tells trade press: 'They [kiosks] are helping to revolutionize the entire sport,' www.kioskbusiness.com/JanFeb02.

page 158. 'We must be careful that Trinidad & Tobago is not used simply to further Mr Warner's business interests,' from 'Not so fast, Jack', *Trinidad Express* Editorial, 24 September 2001.

page 159. Walter Gagg; "We have to be very, very happy to have him (Warner) in the organisation. Garth Wattley, 'Smoking out the truth,' *Trinidad Express*, September 2001.

page 159. 'I'm going to work for transparency.' Blatter press conference (FIFA Under-17 Tournament), Hilton Hotel, Port of Spain, 29 September 2001.

page 160. Blatter's response to press conference questions was dated 17 October 2001.

page 161. Warner letter to Blatter – 'all member federations of CONCACAF are fully supportive of your re-nomination,' 5 October 2001.

page 161. Blatter replies to Warner, 'It is with an immense pleasure,' 9 October 2001.

page 162. Warner warns Blatter there will be a deficit on the FIFA Under-17 tournament, 25 October 2001.

page 163. Jamal Warner selected for Trinidad: 'Two Warners fingered in La Foucade sacking,' *Trinidad Express*, 28 September 2002.

Chapter 18

This chapter draws heavily on ISL company's documents which were made available to me by Jens Weinreich and Thomas Kistner following the company's collapse.

page 169. Weber letter to Helio Viana hoping to buy rights to Pelé, dated 4 January, 2000.

Chapter 19

This chapter also draws heavily on ISL's documents from the last year of the company's existence.

page 174. Letter from the Vatican thanking Blatter for FIFA's CHF50,000 donation, 11 January 2001.

page 175. Article 158 of the Swiss Criminal code covers 'disloyalty to an employer in financial circumstances.'

page 178. Memo 'Financial Overview' by Michel Zen-Ruffinen and Jon Doviken, 19 May 2001. Urs Linsi's response followed on 6 June 2001.

Chapter 20

page 182. Blatter's knowledge of ISL's failure to pay FIFA its share of the Globo TV money claim: 'It was only on 21 April [2001] that we discovered one payment didn't reach the right place' was made on 25 May 2001. Reported by *AP* and *Reuters*.

page 182. The Globo recriminations are contained in the memo 'Financial Overview' by Michel Zen-Ruffinen and Jon Doviken, 19 May 2001. Urs Linsi's response followed on 6 June 2001.

page 182. FIFA's criminal complaint against ISL was filed in Zug on 28 May 2001.

page 184. Johansson's 25 Questions to Blatter were sent on 11 June 2001.

page 185. The Buenos Aires FIFA Congress of July 2001 was covered by the wire services and many newspapers and of considerable assistance was an article by in *Alarco* magazine in Argentina.

Chapter 21

page 188. Blatter's letter to Chung calling on South Korea to stop the mistreatment and eating of dogs, 6 November 2001.

page 189. Johansson's new list of questions sent on 14 December 2001. They dealt with securitisation issues and the promised audit.

page 189. The dissidents letter to Blatter, 18 December 2001.

page 189. Warner letter, 'My dear President, I have taken note of your pain,' 20 December 2001.

page 190. Lennart Johansson to Blatter, 'Coming home from hospital at 5 o'clock in the morning . . . We get flooded with facts and figures,' 22 December 2001.

page 190. David Will to Grondona: 'Honestly, I expected a 200–300 page document and could scarcely believe the two-page "review" that we finally received,' 22 January 2002.

page 191. Villar Llona announced support for Blatter, *Reuters*, 6 March 2002.

page 193. Juca Kfouri comments on Ricardo Teixeira's appointment to FIFA's internal audit committee, 'Yet again the fox is being put in charge of the chickens', *Guardian* 12 March 2002.

page 194. Chuck Blazer went to his keyboard and wrote to David Will. 'At the opening session I made the statement that this Committee was the formation of a political process,' 24 April 2002.

page 194. Blatter suspends FIFA's Internal Audit Committee. *Reuters*, 11 April 2002.

page 195. Blatter quote, 'It has become personal, especially with Mr Johansson attacking me,' *Reuters* and BBC Sport, 25 April 2002.

page 196. Blatter's letter to Johansson: 'It is in your hands, Lennart, to set the tone for the coming weeks,' 22 March 2002.

page 196. Blatter to Chung: Dear Colleague (then in handwriting) dear MJ,' 16 April 2002.

page 196. 'Those who have known me for the past thirty years,' Blatter hits out at "campaign of hatred," *Reuters,* 23 April 2002.

page 197. Michel Zen-Ruffinen in *Le Temps*, 18 April 2002.

page 198. Zen-Ruffinen's presentation of 3 May 2002 soon found its way to the media.

page 198. Bollman booed. FIFA Executive Committee meeting. Many sources inside the room; and *Daily Telegraph*, 4 May 2002.

page 198. Hayatou, one of the five, said later, 'He looked stunned, quite shocked. But he refused to go and said he was answerable only to the congress,' *Reuters*, 6 May 2002.

page 199. Blatter took the opportunity to attack Hayatou. 'In the beginning, I considered him to be a fair man,' *Reuters*, 14 May 2002.

Chapter 22

page 200. Blatter in Monrovia – published by *FIFA News*, December 2000.

page 200. Snowe sets up 'Friends of Blatter in Africa,' 19 March 2002.

page 201. Weah: 'It's unfair to the football programme of the country' and FIFA confirms $50,000 grant to Snowe; BBC, 21 February 2003.

page 201. On 3 January 2006 the UN announced it was continuing its travel ban on Edwin Snowe because of his alleged continuing association with Charles Taylor.

page 202. Gadhafi meeting in late April; *The Monitor*, Kampala, 2 May 2002.

page 202. Champagne: 'President Blatter has not come here to campaign,' *AP*, 25 March 2002.

page 202. One reported, 'Blatter used the opportunity to lobby for votes,' *All Africa Global Media*, 25 March 2002.

page 203. 'Investigations have been conducted and all allegations proved wrong,' *AP*, Lusaka, 6 April 2002.

page 203. Bin Hammam: 'This jet has been provided by a friend of mine, Saleh Kamil,' 9 April 2002.

page 205. 'We would kindly like to draw your attention to the fact that a member of a FIFA standing committee may only be replaced by the body that appointed him, the Executive Committee' wrote general secretary Zen-Ruffinen to Warner, 13 March 2002.

page 205. Blazer erupted, calling for Zen-Ruffinen to be sacked or suspended,' *Bloomberg*, 7 April 2002.

page 206. 'While I acknowledge that English is the first language of the FIFA,' Warner to Zen-Ruffinen, 16 April 2002.

page 207. Grondona to Buenos Aires radio station, 'Zen-Ruffinen isn't fit to run a troop of boy scouts', *AP*, 9 May 2002.

page 207. Blatter's 'Rectification' document, 17 May 2002.

page 210. Blatter: 'Those, who have made allegations and cannot prove them, they will go to prison,' *AP*, 22 May 2002.

page 210. Contiguglia. 'President Blatter should continue as FIFA President!' *AP*, 23 May 2002.

Chapter 23

page 212. The World Cup 2002 Press Conference, Seoul, of the five FIFA vice-presidents was covered by hundreds of reporters from the wire services and other media.

page 217. Monnier memo warning of costs of Special Congress; 22 April 2002.

page 217. All statements made in the FIFA Congress – attended by the author – have been checked against the FIFA official video.

page 230 'Tomorrow we take care of Mr Clean,' *PA* and other wire services, 30 May 2002.

Chapter 24

page 232. The World Cup began in Seoul on 31 May 2002. Warner was photographed by the *Trinidad Express* on the evening of 4 June 2002, back in Trinidad, outside the Port of Spain jail.

page 233. Warner to Blatter: 'My Dear President and Friend,' 7 February 2002.

page 233. Warner: 'A travelling companion for whom a separate room shall not be needed,' 12 February 2002.

page 235. FIFA drops requirement for names on tickets; *AP*, 24 May 2002.

page 236. FIFA spokesman on Bin Hammam's shock that tickets with his name on are circulating; *AP*, 8 June 2002.

page 237. Cooper fired, *PA*, 10 July 2002.

page 238. Tognoni sacked, *Daily Mail*, 28 March 2003.

page 240. Blatter threat to suspend Brazil, Agencies, 30 October 2000.

page 241. 'Critic of Marxist regime, awaits trial amid threats,' *AP*, 12 August 1999.

page 247. Grondona's anti-Semitism; http://www.wiesenthal.com/site/apps/s/content.asp?c=fwLYKnN8LzH&b=253162&ct=286023

Chapter 25

page 249. Blatter threatens sanctions; 'World Cup Ticket Scandals Widen,' *AP*, 19 June 1998.

page 249. Greene order for 2,964 World Cup tickets, faxed to FIFA on 15 January 1998. Seen by author.

page 250. Johansson's office faxing Greene about tickets; 10 July 1998.

page 250. The 57,526.70 francs owing for tickets Greene ordered in 1998 is shown as outstanding in Antigua's account with FIFA in 2002.

page 250. The 'hungry' businessman's fax was sent from a Seattle address on 27 February 2002.

page 251. Umbro and Admiral correspondence discovered in the Antiguan Association's files after Greene was ousted.

page 255. Jerome Champagne letters dated 22 and 23 of January 2003.

page 255. Warner 'nothing short of exemplary' letter; 3 February 2003.

page 261. Crump counter-attacks; *Antigua Sun*, 1 March 2004.

page 262. Burrell fires Jamie Lawrence; *Jamaica Gleaner*, 1 June 2000.

page 263. Blatter visits Jamaica to support Burrell; *AP*, 16 November 2003.

page 265. Horace Reid prepared to die for his 'principles,' *Jamaica Observer*, 14 February 2005.

Chapter 26

page 269. Guenter Netzer, a Kirch manager quote, *AP*, 19 April 2003.

page 270. Warner invited to Mala Mala game lodge, 1 June 2000.

page 272. Warner 'Winter of your football career' letter to Dempsey; 10 July 2000.

page 272. Al-Saadi Gadhafi in *Super* Magazine, September 2003.

page 273. Al-Saadi Gadhafi fails dope test; *Reuters*, 8 January 2004.

page 274. Zagallo story in Brazil – ISTOÉ São Paulo, 18 September 2002.

FOUL!

page 275. Blatter tells Tunisia 'Your sports infrastructure is impressive.' Tunisia Online, 19 November 2003.

page 276. Morocco and the Western Sahara – see Toby Shelley – 'Endgame in the Western Sahara: What future for Africa's last colony' (ZED Books, London, 2004)

page 277. The hotel Winston Churchill loved; *Daily Telegraph*, 11 March 2004.

page 278. 'They know I'm Jewish . . .' Alan Rothenberg quoted in the *New York Times*, 23 September 2003.

page 278. 'He [Rothenberg] clearly believed that Elvis Presley was alive and living on the moon . . .'; evidence of the late Tony Banks MP to the Select Committee on Culture, Media and Sport Minutes of Evidence.

page 279. *Spiegel* profile of Sheikh Saleh Kamil; June 2003.

page 279. 'If we don't give the poor free bread,' *Al-Ahram*, 22 March 2001.

page 280. Patrick Manning: 'This visit is being unnecessarily politicised,' *Trinidad Guardian*, 23 April 2004.

page 281. 'He is our guest. We are not budging on Mr Warner greeting Mr Mandela,' *Trinidad Guardian*, 23 April 2004.

page 283. Warner: 'Unfortunately, CONCACAF is still undecided,' *Cape Argus*, 14 May 2004.

page 283. Rothenberg: Mandela is not a man of the future. He is a man of history,' *Reuters*, 14 May 2004.

page 284. Ali El-Din Hillal claimed he'd been asked for bribes amounting to $67 million. *Al-Ahram*, 27 May 2005.

page 285. Mandela wishes to retire. SouthAfrica info reporter, 2 June 2004.

Chapter 27

page 290. I took screenshots of Hargitay's ECN website before the pages were erased.

page 291. Allegations about stock swindle in Hungary. *Blick*, 23 August 1995.

page 292. Letter from J. Michael Houlahan, Director of the US Information Service. *Jamaica Herald*, 21 March 1996.

page 292. I made screenshots of Hargitay's ADHOC Group for Human Rights website before it was killed off.

Chapter 28

page 294. ECN invitation to Blatter round-table. Undated but mid-January 2003.

page 297. 'European Communications & Research Think Tank' that delivered 'sensitive investigative data to clients.'

page 300. Hotpants. *Guardian*, Friday 16 January 2004.

Chapter 29:

page 301. The interviewer for the television documentary was Jens Weinreich.

page 303. Author's report in *Daily Mail* revealing Blatter's secret bonus and the instant threat on fifa.com to sue in London. Both on 18 March 2003.

page 304. Siegler bans the author from FIFA premises – email of 25 March 2003.

page 304. Cartier threatens legal action, 25 March 2003.

page 305. Cartier ten-page letter, dated 19 May 2003.

Cartier demands my articles in advance of publication, letter 21 November 2003.

Cartier 'It is not for you to decide to bypass my firm and contact my clients direct,' letter 13 February 2004.

page 307. Cartier, 'responsible journalistic standards require,' letter 17 September 2004.

page 313. Mathier declines to comment on his vote-rigging investigation, 30 March 2003.

page 313. On 11 July 2003 Cartier confirmed in a letter that the vote-rigging investigation was still in progress.

page 315. FIFA's Disciplinary Code and procedures can be downloaded at: http://www.fifa.com/en/organisation/legal/chamber/0,1489,2,00.html

The relevant section is on page 42, 'Art.121 Form and contents of the decision.'

Chapter 30

page 317. *100 years of Football: The FIFA Centennial Book*, by Pierre Lanfranchi, Christiane Eisenberg, Tony Mason and Alfred Wahl (Weidenfeld & Nicholson, 2004).

page 318. Weber and other ISL executives arrested, *Reuters*, 19 November 2002.

page 319. The astonishing story of ISL liquidator Thomas Bauer's legal battle to get the bribes repaid, the account opened for Weber to channel them, the role of lawyer Peter Nobel and the attempts by investigating magistrate Thomas Hildbrand to obtain the list of football officials who took bribes is revealed in an extraordinary judgement by the Swiss Federal Court. http://wwwsrv.bger.ch/cgi-bin/AZA/JumpCGI?id=11.07.2005_1P.32/2005

This judgement was first disclosed by Jean Francois Tanda in *Sonntags Zeitung*, 7 August 2005 under the headline, 'Der lange Arm des Sepp Blatter [The long arm of Sepp Blatter]'.

page 322. Warner 'I have never seen one iota of corruption,' from 'Jumpin' Jack Flash,' *Trinidad Express*, 12 December 2004.

page 326. Linsi's letter to Blatter, asking him to sack Champagne, quoted in *Sonntags Zeitung*, 16 October 2005.

page 328. Hildbrand raid on FIFA House revealed in *Daily Mail*, 28 November 2005.

Chapter 31

page 336. Fascinating information about the Warner family activities at the Joao Havelange Centre of Excellence, is at http://www.concacafcentre.co.tt/index.htm

page 337. Giving away the keys to the CoE; weekly column by Managing Editor Keith Smith, *Trinidad Express*, 8 September 2006.

page 337. Keith Rowley and the budget for 2001, *AP*, 23 February 2006 and regional media.

page 338. The report of the meeting of FIFA's Ethics Committee on 15 February 2006 that discussed Warner and Simpaul can be downloaded from www.transparencyinsport.org

page 342. The Ernst & Young reports on the Warners and Simpaul can be downloaded from www.transparencyinsport.org

page 343. The script of the BBC Panorama is at http://news.bbc.co.uk/1/hi/programmes/panorama/5076282.stm

page 345. Warner's racist abuse of the author, *Trinidad Express*, 10 May 2006.

page 345. Prices of tickets for Peru game, *Trinidad Express*, 14 April 2006.

page 346. Warner insisting that a non-existent microphone had hit his face, *Trinidad Express*, 24 May 2006.

page 346. Warner's lawyer sent a selection of ticket documents, letters and emails to the Caribbean media on 15 September 2006.

page 350. Soca Warriors threaten to strike, *Trinidad Express*, 7 October 2006.

page 350. Groden's concession to 'repatriate' money to the Soca Warriors, T&TFF press release, 17 November 2006.

page 351. Daryan Warner penalised by FIFA executive committee; confidential minutes of their meeting of 5 December 2006 can be downloaded from www.transparencyinsport.org

Chapter 32

page 353. During the investigation other ISL executives confirmed all of the information from 'Mr Brown'.

page 356. The judgment of the Liechtenstein Royal Court, *Sonntags Zietung*, 14 May 2006.

Chapter 33

page 373. Judge Preska's rulings and all other documents are filed at the US District Court, Southern District of New York.

TIMELINE

1904: FIFA founded in Paris.

1954: FIFA moves to Sonnenberg – Sunny Hill.

1961: Sir Stanley Rous becomes FIFA President.

1974: June: With assistance of Horst Dassler of Adidas, Joao Havelange becomes FIFA president, replacing Rous. World Cup in Germany.

1974: July: For the last time, in public, future IOC president gives fascist salute in Barcelona.

1975: Sepp Blatter joins FIFA to organise Coca-Cola-funded development programmes.

1978: World Cup in Argentina.

1980: With assistance of Horst Dassler former Franco fascist Juan Antonio Samaranch wins presidency of IOC.

1981: Dassler operatives lever Primo Nebiolo into presidency of IAAF.

1981: September: Helmut Käser resigns as FIFA General Secretary, replaced by Sepp Blatter.

1982: Horst Dassler sets up International Sport & Leisure (ISL). Wins FIFA contracts up to and including 1998 and similar from IAAF and IOC.

1982: World Cup in Spain.

1986: Michel Zen-Ruffinen joins FIFA legal department.

1986: World Cup in Mexico.

1987: Horst Dassler dies.

1989: November: USA defeats Trinidad & Tobago to qualify for World Cup. Controversy over number of tickets printed by T&TFF General Secretary Jack Warner.

1990: World Cup in Italy.

1990: Lennart Johansson becomes president of UEFA.

1990: Warner becomes president of CONCACAF.

1993: December: Havelange bans Pelé from World Cup draw in Las Vegas.

1994: Havelange and Weber secretly plan FIFA gambling business.

1994: World Cup in USA.

1994: Blatter puts himself forward to replace Havelange.

1994: August: Brazilian tycoon Matias Machline dies in New Jersey helicopter crash.

1995: Michel Zen-Ruffinen appointed FIFA deputy General Secretary.

1995: August: IMG's Eric Drossart offers US$1 billion to take FIFA World Cup television and marketing contracts from ISL.

1995: August: Jamaican police discover cocaine on ship belonging to Peter Hargitay. He is cleared and in 2002 becomes Special Advisor to Blatter.

1995: November: Havelange bolsters Nigerian dictator Abacha while executioners prepare scaffold for the Ogoni Nine.

1995: December: IOC cancels contract with ISL.

1996: December: Havelange announces retirement.

1996: July: Jamaica's Vincy Jalal sits in at FIFA's Zurich Congress for absent Haitian delegate.

1996: July: ISL retain FIFA television contracts, for 2002 and 2006, with funding from Leo Kirch.

1996: Julio Grondona takes chair of FIFA Finance Committee.

1997: September: Johansson announces he will run for FIFA presidency

1997: December: ISL awarded FIFA marketing contract for 2002 and 2006.

1998: ISL bribe to a senior football official sent, mistakenly, to Sunny Hill.

1998: January. Antiguan official Chet Greene orders 2,964 tickets for World Cup.

1998: March: Sepp Blatter announces he will run for FIFA presidency.

1998: June: Sepp Blatter defeats Lennart Johansson to win FIFA presidency. Trinidadian Neville Ferguson takes place of absent Haitian delegate.

1998: World Cup in France.

1998: July: After the World Cup Blatter returns to Sunny Hill and charges his election costs to his FIFA expenses account.

1998: September: FIFA demands that ISL hand over Globo television rights payment. They don't.

1998: December: Michel Zen-Ruffinen appointed FIFA General Secretary.

1999: April: ISL agree to spend US$1.2 billion buying rights to the ATP tennis tour. ISL begins to haemorrhage money.

1999: July: Urs Linsi becomes FIFA's head of finance.

1999: Management consultants McKinsey begin the work of reshaping FIFA.

1999: November: Blatter embraces President Charles Taylor as he opens first Goal project facility in Liberia.

1999: December: On the eve of KPMG taking over audit, FIFA accounts clerk Guy-Philippe Mathieu converts Blatter's expenses repayment into a possible claim for 55 per diems at US$500 a day.

2000: February: Bad Ragaz therapy session for FIFA employees.

2000: Chuck Blazer sets up GIG sports gambling company in London.

2000: May: FIFA advised to force ISL to hand over Globo money. They don't.

2000: July: Germany defeats South Africa to host 2006 World Cup. Charles Dempsey declines to vote.

2000: August: Jamaica's Captain Horace Burrell receives FIFA's highest honour, the Order of Merit.

2000: December: Guy-Philippe Mathieu, exasperated by the demands of an Executive Committee member, scribbles 'Last year he defrauded us' and 'Ripped off' on the man's expenses claim.

2001: May: ISL declared bankrupt. FIFA makes criminal complaint to authorities in Zug alleging ISL executives embezzled Globo money.

2001: July: Liquidator Thomas Bauer confirms to author that ISL paid bribes to football officials and he would litigate if necessary to reclaim the money for creditors.

2001: July: Blatter triumphs at FIFA congress in Buenos Aires.

2001: September: FIFA Under-17 World Youth Championships staged in Trinidad & Tobago. Controversy over allocation of contracts to Jack Warner's family businesses.

2002: Spring: Issa Hyatou challenges Blatter for FIFA presidency.

2002: March: Blatter agrees to set up Internal Audit Committee. The following month he closes it down.

2002: May: FIFA General Secretary Michel Zen-Ruffinen speaks out against Blatter. Corruption allegations against Blatter referred to Zurich authorities by members of Executive Committee.

2002: May: Blatter re-elected at Seoul FIFA congress.

2002: June: World Cup in Korea and Japan. Blatter sacks General Secretary Michel Zen-Ruffinen and several FIFA staff.

2002: November: Zurich Magistrate Urs Hubmann finds 'insufficient evidence' to prosecute Blatter.

2002: November: Weber and other ISL executives detained for questioning by Zug Investigating Magistrate Thomas Hildbrand.

2002: December: Urs Linsi appointed FIFA General Secretary – and retains his post as head of finance.

2003: January: Blatter's Special Advisor Peter Hargitay hosts media Round Table meeting in London. Blatter promises to investigate allegations of vote-rigging at 1996 and 1998 FIFA congresses.

2003: March: FIFA announces on fifa.com they will 'sue Andrew Jennings' on day of publication of story revealing undisclosed Blatter bonus. They didn't.

2003: May: ISL liquidator Bauer files writ in Zug court against former company executives, demanding repayment of bribes to football officials.

2003: May: FIFA suspends Antigua and Barbuda national association.

2003: June: At a secret hearing in Paris FIFA Disciplinary Committee confirms vote-rigging at Paris Congress that elected Blatter. Verdict never published.

2003: June: Blatter hires Jerome Valcke to be new head of FIFA Marketing.

2003: July: Grondona makes anti-Semitic remark on Argentine television.

2003: November: Jamaica FF president Captain Horace Burrell ousted by Crenston Boxhill.

2004: January: Author asks Blatter about the wrongly addressed bribe at a Tunis press conference.

2004: February: Swiss lawyer Peter Nobel opens a bank account in Zurich of behalf of ISL's Jean-Marie Weber for the return of bribes to liquidator Bauer.

2004: April: Mervyn Richards defeats Chet Greene for presidency of Antigua and Barbuda national association.

2004: April: Nelson Mandela and Desmond Tutu travel to Trinidad at request of Warner.

2004: May: South Africa awarded 2010 World Cup.

2004: June: Without publicity, FIFA withdraws criminal complaint accusing ISL directors of embezzling Globo television money.

2004: August: BBC *Panorama* programme reveals IOC member and Blatter ally Ivan Slavkov soliciting bribes.

2004: August: Zug Magistrate Thomas Hildbrand demands that Peter Nobel hand over details of the bank account set up for Weber and the names of the officials who repaid bribes.

2004: November: Zug court orders Nobel to hand over bribes documents.

2005: January: Nobel appeals Zug ruling to Swiss Federal Court in Lausanne.

2005: February: FIFA General Secretary Urs Linsi demands that Blatter sack deputy General Secretary, Jerome Champagne.

2005: May: Magistrate Hildbrand indicts Jean-Marie Weber and other ISL executives for allegedly embezzling Globo money.

2005: June: Warner family started organising sale of more than 5,000 World Cup tickets to travel agencies.

2005: July: Linsi repeats demand that Champagne is sacked.

2005: July: Swiss Federal Court upholds Nobel's appeal that he need not hand over bribes documents to Hildbrand. However, judgement discloses how bribes were repaid.

2005: September: FIFA congress in Marrakech. Jean-Marie Weber, awaiting trial on allegations of embezzling FIFA money, accredited as a guest.

2005: September: Blatter's lawyer Peter Nobel asks a Zurich court to impose a global ban on this book.

2005: November: Hildbrand launches a new ISL-related investigation and raids FIFA House seeking documents.

2005: December: Lawyer Karl Wüthrich replaces Bauer as ISL liquidator.

2005: December: Trinidad travel company Simpaul offers 'exclusive' tickets for World Cup. *Trinidad Express* investigative reporter Lasana Liburd reveals Simpaul is owned by Warner family.

2006: January: Warner claims Liburd is an 'unrepentant and inveterate liar.'

2006: February: FIFA's Ethics Committee decide that Warner has violated their rules and send his case to Executive Committee for punishment.

2006: March: Zurich court rejects Blatter's attempt to ban this book.

2006: March: Warner claims to have sold his interest in Simpaul travel company and so escapes punishment by FIFA's Executive Committee.

2006: April: Blatter signs sponsorship deal with VISA. MasterCard sue immediately in New York.

2006: April: Investigating Magistrate Thomas Hildbrand in court in Vaduz, Liechtenstein. He receives permission to use documents seized from ISL-owned offshore company Sunbow Ltd in his investigation into allegations that FIFA repaid bribes demanded by the ISL liquidator.

2006: April: First report from Ernst & Young about Jack Warner's ticket deals.

2006: July: Second report by Ernst & Young on Warner's ticket orders.

2006: July: Italy win World Cup in Berlin. Blatter absent from ceremony, admitting fans would whistle him.

2006: July: Lord Sebastian Coe appointed FIFA's new Ethics Chief.

2006: December: In public Warner and son Daryan given mild rebukes by FIFA's Executive Committee for their ticket operations. Secretly, Committee is told that Daryan and Simpaul have been fined nearly US$1 million for their profiteering at the World Cup – but have only paid US$250,000.

2006: December: Judge Loretta A Preska in New York awards MasterCard a permanent order compelling FIFA to give them the 2007–2014 credit card sponsorship contract. She states that FIFA's witnesses were 'generally not credible' and repeatedly lied during commercial negotiations. Blatter fires four FIFA marketing executives.

2007: January: Michel Platini ousts Lennart Johansson to become new President of UEFA – with huge backing from Blatter.

CAST LIST A-Z

Farah Addo. Former international referee and vice-president of African Football Confederation who alleged bribes had been paid to elect Blatter in 1998.

Flavio Battaini. Former FIFA lawyer, now with International Sports and Entertainment company who have the commercial hospitality contract for World Cup 2006.

Thomas Bauer. Accountant at Basel office of Ernst & Young. Appointed to liquidate ISL in 2001, he found evidence of illicit payments to sports officials.

Mohamed Bin Hammam. President of Asian Federation, backed by Emir of Qatar. Member of Executive Committee, Finance Committee and chairman of Goal Bureau. Bin Hammam is a powerful Blatter supporter. Expected to either run for the presidency or be king-maker when Blatter steps down.

Philippe Blatter. Nephew of Sepp Blatter, resigned from McKinsey management consultants in December 2005 to become CEO of marketing agency, Infront. Controls hospitality rights and oversees World Cup broadcasts for Germany 2006.

Sepp Blatter. FIFA President since 1998. Up for re-election 2007. Close friend and protégé of Horst Dassler. Apprentice and General Secretary to Havelange for 17 years.

Chuck Blazer. Jack Warner's bright, entrepreneurial sidekick and General Secretary. Runs CONCACAF from Trump Tower in New York.

Horace Burrell. Former president of Jamaica Football Federation, member of FIFA Disciplinary Committee.

Jerome Champagne. Deputy General Secretary and astute behind-the-scenes fixer for Blatter. Engaged in battle with Urs Linsi. FIFA insiders suggest Champagne wants the presidency – or a stake in it by backing Michel Platini for the job.

Keith Cooper. Former FIFA Director of Communications, sacked in July 2002.

Horst Dassler. Inherited and transformed the Adidas company. Created ISL, the sports marketing company that grew to dominate world sport. A brilliant innovator, the architect of modern sports politics, marketing – and sleaze. Dassler died in 1987. His methods, morality and protégés live on.

Charlie Dempsey. FIFA Executive Committee member who abstained in vote for who would host World Cup 2006.

Raymond Doorgen. Antiguan accounts clerk who was given control of FIFA grant.

Eric Drossart. Senior executive of IMG company who tried to buy television and marketing rights to World Cups 2002 and 2006.

Neville Ferguson. Trinidadian football official who sat in Haiti's seat at FIFA congress in June 1998 in Paris that elected Blatter president.

Chet Greene. Former General Secretary, Antigua & Barbuda Football Association.

Julio Grondona. President of Argentine football for a quarter of a century and FIFA's most senior vice-president. Loyal to Blatter. Chairs the Finance Committee.

André Guelfi. French wheeler-dealer, helped finance Dassler in 1970s, later convicted of money laundering in Elf scandal in Paris, 2003.

Peter Hargitay. Public relations man, specialising in clients with image problems. Advises Sepp Blatter and is an Executive Producer of sponsor-supported film, *Goal!*

Joao Havelange. FIFA President from 1974 to 1998, he deployed an effective mix of charm, menace and persuasion to keep world football at his command for decades.

Issa Hayatou. President of African Football Confederation.

Richard Herson. Executive assistant to Mathias Machline.

Thomas Hildbrand. Economic crime investigator probing allegations that ISL embezzled FIFA money.

Vincy Jalal. Companion of Jamaica's Horace Burrell who sat in Haiti's seat in FIFA congress in Zurich, 1996.

Lennart Johansson. Fought Blatter for the FIFA presidency in 1998 and lost. A sometime Blatter critic, weakened by attacks from Blatter allies. Now a FIFA Vice-President and President of UEFA until 2007.

Helmut Käser. FIFA General Secretary forced out by Havelange.

Leo Kirch. German film and television mogul and owner of World Cup rights whose empire crashed in April 2002.

Jean-Marie Kyss. Former president of Haiti Football Federation who was unable to attend FIFA congresses in 1996 and 1998.

Lasana Liburd. Trinidad reporter who broke story in 2005 of Jack Warner and his conflict of interest selling World Cup tickets.

Urs Linsi. Blatter's choice as Finance Chief in 1999. Now FIFA General Secretary locked in power battle with Jerome Champagne.

Fredy Luthiger. KPMG partner, audits FIFA books.

Matias Machline. Brazilian tycoon who hoped to set up 'FIFA Club' lottery on World Cup.

Christoph Malms. Married into Dassler family, became senior executive at ISL.

Antonio Mataresse. Former UEFA member of FIFA Executive Committee.

Marcel Mathier. Swiss lawyer and chairman of FIFA's Disciplinary Committee. Will preside over disciplinary matters at 2006 World Cup.

Guy-Philippe Mathieu. Long-time accounts clerk in FIFA's finance office with responsibility for processing expense claims by Blatter and Executive committee members.

Chung Mong-Joon. Korean member of FIFA Executive Committee, member of Hyundai family.

Peter Nobel. Leading Swiss lawyer who frequently represents Blatter and FIFA.

Helen Petermann. Blatter's long-time and devoted personal assistant.

The Honourable Loretta Preska. District Judge, Southern District of New York. Delivered devastating verdict on the honesty and credibility of FIFA in their dealings with sponsors.

Sir Stanley Rous. President of FIFA, 1961–1974.

Erwin Schmid. FIFA's Chief Financial Officer from the early 1980s until 1999 when he was replaced by Urs Linsi.

Markus Siegler & Andreas Herren. Loyal spokesmen for Blatter and FIFA.

Ricardo Teixiera. Havelange's son-in-law, president of Brazilian Football Federation, dogged by serious allegations of corruption. A member of FIFA's ruling Executive Committee.

Jérôme Valcke. French sports business executive hired by Blatter to re-organise FIFA's marketing, under the leadership of the President. Fired in December 2006 after admitting lying to VISA and MasterCard.

Daryan and Darryl Warner. Sons of Jack Warner, involved in several of his football businesses.

Jack Warner. Warner rules the CONCACAF football region that stretches from Central America, through the Caribbean to Alaska. Dogged by allegations (that he strenuously denies) about ticket scandals and contracts for family members. Julio Grondona's deputy at Finance Committee.

Jean-Marie Weber. Dassler's personal assistant. Weber took over Dassler's political role, persuading sports leaders to take their contracts to ISL. Built a strong personal relationship with Havelange and Blatter.

David Will. Scottish lawyer, represents the four British associations who have an automatic FIFA vice-presidency.

Michel Zen-Ruffinen. FIFA General Secretary 1998–2002. Blew the whistle on FIFA secrets in 2002. Forced out and now practises law in Switzerland.

ACKNOWLEDGEMENTS

You can't chase the bad guys without help from the good guys, and it's the good ones who make my work a joy. Thanks to all of you.

Some brave and principled people have taken personal risks to shine a light into the secret world of international football. For obvious reasons I won't name them here. They have my respect and warmest thanks.

Here are the ones I can name.

Colin Gibson, as sports editor of the *Daily Mail*, commissioned me to travel the world investigating FIFA and had the courage to run stories that scared the pants off other editors.

Thomas Kistner of the Munich *Süddeutsche Zeitung* and Jens Weinreich of the *Berliner Zeitung* shared intelligence, friendship and laughter. I recommend their 1998 book *Das Milliarden Spiel: Fusball, Geld und Medien*. Jean François Tanda at Zurich's *Sonntags Zeitung* broke a string of stories at FIFA in 2005 that were followed world-wide.

Veteran journalist Keith Botsford offered his stories, wisdom and wit on the era of Joao Havelange. Morley Myers, still on the beat, still at every major sports event, recalled Frankfurt in 1974 with gusto.

Barbara Smit shared her painstaking research on the Dassler family. Her *Pitch Invasion* will be essential reading for anyone who wants to learn more about how corporations took over world sport, trained its officials to be obedient and found intriguing ways to bribe them.

Rafael Marques in Angola told me how he was jailed on the demand of Justino José Fernandes, a member of FIFA's internal audit committee. In Kenya, I was guided by newspaperman Elias Makori, Bob Munro of the Mathere project that uses football to help kids from the slums, and agent Simon Wiseman. In Uganda Stephen Ouma Bwire briefed me on who was stealing the national association's money. In Nigeria, Olukayode Thomas told me where to go looking for evidence.

Bob Wagman gave me an education in American soccer and in Argentina Ezequiel Fernandes Moores shared his knowledge of Julio Grondona and the Generals' World Cup of 1978. Rodrigo Mattos in Brazil taught me about Joao Havelange and Ricardo Teixeira and their FIFA gambling business, and generously handed over his cache of letters and contracts.

Fans and administrators in Trinidad told me illuminating stories about life with Jack Warner. Emile Elias of the Contractors' Association and Selby Browne of Caribbean Sports Television Network were especially helpful. Raffique Shah and George Hislop recalled Jack's early days. Journalist Lasana Liburd gave excellent guidance, even as he broke new ground.

In Mexico City and Miami Edgardo Codesal briefed me on his experiences with Warner and Blazer.

Dr Jean-Marie Kyss spared his precious time in Port au Prince to talk modestly about his battles to preserve football's assets from government gangsters. Kalai and Ron Bluntschli interpreted, drove and educated me about Haiti.

Ian 'Magic' Hughes drew me to Antigua with his groundbreaking reporting of the extraordinary abuse of FIFA grants. Alex Tomlinson shared with me his (unsuccessful) attempts to

418

persuade the IOC's president Jacques Rogge to let the island's youngsters participate in the qualifying rounds of the Athens Olympic tournament. Gordon Derrick helped me make sense of the mess of papers that were the national association's accounts and Noel Egan introduced me to the young people at the grass-roots who'd never seen a penny of FIFA's money.

Jens Sejer Andersen in Denmark brings together so many digging reporters at 'Play the Game' conferences; connections made there have produced lots of great stories – for me and reporters all over the world. In Barcelona Xavier Vinyals i Capdepon never gave up in the quest for a picture of Juan Antonio Samaranch doing something he'd prefer you didn't know about. After 15 years, Xavier found it.

Christian Jannette quarried his memories of the Dassler years and Eric Wattez helped me research in France and guided the French translators of this book. Laurent Coadic at *L'Équipe* explained the relationship between France and FIFA. In Tunis, David Barnes, now freelancing in Provence, told me some of the funniest stories of the Dassler legacy.

Switzerland's Christoph Mueller was a great colleague in Mali. We worked and laughed in Bamako and again back in Zurich. Christoph introduced me to his colleague Urs Schnell from the weekly *Rundschau* programme who spent many hours explaining the details of the ISL liquidation. Zora Ledergerber of Swiss Transparency International gave me an insight into Markus Siegler's heavy-handed tactics.

Zurich investigating magistrate Urs Hubmann was generous with his wisdom and time as was ISL liquidator Thomas Bauer – despite a raging toothache.

Osama El-Sheikh, managing editor of *Super* magazine helped in Tunis. Back in England Neil Wilson of the *Daily Mail* generously shared his knowledge of ISL's history. At the *Mail* Matt

Lawton and Martin Lipton, Paul Newman, Charles Sale, John Greechan, Victoria Jackson and the Sports Desk crew gave solid support.

David Bond at the *Evening Standard*, Gordon Farquhar at *BBC Sport* and Brian Oliver at the *Observer* opened my eyes to other aspects of Blatter's FIFA. David Pallister at the *Guardian* remembered Morocco's hasty exit from the Organisation of African Unity to continue plundering the Western Sahara and Toby Shelley of the *Financial Times* shared his deep understanding of the region and its politics.

As always Michael Gillard gave masterly advice. Peter Jackson and others gave me the assistance – and sometimes interventions – of seasoned detectives. Denis O'Connor looked at KPMG's way of presenting FIFA's financial information. Accountant Richard Woods advised me how to interpret KPMG's private advice to Blatter on the curiosities they found when they took over FIFA's audit.

Caroline Wood brought order to my research. Christopher Whiteley enthusiastically led me through heaps of German language documents and Azucena Fernandez Durán explained the Spanish ones. Mathew D. Rose steered me through the intricacies of legal High German. When the Great Cumbrian storm of January 2005 severed my power lines in the hills, Tom and Andri Thwaites gave me shelter and electricity.

Warm thanks are due to my agent Sheila Crowley and my editor Tom Whiting at HarperSport, and to Clare Sambrook for bringing her wit and energy to the editing.

INDEX